Inside Organized Racism

T0367076

INSIDE ORGANIZED RACISM

WOMEN IN THE HATE MOVEMENT

Kathleen M. Blee

UNIVERSITY OF CALIFORNIA PRESS
BERKELEY   LOS ANGELES   LONDON

University of California Press
Berkeley and Los Angeles, California

University of California Press, Ltd.
London, England

First paperback printing 2003
© 2002 by the Regents of the University of California

Library of Congress Cataloging-in-Publication Data

Blee, Kathleen M.
    Inside organized racism : women in the hate movement /
Kathleen M. Blee.
        p. cm.
    Includes bibliographical references and index.
    ISBN 978-0-520-24055-1 (pbk : alk. paper)
    1. Hate groups—United States.   2. White supremacy movements—
United States.   3. White women—United States—Psychology.
4. White women—United States—Attitudes.   5. White women—
United States—Conduct of life.   6. Whites—United States—Race
identity.   7. United States—Race relations.   I. Title.

HV6773.2 .B54 2002
320.5'6'0820973—dc21   2001041449

11   10   09   08   07
10   9   8   7   6   5   4   3

To
my parents and Aunt Nancy

CONTENTS

CROSSING A BOUNDARY

At a racist gathering on the West Coast, Frank, a skinhead from Texas, sidled up to me to share his disgust at an event so mild it was "something you could see on the family channel." At his side, Liz echoed his sentiment, complaining that she felt trapped in a "Baptist church social." We chatted some more. Frank boasted that this was nothing like he expected. He made the long trip to "get his juices going," not to be part of something concocted by "wimps." Liz agreed, pointing with disdain to a group of women hauling boxes of hamburger buns over to a large grill.

I found their reactions baffling. To me, the scene was horrifying, anything but mundane. Frank's arms were covered with swastika tattoos. On his head was a baseball cap with a comic-like depiction of an African American man being lynched. Liz's black skirt, hose, and boots accentuated the small Klan cross embroidered on her white tailored shirt. The rituals of historical hatred being enacted in front of us seemed far from disappointingly "tame," as Frank and Liz's complaints suggested. A cross was doused with gasoline and set ablaze. People spoke casually of the need to "get rid" of African Americans, immigrants, Jews, gay men and lesbians, and Asian Americans, or exchanged historical trivia purporting to expose the Holocaust as a Zionist hoax.

Later that night, the rally's leaders called everyone into headquarters to don robes and hoods. It was then that I regretted not taking notice of people's shoes earlier in the day. After our initial conversation, I decided that Frank and Liz were less scary than the young skinheads screaming about white power, and I tried to stick close to them. But amid all the covered faces and identical Klan garb, I couldn't tell one person from another. I was frightened. Everything was chillingly out of the ordinary.

Only much later did I understand how Frank and Liz could compare a racist rally to a community social gathering. It was years before I could bring myself to read my notes on this rally, written on sheets of paper to which faint scents of smoke and kerosene still seemed to cling. Yet with time and psychic distance from my encounters with Frank, Liz, and others like them, I came to see that aspects of racist gatherings do mirror church socials or neighborhood picnics, albeit in a distorted, perverse fashion. I remember a card table piled high with racist children's books, bumper stickers, and index cards of "white power recipes"; sessions on self-help for disgruntled or substance-addicted members; hymns sung as background to speeches about strengthening the "racialist movement"; and the pancake breakfast and "social hour."

It was with an eerie sense of the familiar colliding with the bizarre that I crossed the boundary that divides the racist underground from the mainstream to write this book. Much about racist groups appears disturbingly ordinary, especially their evocation of community, family, and social ties. One woman gushed that a Ku Klux Klan rally "was a blast. I had fun. And it was just like a big family get-together. We played volleyball. And you had your little church thing on Sunday. For the longest time I thought I would be bored. But I wasn't bored at all." Another woman described a Nazi compound as being "almost set up like a summer camp. There was just a big hall, like a bunkhouse-type thing where you could eat. And then there was the chapel. Only people who lived there and did security got actual places to sleep. Independent women had houses and cabins to sleep in. You pitched tents. The rules were very strict: no drinking, no smoking, no this and that. When the women came together it was real fun. It was like a giant family reunion. It really didn't seem harmful or threatening at all, other than the men [who] would take care of guarding the guests."

Some of the ideas voiced by racist groups can seem unremarkable, as evident in the scary similarity to mainstream right-wing stands on such issues as gun control. Still, the watershed that divides racist activism from the rest of society is striking. The beliefs of racist groups are not just extreme variants of mainstream racism, xenophobia, or anti-Semitism. Rather, their conspiratorial logic and zeal for activism separate members of racist groups from those on "the outside," as racist activists call it. By combining the aberrant with the ordinary, the peculiar with the prosaic, modern racist groups gain strength. To design effective strategies to combat racist groups, we must understand this combination.

Intense, activist racism typically does not arise on its own; it is learned in racist *groups*. These groups promote ideas radically different from the racist attitudes held by many whites. They teach a complex and contradictory mix of hatred for enemies, belief in conspiracies, and allegiance to an imaginary unified race of "Aryans." Women are the newest recruiting targets of racist groups, and they provide a key to these groups' campaign for racial supremacy. "We are very picky when we come to girls," one woman told me. "We don't like sluts. The girls must know their place but take care of business and contribute a lot too. Our girls have a clean slate. Nobody could disrespect us if they tried. We want girls [who are] well educated, the whole bit. And tough as shit."

The groups and networks that espouse and promote openly racist and anti-Semitic, and often xenophobic and homophobic, views and actions are what I call "organized racism."[1] Organized racism is more than the aggregation of individual racist sentiments. It is a social milieu in which venomous ideas—about African Americans, Jews, Hispanics, Asians, gay men and lesbians, and others—take shape. Through networks of groups and activists, it channels personal sentiments of hatred into collective racist acts. Organized racism is different from the racism widespread in mainstream white society: it is more focused, self-conscious, and targeted at specific strategic goals.

Today, organized racism in the United States is rife with paradox. While racist groups are becoming more visible, their messages of racial hatred and white supremacy find little support in the rest of society. Racist groups increasingly have anti-Semitism as their core belief, though anti-Semitic attitudes in America as a whole are at their lowest ebb. Despite proclaiming bizarre and illogical views of race and religion, racist groups attract not only those who are ignorant, irrational, socially isolated, or marginal, but also intelligent, educated people, those with resources and social connections, those with something to lose. Organized racists trade in a currency of racist stereotyping little changed from the views of the nineteenth-century Klan and of anti-Semitism recycled from World War II–era Nazi propaganda, yet they recruit successfully among the young who have little or no knowledge of that history. They seize on racist rituals from the past to foment rage about the conditions of the present, appealing to teenagers whose lives are scarred by familial abuse and terror as well as the sons and daughters of stable and loving families, the offspring of privilege and the beneficiaries of parental attention. Racist groups project a sense of hypermasculinity in their militaristic swagger and tactics of bullying and intimidation,[2] but they increasingly are able to bring women into their ranks.

When I began my research, I wanted to understand the paradoxes of organized racism. Were, I wondered, the increased numbers of women changing the masculine cast of racist groups? Why, I asked myself, did racist activists continue to see Jews, African Americans, and others as enemies, and why did they regard violence as a racial solution? Convinced that we can defeat organized racism only if we know how it recruits and retains its members, I also wanted to learn why people join organized racism and how being in racist groups affects them. My approach makes four basic assumptions:

- **The members of racist groups are as important as the leaders.** When we look at the members of racist groups we find a surprising diversity—a point often missed because of the tendency to emphasize their similarities. The sociologist Norman Elias observed that individuals can be larger than groups.[3] Every person has multiple identities and social positions, some of which tug in different directions, such as mother, worker, daughter, citizen, and friend. Voluntary social groups, in contrast, cluster people according to what they have in common, as do churches, parenting groups, or labor unions. If we focus on the homogeneity of a group, we can lose sight of the more complex nature of the people in it. Concentrating on the organized facade of racism—the structure, leadership, and propaganda issued by racist groups—creates a strong impression of uniformity, which may be undermined by an examination of *individual* racists. Only by paying attention to the members can we assess the varied backgrounds, worldviews, identities, and racial loyalties that are found in racist groups.

Racists may not be who we expect. One woman told me, "I was a hostess at a restaurant. . . . Someone gave me a tip one time as they were leaving because they had requested a special booth near the fireplace. And I got it for them. And they gave me a tip as they were leaving. And it was a five-dollar bill folded in half. And inside the five-dollar bill was a card that said, 'You have been patronized by the KKK.' You can't tell. It's real surprising."

The usual focus on a few prominent leaders gives the mistaken im-

pression that organized racism is made up of forceful leaders and compliant followers. The handful of men who proclaim themselves leaders
or spokespersons for organized racism—including David Duke of the
National Association for the Advancement of White People, William
Pierce of the National Alliance, Robert Miles of Aryan Nations, and
Louis Beam of the Ku Klux Klan—make headlines, but most men and
virtually all women occupy hidden niches in racist groups. Paying attention to members enables us to explore when members exercise power
over their leaders by granting or withdrawing their support as well as
how leaders secure loyalty from recalcitrant followers.

In addition, focusing on members helps us avoid the common but
fallacious tendency to use macro (societal) patterns to understand micro
(individual) behavior. We cannot assume that the same factors that explain mass social movements also supply the motivations of all those
who join the movement. For example, Germany's interwar economic
crisis fostered the Nazis' rise to power. But it does not follow that every
member joined the Nazi Party for economic reasons. Similarly, to explain individual recruitment into the far right today we must look at the
actual motives and experiences of its participants rather than make
sweeping generalizations about social trends.

• **People receive racist messages differently.** It is not possible to understand how people are attracted to organized racism simply by reading
racist propaganda or listening to the speeches of its leaders. Texts are
read in various ways by different readers—sometimes in ways contrary
to the author's intentions. Thus, it can be dangerously misleading to
presume that we can understand the motives of racist activists by looking at the ideologies of their groups. Nor can we understand racist
groups by simply examining their propaganda. Rather, we must consider how members *receive* the cultural, political, and ideological messages projected by racist groups. Although racist groups display great
similarity in their ideological messages and stylized pageantry, the members to whom these are directed are heterogeneous and their reception
of these messages is uneven.[4] As we will see, racist individuals actively
mold the messages of racist groups to fit their own lives and agendas.

• **Organized racism is a social movement.** Racist activism is more than the
sum of racist people or racist groups. It is a *social movement,* a "family"
of overlapping groups organized to spread racist and anti-Semitic ideas
and terrorist tactics.[5] And as a social movement, whatever its goals,

organized racism shares features with other, more benign, social movements. For example, it is shaped by the larger political environment in which it operates. Today's racist movement is politically and socially marginal, scorned in almost every sphere of mainstream society, from the media, education, and organized religion to electoral politics. Given such sentiments, it is not surprising that racist activists view the outside world as conspiring against them, that they embrace terrorism over electoral politics, and that they favor secretive and hierarchical groups. As one skinhead woman indicated, as a member of the racist movement, you have to "prepare yourself for war constantly. Don't speak if you can't defend yourself in every way. Prepare by knowing, first of all, then work on guns and amass food and water supplies, first aid kits, medication, clothing, blankets. Try to become self-sufficient."

In addition to being affected by the larger political milieu, organized racism has other features oddly similar to those of what scholars term "new social movements" (NSMs), such as the environmental, gay/lesbian rights, and feminist movements. Like these new social movements, organized racism draws members from diverse backgrounds, pays attention to issues of individual identity and daily life as well as abstract policies, and incorporates personal relationships into collective action. Also, like progressive NSMs, today's racist groups occupy what the social movement scholar Alberto Melucci describes as the "intermediate space of social life where individual needs and the pressures of political innovations mesh," and in a perverse way they expand civil society—although certainly not, as is characteristic of NSMs, in the direction of democratization.[6]

• ***Organized racism is emotional but not irrational.*** Emotions play an important role in all social movements,[7] including racist movements. Collective racist agendas depend on emotional relationships among activists to motivate and sustain activism, including intricate dynamics of intimacy, betrayal, dissension, grief, exhilaration, conflict, satisfaction, intimidation, coercion, confusion, and disillusionment.[8] Emotions can overlap in complex ways. For example, loyalty may stem in part from fear, as one skinhead suggested when she declared, "You have to prove yourself and your loyalty. They do, like, a background-type check on you, you know. It's amazing, you know. They know people at the DMV [Department of Motor Vehicles] and they can find out where you live." But loyalty may also be nourished by pride and a sense of accomplishment. One woman explained, "I just kind of got volunteered into a lot of things that I didn't really expect to, but when I got up and spoke at rallies and stuff, people really listened to what I had to say. And it's, like, that I owe them. It is a responsibility."

That racist groups have an emotional dimension does not mean that they or their adherents are irrational.[9] As the historian of Italian fascism Mabel Berezin argues, "Emotion is nonrational, but it is not irrational."[10] Certainly, many racist activists exhibit paranoia, conspiratorial thinking, social isolation, obsessive xenophobia, and emotional attenuation. But, like racist identities themselves, these may be *outcomes* rather than *predictors* of joining a racist group.

FOCUSING ON RACIST WOMEN

To understand organized racism from the inside—from the experiences and beliefs of its members—I decided that I needed to talk with racist activists. I chose to interview women for a variety of reasons. On a practical level, I found that I could get access to women racists and develop some measure of rapport with them. More substantively, I wanted to study women racists because we know so little about them. Since 1980 women have been actively recruited by U.S. racist groups both because racist leaders see them as unlikely to have criminal records that would draw the attention of police and because they help augment membership rolls. Today, women are estimated to constitute nearly 50 percent of new members in some racist groups, leading some antiracist monitoring groups to claim that they are the "fastest growing part of the racist movement."[11] Yet this new group of racist activists has been ignored, as researchers have tended to view racism as male-dominated and racist women as more interested in domestic and personal concerns than in its politics.[12]

Eventually, I persuaded thirty-four women from a variety of racist and anti-Semitic groups across the country to talk to me at length about themselves and their racist activities. Fourteen women were in neo-Nazi but not skinhead groups, six were members of Ku Klux Klans, eight were white power skinheads, and six were in Christian Identity or related groups (see appendix 1 for more on the distinctions among these groups). What they told me shatters many common ideas about what racist activists are like.

Among the women I interviewed there was no single racist *type*. The media depict unkempt, surly women in faded T-shirts, but the reality is different. One of my first interviews was with Mary, a vivacious Klans-woman who met me at her door with a big smile and ushered me into her large, inviting kitchen. Her blond hair was pulled back into a long ponytail and tied with a large green bow. She wore dangling gold hoop earrings, blue jeans, a modest flowered blouse, and no visible tat-toos or other racist insignia. Her only other jewelry was a simple gold-colored necklace. Perhaps sensing my surprise at her unremarkable ap-pearance, she joked that her suburban appearance was her "undercover uniform."

Trudy, an elderly Nazi activist I interviewed somewhat later, lived in a one-story, almost shabby ranch house on a lower-middle-class street in a small town in the Midwest. Her house was furnished plainly. Mov-ing cautiously with the aid of a walker, she brought out tea and cookies prepared for my visit. Meeting her reminded me of the phrase "old coun-try women," which I had once heard from a southern policeman char-acterizing the rural Klanswomen in his area.

I also interviewed Roseanne, a small, lively white supremacist woman with short-cropped black hair who wore a flowered sundress. We got together in the living room of her government-subsidized apartment in a large, racially mixed housing complex. Her apartment was very small and nearly barren of furniture—making her expensive computer and fax and copy machines dedicated to her work "for the movement" stand out all the more.

My encounters with skinhead women were more guarded, although some were quite animated and articulate. Not one invited me into her home—all I got was a quick glance when I picked her up for an interview in some other location. Most seemed to live at or barely above the level of squatters, in dirty, poorly equipped spaces that were nearly uninha-bitable. Their appearance varied. Molly sported five ear piercings that held silver hoops and a silver female sign, an attractive and profession-ally cut punk hairstyle, fine features, and intense eyes. Others were ghostly figures, with empty eyes and visible scars poorly hidden behind heavy makeup and garish lipstick.

Over a two-year period I spent considerable time with these women, talking to them about their racist commitments and getting them to tell me their life stories (see appendix 2 for details on how the study was conducted). Listening to them describe their backgrounds, I realized that many did not fit common stereotypes about racist women as unedu-cated, marginal members of society raised in terrible families and lured into racist groups by boyfriends and husbands. Instead, I learned:

· *Most were educated.* Against the idea that racism is the product of ignorance, fourteen of the thirty-four women were in college or held associate or higher degrees. Another fifteen had finished or were currently in high school. Only five had failed to complete high school.

· *Most were not poor.* People generally believe that racism is most intense among poor and lower-working-class people who compete with racial minorities for jobs, housing, and social services.[13] However, most of the women I interviewed had good jobs. They were occupational therapists, nurses, teachers, engineers, librarians, draftspersons, or phone company representatives. Some were attending college; others were not employed but were married to men with decent jobs. Only about one-third were living in more precarious conditions—as waitresses in pizza parlors, as lay ministers in tiny racist churches, as teachers in racist private schools, or as the wives of men who lacked secure employment.

· *For some, poverty was caused by racist activism.* For almost half of those without good jobs (or married to underemployed men), marginal employment was a *consequence,* not a *cause,* of being active in racist politics. Some women (or their husbands) lost their jobs when employers discovered their racist activities, or when they were caught proselytizing racism to customers or fellow employees. Others decided to work in racist enclaves—for example, as teachers in Christian Identity schools—to escape the nefarious influences of the outside world and to contribute to the racist movement. Despite their fervent hatred for a federal government that racist activists see as the tool of Zionist/Jewish forces, several women admitted that they relied on welfare programs or food stamps to sustain them and their children during rough economic times.

· *Most did not grow up poor.* Most of the parents of these women had decent jobs. Their fathers were laboratory technicians, construction workers, store owners, company executives, salesmen, farmers, repairmen, postal workers, architects, doctors, factory foremen, and inspectors as well as Christian Identity "ministers." Their mothers were housewives and Christian Identity schoolteachers as well as nurses, teachers, secretaries, social workers, clerks, computer consultants, corporate executives, real estate agents, and bankers.

· *Most were not raised in abusive families.* Writers often suggest that racist activists are the product of disorganized, uncaring, or abusive families.[14] Yet none of the women I interviewed were raised in foster homes, by relatives, or in institutions. Several grew up in unstable and violent families, ran away from home, or had intense conflicts with parents or stepparents, but it is not clear that such stresses burdened a significantly higher proportion of these women than the population as a whole. In contrast, some women related stories of idyllic family lives, as did the Klanswoman who recalled her "very happy family background [in which] my parents have been married for thirty-two years and all my brothers and sisters and I are very close." Most described their family backgrounds in more mixed terms, as both nurturing and restrictive. In any case, it is difficult to know how childhood experiences are related to racist activism. The women's descriptions of their pasts may be distorted by memory or by an effort to show themselves in a particular light in the interview. Moreover, a number of women related stories of strife with parents or siblings that they later admitted resulted from their racial activism; thus cause and effect are not always easy to determine.

· *Not all women followed a man into racism.* Racist women often are seen as compliant followers of the men in their lives. But the women I interviewed described many paths into the racist movement. Several said they and their husbands or boyfriends grew up in the racist movement and followed their family's political path. Four said that they and their husband or boyfriend joined a racist group at the same time, as a mutual decision. Another four said they joined racist groups by themselves and met their current boyfriend or husband at a racist event. Seven said a boyfriend or husband encouraged them to join a racist group. Others followed different patterns, including one woman who followed her son into the racist movement, several who recruited male intimates into racist activism, and a handful whose husbands or boyfriends refused to become involved in organized racism.

Why were these racist women willing to talk to me? They had a variety of reasons. Some hoped to generate publicity for their groups or themselves—a common motivation for granting interviews to the media. Many saw an opportunity to explain their racial politics to a white outsider, even one decidedly unsympathetic to their arguments. In a racist variant on the religious imperative to "bear witness" to the unconverted,[15] they wanted the outside world to have an accurate (even if negative) account to counter superficial media reports. As one young woman put it, "I don't know what your political affiliations are, but I trust that you'll try to be as objective as possible." Others wished to support or challenge what they imagined I had been told in earlier interviews with racist comrades or competitors. And, despite their deep antagonism toward authority figures, some young women were flattered to have their opinions solicited by a university professor. They had rarely encountered someone older who talked with them without being patronizing, threatening, or directive.

From the beginning, when I asked women if I could interview them, I made it clear that I did not share the racial convictions of these groups. I explicitly said that my views were quite opposed to theirs, that they should not hope to convert me to their views, but that I would try to depict women racist activists accurately. I revealed my critical stance but made it clear that I had no intent to portray them as crazy and did not plan to turn them over to law enforcement or mental health agencies.[16]

I was prepared to elaborate on my disagreements with organized racism in my interviews, but in nearly every case the women cut me short, eager to talk about themselves.[17] Recognizing the extreme marginalization of the racist movement in the American political landscape, these women had no doubt that an ideological gulf divided them from me—it separates their beliefs from nearly all political ideas deemed acceptable in modern public life. They were accustomed to having people disagree with them, and they rarely tried to sway those who openly opposed their opinions. They were interested in me not as a potential convert, but rather as a recorder of their lives and thoughts. Their desire, at once personal and politically evangelical, was that someone outside the small racist groups to which they belong hear and record their words.

Indeed, such eagerness to talk underscores the ethical dilemma of inadvertently providing a platform for racist propaganda.[18] Studies on racist extremists have the power to publicize even as they scrutinize. The problem was brought to the fore as I considered the issue of anonymity for my interviewees. Although the inclusion of more biographical details about the racist women activists I interviewed would be useful, I decided that doing so would unavoidably reveal their identities and thus give further publicity to them and their groups. For this reason, I have used pseudonyms for interviewees and their groups and changed all identifying details, while rendering quotations verbatim.[19] Most people interviewed by scholars desire to remain anonymous, but these women wanted to be known. Some tried to demand that I use their names or the names of their groups. When an older Ku Klux Klan woman thanked me "for writing an article that might inspire others," however, I was convinced that my decision to disguise identities was correct.

RAPPORT, SEDUCTION, AND FEAR

What is the correct stance for a researcher studying organized racism to take? Reflecting on his studies of the fascist National Front in England, Nigel Fielding noted the lack of guidelines for those who focus on what he termed, with great understatement, " 'unloved' groups."[20] The feminist scholarly principle of basing interviews on rapport and empathy is helpful for groups that are "conducive, whimsical, or at least unthreatening,"[21] but it hardly seems appropriate when the groups are hostile or frightening.

Walking a tightrope in my interviews, I kept a balance between maintaining enough distance to make it clear that I rejected their ideas and creating sufficient rapport to encourage women to talk to me.[22] A successful interview needs some conversational common ground. Each party needs to feel understood, if not entirely accepted, by the other. These racist women were unlikely to reveal much about themselves if they did not have some trust in me, if I could not manage to express interest in their lives and refrain from repeatedly condemning them.[23]

Usually a researcher can establish rapport with interviewees by proffering details of his or her personal life or expressing agreement with their choices and beliefs. Because I was unwilling to do either, I was forced to rely on more indirect and fragile measures. Like those at family gatherings and office parties who strain toward congeniality across known lines of disagreement, I seized on any experiences or values that we shared, no matter how trivial.[24] When they expressed dissatisfaction with their bodies, I let them know that I had the same concerns. I commented positively when they talked of their children in parental rather than political terms—for example, when they worried about having enough time to be good mothers—and hoped that my sympathy would lead them to overlook my silence when they discussed such things as the "racial education" they planned for their children. This approach was not always successful. When one woman with a particularly violent reputation told me in the course of our interview about problems she was having with her infant son, I found it difficult not to offer advice; but fearing to open the conversation to questions about me or my life, I kept my expressions of concern vague. She was clearly dissatisfied, and our rapport began to dissolve. In a later phone call, when I asked about her baby, she dismissed my queries, making it plain that the topic was no longer open for discussion.

A researcher can be simultaneously an "insider" and an "outsider" to the culture of those being studied. As a white person I had access that no nonwhite researcher could enjoy. As a woman, I had a store of shared experiences that could support a stream of conversational banter about bodies, men, food, and clothing in which a male researcher would be unlikely to engage. Certainly, both I and the women I interviewed realized that I was an outsider to the world of organized racism. But even the obvious barriers between us gave me insight into their convoluted racial beliefs. For example, my contradictory status as both a racial outsider (to their politics) and an apparent racial insider (as white) helped me understand their ambivalent descriptions of their racial and racist identities.

Yet a reliance on rapport is problematic when scholars do not share a worldview with those they study. Trying to understand the world through the eyes of someone for whom you have even a little sympathy is one thing, but the prospect of developing empathy for a racist activist whose life is given meaning and purpose by the desire to annihilate you or others like you is a very different matter. And even if it were possible, such empathy would violate the expected boundaries between scholars and intensely "unloved" groups. I am not alone in worrying that the political stigma attached to these groups will sully those who study them.[25]

There are uncomfortable emotional complexities to this kind of research. Interviewing members of racist groups is dangerous but also intriguing, even offering a voyeuristic thrill. Though I'm embarrassed to admit it, I found meeting racist activists to be exciting as well as horrifying. The ethnographer Barrie Thorne captures this sense of fieldwork as adventure: it consists of "venturing into exciting, taboo, dangerous, perhaps enticing social circumstances; getting the flavor of participation, living out moments of high drama; but in some ultimate way having a cop-out, a built-in escape, a point of outside leverage that full participants lack."[26]

Fieldwork with "unloved groups" also poses the problem of seduction. As Antonius Robben, an anthropologist of Argentinean fascism, notes, even when researchers and interviewees begin as wary opponents, scholars can be drawn into "trad[ing] our critical stance as observers for an illusion of congeniality with cultural insiders."[27] Indeed, others who study loathsome political groups cite the pain of discovering that participants in some of history's most dreadful social movements can be charming and engaging in interviews.[28]

My time with Linda, a white power skinhead from the West, illustrates one instance of emotional seduction. Before our formal interview, our relationship was tense. With every phone call Linda insisted on changing the place and conditions of the interview, demanding ever more evidence that I was not with the police. She repeatedly threatened to bring her boyfriend and a gun to the interview, in violation of our agreement. Each of her demands required more negotiation and gave Linda another opportunity to remind me that she would not hesitate to hurt anyone who betrayed her or her group. Indeed, I had ample reason to take her threats seriously: both Linda and her boyfriend had served prison sentences for assault, selling drugs, and other offenses. I came to the interview frightened and prepared for hostile confrontation. In person, however, Linda confounded my expectations. She was charming, soft-spoken, and concerned for my comfort during the interview. Although quite willing to express appalling attitudes, Linda prefaced many of her statements by apologizing for what I might find offensive. My fear eased, replaced by a seductive, false rapport as Linda set the parameters of our interaction and I responded to her. Off-guard, I pressed Linda less aggressively than the other women to explain contradictions in the chronology and logic of her story. In retrospect, the field notes that I taped immediately after the interview make me uneasy. They show how disarming emotional manipulation can be, even when one is on guard against it:

I found the [negotiation and preparation for the] interview with Linda to be the most emotionally stressful, maybe with the exception of [another] interview during which I was fearing for my life. Actually with Linda and [her boyfriend] there was no indication that they might try to harm me at all. In fact, quite the contrary. I actually was afraid of that before they came because they both have very violent reputations, but in person they were extremely cordial and very friendly, not trying to intimidate me in any way. Perhaps trying to cultivate me.

Researchers often talk informally about the emotional side of doing fieldwork, but it is a subject rarely discussed in print.[29] Pondering one's own emotional state may seem narcissistic—yet it also can be analytically revealing. In the early stages of this research, I experienced a great deal of fear. The violent reputations of some of the women I wanted to interview, including the skinhead organizer whose comrades referred to her as "Ms. Icepick," did little to dispel my concerns. As I got to know some people in the racist world, I became somewhat less afraid. As I began to see them in more complicated, less stereotyped ways, I no longer worried that every interaction would end in disaster. It also became clear that as a woman in that male-dominated world I was safer because I seemed to pose little threat: male researchers were seen as more personally challenging to male racists and more likely to be covert police operatives.[30]

But in other respects, I grew more afraid as I became less naive. For one thing, I came to realize that my white skin color would provide me little protection. Many racist activists who have faced criminal charges were turned in by other whites, sometimes even members of their own groups. Moreover, as I discuss later, some racists see race as determined by commitment to white power politics rather than by genetics. I could not assume that those I interviewed would view me either as white or as nonhostile. I could not count on racial immunity from violence.

As I was contacting and interviewing racist women, the structure of the racist movement also changed in two ways that increased my risk. First, the 1995 bombing of the Alfred P. Murrah Federal Building in Oklahoma City occurred midway through my interviewing. In its wake, the racist movement went further underground. Racist groups were subject to investigation and members became increasingly sensitive to the possibility of police informants and infiltrators. Second, as a result of the heightened scrutiny of hate groups after the Oklahoma City bombing, the racist movement became less organized. Some adopted a strategy known as "leaderless resistance," which was designed to make the racist movement less vulnerable to investigation and prosecution. Racist activists began to operate in small units or cells, sometimes in pairs or even alone, to avoid detection by authorities. While adhering to a common agenda of Aryan supremacism, they were able to develop their own strategies, even select enemies, without answering to formal leaders; they used the Internet or other anonymous means to disseminate their ideas rather than relying on organized groups.[31]

Leaderless resistance makes studying the racist movement scarier because it reduces the accountability of individual racists. When I attended a racist rally in the later stages of my research, I came with the permission of the rally's leader. I felt, or at least hoped, that his invitation would ensure my safety. Yet a significant number of those in attendance felt no allegiance to him; they did not care whether their words or actions might reflect on the group or implicate its leader. The *organization* of organized racism, I realized, was double-pronged. It channeled the racist beliefs of members into collective strategies of terrorism, building an agenda of racist practices that could be catastrophic. But it could also curb the violence of particular individuals, unruly members whose actions could bring the collective and its leaders to the attention of the authorities. Without leaders, such restraints do not exist.

My fear was caused by more than simple proximity to racist groups. It was deliberately fed by the women I interviewed, who hoped to limit the scope of my study and shape my analysis. When I have done research on other topics, an awkward inequality in power has separated me, the scholarly authority, from those I interviewed. But here, my feelings of fear put us on the same level. The racist women constantly drew attention to my vulnerability to them, asking whether I was afraid to come see them, whether I was afraid to be in their homes. Others suggested that I risked harm if I did—or sometimes if I did not—interview a particular person in the movement. Even a woman in prison on death row, who was brought to our interview in handcuffs, found a way to undermine any power I had over her by noting that she could call on gangs of allies in and outside the prison walls. "I'm not scared of anybody," she told me, "so I'm not gonna worry about it. I'll say what I got to say . . . 'cause I got the Jamaican Posse and the Cuban Posse all behind me, they gonna kick ass."

Some women were more indirect in their intimidation. Many bragged of their group's violence, making it clear that they treated enemies harshly. An Aryan supremacist boasted that the racist movement attracted people who were "totally messed up and totally mindless," people who were prone to "fight and kill, rip off armored cars, get guns." Others were even more specific about how their comrades retaliated against enemies. A self-proclaimed lesbian neo-Nazi described the aftermath of a conflict she had with two African American women: "And so I called my ex-girlfriend about it, I'm like, 'Well D——, I have a job for you to do.' She's like, 'What's wrong?' I said 'I want you to fuck somebody up for me.' She said, 'No problem, Mommy. I'd do anything for you. I love you Mommy.'" Even now, years after completing the interviews, I receive signed and anonymous letters warning that they "are watching" me, that I had better tell "the truth" about them and their movement.

Often the women saw even the selection of where we would conduct the interview as an opening to use intimidation. Usually, I asked each woman to choose a place where she would feel comfortable, although I reminded her that I did not want to be interrupted by family members or racist group comrades. Several suggested their homes, saying that they would be most at ease there but also warning that their houses contained weapons and that other comrades (presumably less trustworthy than themselves) might appear at the house during the interview. Others picked a public place but indicated that they would station armed comrades nearby in case the interview did not "proceed as planned." On only two occasions did I refuse a suggestion for an interview site, both for safety reasons. One woman wanted me to be blindfolded and transported to an unknown destination in the back of a truck. Another proposed a meeting in a very remote racist compound to which I would have to be driven by a racist group member. And even in these cases, when my concerns for personal safety denied them their choice, they continued the implicit threats. For example, after the woman who had wanted me to be blindfolded agreed on a more visible site, she assured me that I should not be concerned for my safety there because "men with guns" would be hidden along the street "in case of a police raid." Negotiations over terms and settings thus provided the women the opportunity to gain some control over the interview by putting me off balance with allusions to guns, hidden compounds, and the like.

But fear went both ways. These women were afraid of me. I could betray their confidences to the police, to enemies, or to family members who were not aware of their activities. Telling me about their journey into organized racism could feel empowering to them, but it could also expose them to retribution. One Washington racist skinhead worried that I might secretly funnel information to violent gangs of antiracist skinheads about buildings occupied by racist skinheads: "[After you leave], well, uh, I wonder if some skin's house is gonna get Molotov-cocktailed and the [antiracist skinheads] are doing this in retaliation." An older neo-Nazi was concerned that my tape recording of her interview "could be used against me in a court of law." Many expressed suspicions about how I had found them at all. Throughout the interview a woman from the East repeatedly asked, "Just how did you become aware of the group that I'm in?" Worried that such fears could derail the interview, I assured each woman that her interview would be confidential and that I would not ask questions about illegal activities.

Some women used fear as a strategy to protect themselves not from actual jeopardy but from revelations that might reflect badly on them personally. Once fear of exposure was established as a realistic concern, they cited it to justify not answering questions about boyfriends or parents, their performance in school, and even their taste in music. The flimsiness of this excuse was clear from their willingness to divulge genuinely incriminating information: I had to interrupt several of these same women to keep them from telling me about their illegal activities or plans. A young Nazi activist in California, for example, deflected nearly all my inquiries about her family by saying that she was being constantly watched by the police, who could use such information against her, yet she repeatedly returned to an unsolicited story about her friends who "buried their guns in oil drums up in the hills for when the race war comes."

Racists also used their own fear to create rapport to keep the interview moving. Usually the task of creating rapport falls to the researcher, who generally has the most to gain from a successful interview. But many of these women were highly motivated to have me hear their stories. Thus, even as they tried to made me more afraid, they often pointed to their vulnerability to me; a woman might emphasize my exposure in the well-guarded living room of a racist leader, and at the same time observe that I probably had "really good connections to the police." At times, this tempering became nearly comical; one interviewee repeatedly made note of the guns and sketches of lynchings that lay around her living room but then sought to assure me that although "the average person has an idea that the Klan is very military [violent] and they're afraid," she was no threat, because she "wasn't aware of [that reputation] until just recently." But fear did help bring our sense of risk to the same level, making plain the stalemate in which we at least seemed to be equally unsafe.

Although the danger of engaging with racist activists actually increased while I was interviewing these women, I became less afraid over time, for reasons that are disturbing. The first interviews, conducted largely with members of the Ku Klux Klan, left me nearly paralyzed with fear. My field journal is full of notes on how to increase my own safety. Before each interview, I made elaborate preparations, giving friends instructions on what to do if I did not return on schedule. Yet my field notes on the last interviews, conducted largely with neo-Nazis and white power skinheads—members of groups that in recent years have been more likely than the Klan to engage in overt violence—show that my fears had largely abated. I took personal risks that earlier I would have found unthinkable. I had become more numb to tales of assaults and boasts of preparing for "race war."

It is terrifying to realize that you find it difficult to be shocked. But gradually my dealings with racist women became like a business transaction, with both parties parrying for favorable terms. I was not unafraid, but I took fewer precautions based on fear. Perhaps this change in attitude explains why my later interviews were less productive. In the earlier interviews, the tension created by fear made me think hard. As it subsided, some of my analytical edge slipped away as well. I was becoming anesthetized to the horrors of organized racism, a numbness that was personally dismaying and that also signaled my need to regain emotional distance from this research before writing about it—a process that took years.

During his lengthy convalescence from a leg injury, the neurologist Oliver Sacks discovered that his visual depth perception had become foreshortened: "Not the least part of the terror was that I experienced no terror. I had no sense, no realization, of how contracted I was, how insensibly I had become contracted to the locus of my sickbed and sickroom."[32] As I researched organized racism for more than a decade, my perceptions similarly became unconsciously attenuated. At the beginning, my insight was sharp and my emotions were constantly wrenched. Later, my vision and emotions were dulled, worn down by the emotional confinement of studying racism from within.

My experience suggests something about what it must feel to be inside a racist group: how the bizarre begins to feel normal, taken-for-granted, both unquestioned and unquestionable; how Jews or African Americans or gay men might come to seem so demonic and so personally threatening that group members could be moved to actions that seem incomprehensible to those on the outside. This state of mind results from a perceptual contraction that is all but imperceptible to the actor.

My feelings of fear also provide insight into the internal workings of racist groups. Fear is highly salient in the racist movement. Since they are greatly outnumbered by the racial, sexual, religious, and political groups they seek to destroy, organized racists use physical intimidation and the threat of violence to gain power over their opponents. Demonstrations, marches, violent propaganda, cross burnings, and terroristic actions are meant to demonstrate the strength of the racial movement and induce fear among enemies. So are the shocking cartoons and graphics that are the mainstay of racist propaganda. Racists pay close attention to their opponents' reactions, noting with glee any indication that they are feared by other groups or by the public. And fear is wielded within their groups as well. Members are warned repeatedly of the dire consequences that might befall them if they defect, particularly if they betray the group to the outside. These are not idle threats, as those who leave racist groups often risk violence at the hands of their former comrades. While I was doing these interviews, police on the East Coast were investigating the chilling abduction, assault, and near-murder of a young girl by a mixed-sex gang of skinheads who feared that she would defect from the group.

Members of the racist movement also are reminded by their groups and leaders that they have much to fear from the "outside" world. Racist activists incessantly speak of the terrors that they would face outside the protective shelter of the organized racist movement. Even for those whose initial decision to join a racist group was not driven by fear of others such concerns grew over time. In this sense, what is learned in the racist movement is fear of those who are nonwhite, non-Aryan, and nonracist.

The emotional world of organized racism becomes clearer when I consider the emotional work I needed to do to study racist groups.[33] In the course of interviewing, I constantly sensed the need to display certain feelings. Sometimes I mimicked what I did not feel, forcing myself to laugh along with the more innocuous comments, hoping to establish rapport and fend off anecdotes that might be more offensive. At other times I withheld the emotions I did feel, maintaining a blank and studied expression when confronted with cross burnings or propaganda that glorified Nazi atrocities or even the interviewee's warped take on current events. In an interview done right after the Oklahoma City bombing, as the sickening images of the bombing were still in the newspapers and fresh in my mind, a woman told me that the people in her group "were happy about what happened in Oklahoma. There's a lot of anger out there. The people, some felt sorry for the [white] children but the rest of them got what they deserved, the government deserved. The government provoked this. . . . It's like in Germany when the skinheads went on the streets and burned down the refugee centers and the townspeople poured out and applauded. It could reach that point here." Throughout, I had to feign interest in the women's intricate stories of hatred, to ask questions in a neutral tone, and to be responsive when I wanted to flee or scream. But by examining my emotional work, I gained some insight into how the racist movement manipulates the emotions of its members, evoking not just fear but also awe.

Individual and political needs collide in writing about racism. As we acknowledge the rationality of racist women, we must never forget the evil they do. Yet writing from, and about, the stories of racist women runs the risk of personalizing them too much, making their ideas more sympathetic or less odious. It may subtly lend an academic gloss to the importance of racist activists, empowering them to work harder on behalf of their beliefs.[34] These are dangerous outcomes—but the consequences of not learning from and about racists are worse.

If we stand too far back from racist groups and fail to look carefully at the women and men in organized racism, we are likely to draw politically misleading conclusions. Superficial studies simply caricature racist activists and make organized racism a foil against which we see ourselves as righteous and tolerant. We cannot simply comb the backgrounds of racist activists in search of a flaw—an absent parent, childhood victimization, or economic hard times—that "explains" their racist commitment. Moreover, we cannot use Germany in the 1930s as a prototype for all movements of the extreme right. Economic distress and social dislocation may explain the rise of such large-scale, powerful movements as the German Nazis or earlier American racist organizations, but such factors play only a small role in the tiny and politically marginal racist movement in the United States today.

We gain far more by taking a direct, hard look at the members of modern racist groups, acknowledging the commonalities between them and mainstream groups as well as the differences. In this book I tell the story of modern organized racism from the inside, focusing on how racist activists understand themselves and their worldviews. In the first section I explore the process of becoming a racist activist. Chapter 1 examines the creation of a racist self in racist groups, exploring how individuals come to adopt individual identities as racist activists. Chapters 2 and 3 focus on the formation of collective identities in racist groups, as racist group members learn about whiteness and its enemies. The second section of the book explores the world within organized racism. Chapter 4 details the gendered contours of racist groups and the contradictory experiences of women in racist groups. In chapter 5 I examine the cultural foundation of organized racism, particularly the ways in which cultural practices create political loyalties. The conclusion builds on the understandings gained in this study to offer ideas for combating racist groups.

My intent is to present organized racism critically, pointing out its conceptual errors and its loathsome implications. I assume that readers will condemn racist ideas and practices. However, I am not able here to give equal time to the voices of antiracist activists or the victims of racist violence.[35] That work is done much more effectively by antiracist monitoring and activist groups, some of which are listed in appendix 3.

BECOMING A RACIST

THE RACIST SELF

What are racist activists like? The news media typically depict them as semiarticulate, lower-class men (and sometimes women) who spew venomous sentiments about African Americans, Jews, and immigrants. Implicit is the message that people become racist activists because they hold intensely racist beliefs and want to keep racial minorities subordinated. For the same reason that poor people are expected to support welfare rights groups more readily than the wealthy do, racist groups are assumed to recruit most successfully among those who have an interest in keeping racial minorities oppressed, in particular poor whites who compete directly with minority groups for jobs, housing, and other resources.[1]

Surprisingly, recruitment by racist groups in the United States does not fit this pattern. White supremacist skinhead groups lure disaffected youth, including those from affluent suburbs. Some neo-Nazis come from politically progressive families. Even the Ku Klux Klan, traditionally the closest to the stereotype of lower-class racists, is attracting middle-class members. Interestingly, many racist groups find overwhelmingly white areas like the Pacific Northwest to be more receptive to their message than are more racially mixed regions.

Consider Jill, a young white supremacist skinhead active in neo-Nazi violence in a small western city. Jill's early life does not fit the media stereotype. Her parents were racially tolerant Democrats, she admitted to me with some embarrassment. Moreover, Jill described her family as emotionally stable and supportive. Although some interviewees distort their depictions of past family life to justify their current situations, I found Jill's account believable because she was estranged from her parents and had little reason to speak of them so warmly.

When I met her, Jill lived with a shifting group of young skinheads in a nearly empty warehouse near the center of a city. In every respect, Jill had severed her connections with mainstream society. She had no regular job, had dropped out long before completing high school, and hinted at a lengthy arrest record, mostly for minor offenses. Her life was consumed by parties with friends and the struggle to fend off what she regarded as legions of enemies—the police, landlords, African Americans, and disapproving family members. Despite her sullen and hostile demeanor, Jill talked to me at great length, perhaps passing the time until something more exciting happened.

Describing how she became a skingirl, Jill recalled, "I'd always had long beautiful hair. Everyone loved it. I went to a party and for some reason a man I'd had a crush on for a little over a year said to me, 'You would look great with a chopsie [haircut],' and I said okay, and I shaved my head." Note that at this point in her story, Jill does not connect ideas of race with her decision to shave her head. Rather disingenuously, Jill suggests that she adopted a skinhead hairstyle without considering its larger implications. "For some reason," she relates dreamily, a hoped-for boyfriend suggested that she shave her head (here, only the word *chopsie* hints at his racist affiliation). And, seeking his approval, she complied.

This minor action—cutting her hair in deference to another's tastes—is pivotal to the larger story that Jill tells. It is her shaved head, she says, that sparked a cycle of reaction that deepened her connection with members of a skinhead group:

That's when it all became very real. My parents had always known, "She's just rebelling but she's keeping up her grades and she's still working part-time and there's no problem. You know we can't control her life." Then I shaved my head. People that I worked with, you know, obviously gave me a hard time. They never said I could no longer work there, they were just teasing me, [but] I quit. My grades started to drop. My parents gave me the ultimate, "No more of this." . . . And I made the choice to leave [home] and join [the skinheads].

As she elaborates her account, Jill tells the story of her head-shaving differently, now positioning herself as the main character. The decision to cut her hair is recast: no longer simply reflecting acquiescence to an intended boyfriend, it takes its place as one in a series of rebellions from her parents. In this telling, the act of haircutting marks a boundary, signifying that Jill's parents have lost control over her life. Jill decides to quit her job, leave home, and become a white power skinhead. Neither version of the story suggests that Jill was propelled into white supremacist politics by her racial beliefs. Nor did her life circumstances (good grades, nonracist parents) appear to push her toward particularly racist ways of thinking. Indeed, Jill's entry into organized racism seems to have had the most trivial causes—teenage rebellion and a man's comment on her hairstyle.

Although Jill's story might be dismissed as an example of the political vicissitudes of youth, women commonly talk in these terms about joining racist groups. Janice, a middle-aged Aryan supremacist from the Midwest, described her move into organized racism with similar dispassion: "I met people that I knew who were white supremacists, but it didn't faze me. I guess it didn't really seem real at that point. And it was just a social thing at first and you met more people. Then I joined." Her story, like the younger Jill's, is split into two stages—an earlier period marked by her *passivity,* lack of agency, and unreality ("it didn't faze me") and a later period marked by her *choice* ("then I joined"). The dividing point is the experience of meeting racist activists. Like Jill, Janice did not characterize her entry into organized racism as a heartfelt search for a way to express her beliefs or safeguard her interests. Rather, she presented becoming a white supremacist as something that just happened, tied more closely to her social life than to her ideology.

Hardly any white supremacist women I met talked about joining organized racism as finding an outlet for long-held beliefs. Instead, their stated reasons for enlisting in racist groups appeared to have little to do with racist ideology. Nor did all these women come from backgrounds that might favor racist careers. Although some came from racist families or mixed neighborhoods filled with racial tension, others grew up in racially tolerant families or all-white suburbs. Indeed, more than one-third of the women I interviewed identified their parents as Democrats, progressives, or even leftists. Many of the other two-thirds described their parents as moderate or nonpolitical, and only a handful called them right-wing or racist.

Apparently, racist beliefs and a racist upbringing are not prerequisites for joining a racist group. As accounts by racist recruiters suggest, people can learn racist views *after* joining. Intense racism can be the result, not the cause, of involvement with organized racism. In his confessional autobiography, the German former neo-Nazi skinhead Ingo Hasselbach describes his efforts to recruit young boys: he sought not right-wing zealots but youngsters who would be attracted to the exclusive and forbidden nature of extremism. Once potential recruits were identified, Hasselbach set out to teach them racist ideas:

I liked to approach 14- to 16-year-olds after school. We looked for kids wearing bomber jackets and Dr. Martens. Usually they didn't really have a political position, but for whatever reason they'd decided it was cool to be right-wing. The first thing I did when I met one of these boys was to show that I wanted to be his friend, to hang out with him, which, coming from someone older, especially someone over 20, was a real compliment. I'd act a lot like an older brother; we'd go into the woods together and do things like Boy Scout exercises, building forts and making trails. I'd always slip in a bit of ideology against foreigners along the way. . . . But only casually at first.[2]

Similarly, the women I interviewed more often described their sense of racist urgency as a *consequence* of associating with members of racist groups than as its *cause*. Much like male and female participants in a wide variety of social movements and groups—from political parties to civic groups to bowling leagues—women in racist groups tend to be recruited by meeting someone who already belongs to the group, and they may have little prior connection to the group's ideas.[3] Fewer than one-fourth of my interviewees said that they took any action to seek out a racist group. Most had some baseline of negative sentiments toward African Americans—but given the pervasiveness of racism in the white mainstream population, that hardly explains why these particular white women entered the racist movement. In general, they became committed racists only as they got to know racist activists and began to participate in racist actions.

The most common route into organized racism clearly is through contact with a racist group member. But how does that contact occur? And why do some women cross the boundary into organized racism while others do not? Though we may never know for certain what makes any person choose to follow a specific path while another, identically situated, does not, my interviews with racist women suggest that opportunities for contact with a racist group member depend in part on social *location*. Some people are in positions and places in society that make them more likely to meet those from racist groups.[4] Those with racist activists in their families have a natural link. Those connected to groups that serve as recruiting grounds for racist organizations, such as clubs of gun owners, survivalist networks, or some hard-core music scenes, have a greater chance of meeting racist activists. The same is true for people in prisons or in those workplaces and schools where racist groups have a foothold. Even geography can play a part, as it did for Ken Loff, a convicted member of the terrorist group known as The Order: he was raised Catholic and had a Jewish best man at his wedding but drifted into the racist underground when he moved to the Pacific Northwest and met people from Aryan Nations.[5]

Of course, not all those who come into contact with racist group members join their groups. Indeed, only a small minority do so. While a few find the proffered images of community, identity, hope, and purpose very alluring, others reject such claims as fraudulent. That is, people vary in their *receptivity* to racist messages. The sociologist James Aho found that Christian Patriots in Idaho were what he termed "active seekers," poised to find a racist message persuasive.[6] The stories that racist women told me can be interpreted in the same way. As I discuss later, many women paint their lives prior to joining a racist group as a search for meaning, suggesting they would be receptive to the simplistic "answers" provided by organized racism. But dissecting people's pasts to discover motives is a tricky undertaking. These women may have been receptive because they were seeking answers—or they may be presenting themselves as seekers only in retrospect. The events in most lives can be seen as fairly haphazard or can be arranged to look like a quest for answers to personal or social problems. We must be careful not to create explanations that become a template to which all evidence can be shaped.

Ultimately, location in society, like differences in receptivity, cannot fully account for the entrance of certain women into racist groups. Some of the women I interviewed drifted from one extreme cause to another, but others came into organized racism from a life seemingly in the mainstream. Some had friends who steadfastly refused to be involved in racist groups even when those closest to them joined, but other women gravitated to racist groups on the strength of a brief acquaintance with a group member. A nineteen-year-old skinhead described her first encounter with white supremacists:

Well, they used to have like Bible studies here, the white supremacists here. . . . I went to them even though I'm not necessarily all for the

Bible but I went there and started getting involved with them, and they would have like demonstrations and marches and stuff around here. So I started going with them to offer support and then. . . . Well, a friend of mine went to one of their meetings one time and she told me about it and then I went to it the next week, and then I started getting involved in it.

This skingirl came in contact with racist activists through an interest in Bible studies, which might also indicate her receptivity to their dualistic visions of good and evil. But nothing in her story suggests that she was seeking an outlet for racist politics when she began going to white supremacist meetings. Rather, she presents organized racism as something that just happened *to* her, the result of a series of minor actions pursued without a particular political objective.[7]

She is not the only woman who drifted into a racist group because of an accidental encounter. Many recount connecting up with old friends who had taken up with racist groups or chancing to meet someone involved in the racist movement. One woman told me of becoming reacquainted with Bill, a former classmate active in organized racism, while she was on vacation: "I'm thinking, 'Oh, well. I haven't seen him for a while. I wondered what's going on with him.' Went up and talked to him. Now, he always used to be known as 'Nazi Bill.' I could take it or leave it, didn't matter. Now, Bill seemed like he was pretty good people. He was a cool guy." It is disturbing to think that becoming racist may be even partly a matter of chance. Yet accident clearly plays a role in leading many of these women into racist politics. The places they lived or worked, the kinds of friends they had, how they spent their time, where they partied, and their general susceptibility to racist appeals all were important in their becoming racist activists. But these factors alone do not predict who will come into contact with a racist group and who will not, who will find their life transformed by organized racism and who will not. Simple happenstance is often an element of racist affiliation.

It is hard to reconcile such casual motives with the dangers of joining organized racism. Though being on the fringe of society is appealing to some, most women find that the cost is high. Enlisting in the Klan or neo-Nazi groups can mean the loss of a job or career. Nearly everyone who joins loses friends and family members, and some risk their lives. Scholarship on right-wing extremist groups suggests three possible explanations for why women like Jill or Janice embark on a life of racist activism for reasons that, on their own account, appear so flimsy.

First, these women could be the victims of "brainwashing." This notion, commonly found in studies of prisoners or kidnapping victims who come to identify with their captors, is used to explain how groups can command allegiance, even loyalty, from originally recalcitrant or hostile individuals. Although the simplicity of this explanation is appealing, the women I interviewed showed no signs of having been coerced into racist activism; their statements gave no hint of intense pressure to join racist groups or adopt racist ideas. To the contrary, Jill and Janice describe being in white supremacism as an *option* in their lives, a path chosen rather than imposed.

Second, they (and all adherents to right-wing extremism) could be crazy or ill-adjusted.[8] Certainly, some women I interviewed showed signs of personal pathologies or had troubled family histories. But I could not determine whether their psychological disorders were a cause or an outcome of their being in a racist group. And the racism of Jill and Janice, the educated and articulate products of stable middle-class families, cannot be explained by a deficient family life.

Third, Jill, Janice, and the others could be rational (if deplorable) political actors trying to gain advantages or stave off threats to their social, political, or economic status.[9] Such an explanation, an interest-based account of racist activism, has several advantages. It acknowledges that racist groups vow to safeguard white and Christian dominance, a promise that appeals to the self-interest of many in the racist movement. It enables us to consider how some women might see organized racism as personally beneficial. It suggests that some aspects of racist groups, however odious to outsiders, might reasonably be found compelling. And it moves us beyond assuming, without evidence, that racists are brainwashed or crazy. Yet it cannot fully explain the motivations of racist women, since the advantages of organized racism for its members are less clear for women than for men. In addition to espousing racial and religious superiority, racist groups promote ideas of individualism, antiegalitarianism, nationalism, and traditional morality that are arguably harmful to, or at least problematic for, women. Individualism evokes the authority of self-reliant men over dependent women and children. Antiegalitarianism opposes efforts to curb the dominance of white men in workplaces and schools. Nationalism strengthens political identities of citizenship to which women are less securely attached. Traditional morality evokes a white patriarchal past.

Because women's interests and the agendas of racist movements do not clearly match, even an interest-based account must fall back on another, less satisfactory explanation—that men enlist in right-wing and racial politics to preserve or extend their obvious, identifiable interests and privileges, while women join because they are confused, are led astray by male intimates, or misidentify their interests. Thus, in a familiar pattern, women's actions are explained by appealing to psychology and men's to politics,[10] even though there is no reason to assume that psychological factors are more salient for the women than the men in organized racism. In fact, the life stories of racist women suggest no difference in political commitment, knowledge, or gullibility: women, like their male counterparts, are drawn into racist groups through personal contacts with racist activists. Jill, Janice, and other women racists are better understood as rational social actors, a characterization long applied to men, than as idiosyncratic and peculiarly compliant racist followers.

But how can racist commitment be both rational and the product of casual acquaintance with a racist activist? How can women stumble into and yet embrace such a risky life? To understand this, we must modify the interest-based account of racist activism. We must consider how someone's understanding of what is in their self-interest—what is a rational political act—can be shaped in a social context. In other words, we must think of self-interest as socially constructed.[11] The racist women I interviewed joined male-dominated racist groups not because they were unaware of what was in their interests as women but because, as part of becoming racist activists, they reassessed their self-interests to fit the agendas of these groups. As they became involved with organized racism, they remade themselves in a racist mold. Men in racist groups also undergo social construction of a racist self, but their initial sense of their self-interest is much closer than the women's to the goals of racist groups.

Originally, neither Jill nor Janice was very focused on racism. Both held only ill-defined ideas, if any, about their self-interest as whites.[12] Once involved with racist group members, however, each began to consider herself and the world in more racialized terms. Jill changed from a stance of political apathy to what she described as "racial awareness," Janice from skirting the edges of white supremacism to speaking on its behalf. In the process, both Jill and Janice came to see their interests as diametrically opposed to those of non-Aryans.

The definition of self-interest is influenced by social interactions.[13]

Such influence can be seen in racist women's lengthy responses to my request that they describe themselves and their lives, that they provide their "life stories." As Jill became involved with racist skinheads, ideas about race became more important to her. She came to see her self-interest as opposed not so much to parents or school authorities as to racial minorities. Janice, too, responded to the shifting social contexts in which she found herself by reassessing her self-interest and identifying more strongly with organized white supremacism.

Because self-interest is not static, we cannot deduce the motives of racist activists from their backgrounds or current circumstances. Too often, commentaries on right-wing extremists are based on what the sociologists John Lofland and Norman Skonovd label "the fallacy of the uniformly profound"—the assumption that dramatic life outcomes must have dramatic causes.[14] Thus analysts comb the past lives of racist activists, searching for the unusual events that can explain their subjects' present racial beliefs. Yet it is impossible to account for the racist activism of Jill, Janice, or most of the other women in this study by scrutinizing the events of their lives, which are mostly unremarkable. Even the circumstances that led them into encounters with racist activists are highly variable, fortuitous rather than predictable. The dramatic political outcomes of racist activism typically had quite mundane beginnings.

In their life stories, racist women reveal more than changing definitions of self-interest. They also relate the alterations in their very sense of who they are, their sense of self. Over time, Jill began to define herself through her racist activism. No longer "just another teenager," she was "someone who is proud to represent and protect my race." Janice, too, changed her sense of self; from someone with no particular political vision she became a person deeply committed to "make the world right."

The stories of racist women are important because it is through storytelling, or what scholars term "narrative," that people create a sense of themselves. Narratives integrate the various threads of life. They assemble incidents of the past to fashion a self in the present. Life stories thus are retrospectively "sense making," making the self coherent over time.[15] At the same time, however, life stories can be unreliable. Accounts of the past are tinged by the commitments of the present. The sociologist C. Wright Mills's insight that motives often are furnished "after the act" should caution us against taking expressed motives at face value. As the sociologist David Snow and his colleagues find, in social movements " 'motives' for joining or continued participation are generally emergent and interactional rather than pre-structured."[16]

Events and circumstances in the past are highlighted in memory when they seem to lead to the circumstances of the present and ignored when they do not: "some aspects of the past are jettisoned, others are redefined, and some are put together in ways that would have previously been inconceivable."[17] Thus women for whom racist activism was an abrupt change from their past lives paint their backgrounds bleakly, as inadequate or confusing. Those few for whom racist activism was lifelong speak of their past more positively.

Life stories also create templates of action. The sociologist Margaret Somers notes that narratives "can be a precondition for knowing what to do." When people tell stories about themselves, points out the social psychologist Margaret Wetherell, they "are attempting to develop positions which might relate their current lives to what has gone before, rendering the past, the present and the future plausible and meaningful." Life stories thus justify and make sense of current political directions that might appear inconsistent with the values and directions of an earlier life. Moreover, the relationship between storytelling and other action is dynamic. Actions shape new stories, just as narratives create new directions for action.[18]

To align themselves with racial goals, racial activists transform their understandings of self. As one southern Klanswoman put it: "It is not so much that I am in the Klan, it is the fact that the Klan is in me. By the Klan being in me I have no choice other than to remain, I can't walk away from myself." Another woman, from a neo-Nazi group, commented: "[The movement] helps, especially at that awkward stage when no one exactly knows who they are. It gives you an identity, it says you're special, you know, because you're white."

By constructing a racial sense of self and self-interest, and by learning racist group ideologies (discussed in the following chapters), fairly ordinary women, most from typical families and places, become wedded to dangerous and bizarre racist agendas.

STORIES OF A RACIST SELF

The life stories of racist women vividly exemplify how notions of self and self-interest can be fashioned in a racist social context. Their accounts offer two different stories of the self. What I call *stories of becoming a racist* tell of transformations in the story of the *past* self; what

I call *stories about being a racist* detail changes in the *current* and *future* self.

Stories of Becoming a Racist

Some women explain their involvement in organized racism by presenting it as the result of dramatic personal transformation. These are stories of *becoming* a racist. Although a few women I interviewed grew up in racist activist families, most did not, and their stories of coming to the racist movement reflect this change.

For racist women, accounts of personal transformation typically take the form of a conversion story, not unlike stories told by converts to religion, sobriety, or feminism.[19] In his studies of the fascist British National Front, Michael Billig discusses this conversion as a process of adopting the official personality of the group, of redefining reality in accord with their new values and beliefs.[20] Similarly, racist women recount a change in their total worldview, a shift in their "sense of ultimate grounding."[21] As converts to racial activism, they describe moving from racial naïveté to racist enlightenment. In their life stories, the more mundane details of actual recruitment to racist groups are glossed over or omitted. What they stress—indeed, what they remember—is a sense of the changed self.

Conversion stories are a narrative genre. Typically, they involve three elements: autobiographical incidents, themes from the larger culture, and ideas from the group to which the teller is converting.[22] Thus a religious conversion story generally details the sense of meaninglessness or family problems that dominated the nonspiritual life; the power of religious faith to help the convert achieve greater personal happiness, inner strength, or other goods valued in the culture generally; and the spiritual enlightenment made possible by the newly acquired religious beliefs. The racist conversion stories related by women in my interviews similarly draw on autobiography, mainstream culture, and racist ideologies.

Events of the Individual's Past Autobiographical elements dominate racist conversion stories, as the women string together what they now see as the most significant incidents of their past. In selecting the events that give shape to their life stories, racist women are strongly influenced by their current racist commitments. The importance of events that illustrate racial conflict—even those that perhaps seemed insignificant at the time—is magnified. For example, clashes with children from other races on school buses or playgrounds that seem trivial to me frequently loom large in racist women's stories. Such incidents probably take on their personal significance, or perhaps are seen as racial at all, only in retrospect. The racist world in which these women now live shapes what they tell about their past.

Themes from Mainstream Culture Four themes from mainstream culture appear frequently in these conversion stories: religion, body, boundaries, and quest. The first is the most common: even women in racist groups that virulently reject mainline religion for favoring racial equality construct their life stories as a spiritual conversion. They recount their turn to racism as moving from evil to ultimate good, prompted by the promise of personal and collective salvation. Such stories, like the accounts of religious transitions examined by Virginia Brereton, have at best a "complex relationship" to the real ordering of life events;[23] but they do attest to the power of religion as a narrative genre.

Too, the body figures often in conversion stories. Some describe an assault on the body—an invasion, attack, or trauma—as moving them to active racism. Others express the absorption of racial commitment into the body—"I am in the Klan [and] the Klan is in me"—as marking conversion to the racial movement.

Boundaries also play a crucial role, because racist women present their commitment to racism as a move across the divide separating their earlier and subsequent life worlds. Sometimes they emphasize their informed decision to move away from one world and embrace another. One woman told me, "Being part of the movement, I have more of a commitment to want to separate [from minority groups] and do what I believe is right and stand together with people and not be so quick to be divided by other people." Others stress the boundaries imposed from the outside, seen as forcibly separating them from their earlier life. Laura, for example, remarked: "[After I became a Nazi], I was very surprised when one of my friends from church stopped calling. I said [to a mutual friend], 'How is she? She hasn't called me or returned a call that I had made to her,' and he said, 'She's afraid to come here.' I said, 'What? How can that be?'"

The idea of a quest is important in all conversion narratives. In her study of women's conversion to holiness and Pentecostal religions, Brereton identified two such stories. One is constructed as "a series of quests, with each quest becoming more intense, more extreme, the result more rewarding." The other features "a deep dark valley (conviction) followed by a high bright peak (conversion), followed in turn by a series of progressively less extreme valleys and peaks (periods of backsliding and renewal)."[24]

The story related by Nancy, a white supremacist skinhead and neo-Nazi organizer from the Southwest, mirrored Brereton's plot of successive enlightenment: "It was pretty gradual. I gradually started writing to other organizations and I started getting other publications and newsletters and started writing articles of my own and then I just gradually got into more and more until I opened the post office boxes [for a neo-Nazi group]. It was really gradual. It wasn't just like I woke up one day and decided, 'Oh I'm gonna go and do that.' I slowly got into it." In contrast, a long account by Lillie, a midwestern supporter of a national Nazi group, typifies a conversion story of valleys and peaks. Her entry into organized racism was a decade-long struggle to accept "the truth" of Nazism. Despite her initial "excitement" at finding "the truth that made sense" and her insistence that Nazi doctrine should be credited with "freeing" her from a life of drugs and confusion, Lillie joined and then quit a number of racist organizations because she feared the possible consequences of being an active Nazi; she had repeatedly reverted to her old life of apolitical partying before finding her current group.

Ideologies of Racist Groups Just as religious organizations provide specific frameworks that teach people how to think about their spiritual conversion,[25] so, too, racist groups shape the individual stories of their converts. Because racist ideologies starkly separate "us" from "them," racist conversion stories tend to split into two parts. They begin with a weak, ignorant, directionless, and naive self that is abandoned and replaced by a newly constructed all-knowing, committed, impassioned self.

The racist group message that racial "enemies" are everywhere and that Aryans are victims also permeates the life stories of racist women. For example, racist women talk of their fear that they will be victimized if they are identified as Nazis, sounding a theme of persecution that is common among racist groups. Their conversion stories are filled with episodes of social sanction, describing how "I lost a lot of friends at first because my friends were antiracist" or how "people pass judgment on [white power] skinheads. Just because their heads are shaven, they are looked down on," and insisting that "you get pulled over by the cops around here because they saw your face on TV and they know you're a racist. And they write you a ticket just for the heck of it." The more violent incidents that they recount eerily mirror the experiences of minority group members at the hands of avowed racists: "A friend of mine had a friend who was shot simply for being a skinhead. He had done nothing provoking others and a Negro came up to him and asked him, 'Are you a skinhead?'—I suppose because he had a shaved head. All he did was reply, 'Yes,' and he was shot and killed."

The interweaving of autobiographical episodes, themes from mainstream culture, and the ideologies of racist groups informs both the general shape of these conversion stories and the women's understanding of specific turning points in their lives. As they reflect on their earlier, nonpolitical life, many seize on a single sensational event or tightly linked series of events to explain how their personal goals and beliefs became fused with the agendas and ideas of the racial movement. This dramatic pivot might have had little significance in their life stories before they joined a racist group. After joining, however, it is seen as a moment of decisive awakening that reveals the essential difference between clarity and confusion and between likeness and otherness, making them acutely aware that Jews, African Americans, or agents of the federal government control the economy, politics, even the minutiae of daily life.

Heidi, a Christian Identity adherent, described to me her "awakening" after seeing the biased news coverage of a criminal trial of white separatists: "I realized that what you hear on the television and everything is not the true story. They don't tell you all the persecution that's happening to people who want to [racially] separate today. We just hear little snippets of it and then if you investigate you find out the *true* story."

Though they present abstract rationales for subsequent racial activism, conversion stories imply a personal experience that crystallizes understanding and prompts a voyage of discovery—even when that pivotal event bears no recognizable connection to the individual's life. An elderly Nazi woman recalled that her turning point came when a federal commission investigating her local schools, to which she had no personal link, concluded that "there was no racial animosity or hostility" in them: "They just whitewashed it. Even the school officials would not return the calls of upset parents. The school board members would not see parents in their office or anything during that time."

Strikingly, many stories of conversion to racist activism pivot around dramatic encounters with death—a personal near-death experience, the loss of a loved one, even the death of a pet. Individual stories of bodily trauma and pain are transformed into a story of racist conversion. They are recast as ordeals that clarified racial perception, sharpened values about race, and revealed the racial dynamics of history.[26]

Amanda, a twenty-three-year-old racist skinhead on death row for murder and robbery in a southern state, cited a car accident as her personal turning point; after she was injured, "it's like, my whole attitude changed . . . my mind focused more on white supremacy." In contrast to Jill, the skinhead who had nonracist parents, Amanda recalled being taught racism by her parents "since the day I was born." However, she never felt inclined to act on those beliefs until she awoke from a coma. Amanda's descriptions of the loss of control she felt as a hospital patient—"IVs in my arms, tubes in my nose"—blurred together with images of African American nurses surrounding her bedside, probing and invading her body. Her assertions of self against the dehumanization and bodily invasion of the hospital thus took on a racialized cast for which her earlier belief system had prepared her: "I said [to the African American nurses], 'Don't touch me. Don't get near me . . . leave me alone.'" It was this incident, she concluded, that brought her into a "racial awareness" that made her get involved with neo-Nazi gangs. And, indeed, what Amanda tells of her life after hospitalization reflects a new racial commitment. Speaking of a cousin who had married an African American man, she said that before the accident she had been cordial to her, seeing family loyalty as more important than race; but afterward, "that was it. . . . I walked out the door and I haven't spoken to her since."

Other conversion-by-near-death stories put the antecedents rather than the outcomes of personal catastrophe in racial terms. That of Judy, a prominent middle-aged Aryan leader on the East Coast, was typical. Her racial commitment was born when she was seriously injured in a hit-and-run accident while living in a impoverished area of Cleveland. The beginnings of her life story provided little hint that racism would become so important to her. The daughter of middle-class parents, Judy began her marriage to an upwardly mobile professional man optimistically. As she spoke of those years she focused on domestic events—marriage, pregnancy, child rearing. She said she was determined to stay away from social problems by staying close to home and following her parents' advice: "don't be prejudiced, try to get along, do your best you can do." Even as she described a series of personal calamities—a miscarriage, divorce, and her rapid downward economic slide, with her two small children—Judy continued to present herself as determined and self-possessed.

But when she spoke of taking her children to Cleveland in search of better employment, Judy's story shifted. The accident—and its racial ramifications—became the core around which her life story unfolded. Judy took nearly an hour to tell me about her accident, as she tried to convey how her racist ideas had resulted from her personal experiences.

As she began her story about Cleveland, Judy described at length her struggle to maintain a "decent" life in squalid surroundings, providing a bridge between her self-assurance before the accident and her racial awareness after it. She presented herself as confident but also, in retrospect, as innocent about "the neighborhood": "Now mind you the neighborhood is not good at all. But I'm thinking, okay, no problem, I just started this job . . . I'll stay here till the end of summer, by winter I'm straight, I got myself a good job. I can transfer my job. I reestablish myself and then I'll be back on towards [another neighborhood] which is a very good area." To this point, the neighborhood's problems appear to be economic, not racial. But as her story progresses, it becomes less abstract and more racialized: the hard work of whites (to get to work, to keep a job, to find babysitters) is set against the inactivity of her African American neighbors. Now, racial factors are clear: "they" are responsible for the "bad" neighborhood, and Judy sees "them" as black.

I want to make my money and get the hell out of this bad neighborhood. And it was bad, but I thought, "Oh I can do this, I'll just be real quiet and they won't mess with me and they won't have no problem with me anyway." (laugh) Well, then the blacks started to holler after me when they catch me coming in and out. . . . And it's like, "Hey," you know, "Hey, woman, we want you come on down here. What you got, don't talk to black people?" You know, I was just trying to mind my own business.

Judy's racist views, though increasingly pronounced, here differ little from those of many other whites. According to her, they shifted into racial activism because *she* changed. Her ability to coexist with her African American neighbors and ignore their now-obvious crime and indolence had depended on racial naïveté. Once she became more "aware," such unconscious acceptance was no longer possible. Being struck by a car was the event that destroyed Judy's innocence and began her transformation. Key to this process was her certainty that "they" were responsible for the accident. Although she acknowledged that she did not see the driver who hit her, Judy nonetheless maintained that it "must have been" an African American man from a neighboring house: "I ignored them but then I was hit by that car . . . I swear they hit me on purpose . . . because I would not have anything to do with them."

Like Amanda, Judy described her racist action as following, almost unbidden, from her racial awakening: "Of course after I got hit by a car, that was *it* . . . I started getting into politics." By assuming that the driver was African American, she made sense of this otherwise random tragedy, according it intent and purpose. Moreover, such a racial lens made sense of the financial and other hardships that she faced as a divorced mother with limited opportunities. But such racialized understanding did not come incrementally, or as the result of economic frustrations alone. Rather, for Judy becoming a racist was a sudden metamorphosis. She now saw the world as a racial battleground, and she had a sense of purpose. From that point on, Judy told me, her life was devoted to furthering Aryan supremacy.

The life story of Greta, a fifty-five-year-old Nazi from a small northern city, had a similar structure of racial awakening. The daughter of a wealthy doctor, Greta was herself a well-paid engineer; she admitted to me that for most of her life she did not hold racist or anti-Semitic views, an oversight she now sees as demonstrating her earlier "ignorance." Part of her life story involved a complicated medical history. For her, the pivotal moment came in an operating room when she was being prepared for surgery. Note Greta's increasingly conspiratorial tones, as she comes to see her situation as embodying the struggle between Aryan and Jew:

There was nobody in there. No instruments, nothing. Then a man appeared from behind me and said he's my anesthesiologist. We started talking, I sat on that operating table, that iron metal thing, and he said, "Where are you from?" I said, "I'm from Germany." I had long blond hair and my face was clear, wonderful complexion. At that time still I believed and trusted completely. . . . He said "Well, I'm gonna give you the anesthesia now." I inhaled and realized that I couldn't exhale . . . he was just sitting there watching me . . . I wanted to say, "I can't breathe," [but] I had no more voice.

In this account, German (Aryan) innocence is counterposed against a disembodied but menacing presence who can literally take away voice and breath. Much later in the story, Greta interprets the encounter in a way that simultaneously explains and structures her life story. As she attempted to build a medical malpractice case against the doctor and hospital, Greta met a woman who encouraged her to see her experience as one incident in a larger but vague conspiracy and who later introduced her to a local Nazi member from whom she learned the specifics of the conspiracy. These meetings led Greta to the "discovery" that her anesthesiologist was Jewish and that the hospital—along with the media, the government, nearly everything—was owned and controlled by Jews. Jews are both sinister and invisible, Greta concluded. That invisibility is the key to their awesome power to control the fate of unsuspecting Aryans.

The emphasis on pivotal personal events in the stories of Amanda, Judy, and Greta both reveals and conceals. It reveals how racist women reshape stories, even memories, of their past to fit their present racist activism. But it conceals how racist recruiting and conversion actually occur incrementally. Research on other extremist groups has demonstrated that slow changes are often buried in stories of dramatic transformation. In their study of terrorists, for example, Maxwell Taylor and Ethel Quayle find that personal events can establish "a boundary in many terrorist careers that marks a movement away from normal society," yet "the identification of a precipitating event can also be a convenient post hoc rationalisation for a much more mundane process of gradual involvement."[27] Indeed, Greta's story illustrates how minor events can shape a racist career. A chance encounter with the conspiratorial woman precipitated a series of events that eventually culminated in her recruitment into a racist group. Greta's subsequent, and decisive, meeting with the local Nazi member depended on that prior, accidental meeting.[28]

The life stories of racist women are useful but complicated. While they show how activists mold themselves to the ideologies of racist groups, they are unreliable as accounts of actual political recruitment or ideological conversion. In fact, almost all the women interviewed, when pressed to construct detailed chronologies of their lives, reveal a pattern of recruitment to racial politics quite at odds with conversion-by-striking-event. Judy's accident, for example, brought her not simply a blinding moment of awareness, as she first recounted, but contact with a locally prominent neo-Nazi who, she later told me, took care of her during her convalescence. Similarly, pursuit of a medical malpractice claim—not a sudden realization in the hospital—brought Greta together with local white power activists.

James Aho documents a similar pattern of incremental, personal recruitment among Christian Patriots. Cindy Cutler, the wife of an Aryan Nations leader, discovered Christian Identity after meeting her future husband at a Baptist church service. Lisa Minor, also in Aryan Nations, found racist activism when she met her husband after she had renounced her drug-centered life and had become "born again." Men typically entered the movement in roughly the same way. As Aho notes, "with few exceptions, social bonding with the recruiter preceded the respondent's intellectual commitment to the cause." Aho's conclusion, consistent with my findings, was that Christian Patriots "joined with others and only later began articulating [the cause's] dogma."[29]

Thus, racial conversion stories are best understood not as literal accounts of the process of ideological transformation but as *learned* accounts, shaped retrospectively by mainstream cultural themes as well as by the political, ideological, and even stylistic conventions dominant in racist groups.

Sarah's Story The story of Sarah, an older neo-Nazi activist, is worth exploring in some detail as an example of the construction of self along racist lines. Despite Sarah's reputation as a "hard-core" Nazi and her numerous arrests for violent acts over a lengthy career in organized racism—both factors that might have made her reticent in the interview—she needed little prompting to give an elaborate account of her life, which she organized as a series of passages.

Sarah's opening statement, "You know, my views have changed tremendously over the years," established the recurrent theme of ideological change. It was illustrated by groups of incidents bundled together. The sequence of events in each episode was the same: Sarah experienced unjust treatment, perceived its unfairness, initially did nothing, and ultimately was forced to defend herself. Over time, Sarah changed: her responses to this pattern altered. She saw herself as getting smarter through experience, as she became more adept at finding the racial causes of her problems.

Sarah began with her childhood: "I was raised in Chicago. In order to get an education you literally had to beat, no, let's not be nasty (laugh), you had to be adept to get an education because if you didn't then the blacks would just keep beating you and robbing you." She described the injustice of having to walk miles to school every day in snow and rain while African Americans were bused to school in a "nice warm bus" and of having to suffer assaults by African American girls who would "not allow" her to enter the school lavatory "without a black eye, a bloody nose, or [being] stabbed." Sarah wasn't sure what to do: "Finally one day I got sick of it. Finally one day I decided it was enough. This was bullshit. I'm going to the ladies' room. I have every right as much as they do. I continue to try to mind my own business. I decided I'm not gonna speak about it any more. I'm gonna do it. . . . I decided I was gonna put my makeup on."

Sarah's decision was sparked not by a sense of racial injustice but by her emerging adolescent sexuality, what she termed "new thinking about boys." She decided that she needed access to the ladies' room to remove her leggings and straighten her skirt ("put your skirt down right") and to fix her makeup ("a little mascara, not too much makeup, but enough") in order "to be somebody." When she entered, seven African American girls verbally harassed her: "And Jessie said, 'Well, you going to have to fight.' I said, 'Yeah, I figured that's all you are. I have to fight seven of you, one of me.' And I never wanted to start none of this crap to begin with." This incident settled a racial grid on Sarah's life. Jessie, one of the African American girls, had been her friend but now regarded her in a racial way that made them antagonists. "We're not friends anymore. Why not? Because I'm a honky now." A fight ensued and Sarah was stabbed—presumably by one of the African American girls, though her story did not make this point clear.

This theme, established in the elementary school drama, recurs in three more episodes in Sarah's story: as a high school student, as a young working woman, and as a new mother. Each time, Sarah contends, her efforts to maintain racial harmony were thwarted by African Americans who reacted to her solely on the basis of color. Although similarly structured, each episode conveyed Sarah's growing sense of racial, and racist, awareness, demonstrating a racial "learning" culled from prior episodes.

In high school, for example, Sarah portrays herself as trying to maintain her distance from the African American students in her school ("I was cool with a couple of them"). Again, circumstances—this time, the changing racial demographics of her high school—intervene to prevent her strategy from working: "Everything was fine until more moved in." Again, she portrays herself as unfairly cast in sharply racist terms ("Then I became a nobody. Then I was like I was a honky") and forced into racial action: "Enough is enough. I gotta do what I gotta do. . . . It got to a point I had to fight." In this way personal narratives absorbed the structure of a racist ideology that depicts the world as sharply divided between friend and foe and history as controlled by enemies.

Accounts like Sarah's share with other conversion stories a retrospective construction of self, a creation of autobiography. They impart an order to what otherwise might seem a disorderly, even chaotic, series of life events and decisions.[30] Moreover, they accord intent, calculation, and meaning to radical changes in identity.

Racist conversion stories fashion autobiography by relying on clues from earlier experiences to explain the present racist self. They thereby accord an essential authenticity to the racist self, making current racist ideas seem to be an expression of lifelong inclinations:

I was like really angry when I was about fourteen, right before I started getting involved with white power. And then in the past couple of years, I mean, I study a lot and I kind of changed from, like, anger to, like, pride. And now I'm proud of race [rather than only] being angry about society.

[When I found] the pro-white movement from my cousins and then started thinking, you know, that they had a lot of good stuff to say, I knew [it was true] that race mixing hurts not only society, but it hurts the offspring of it.

The emergent self becomes defined as the normal and true:

I met with these Klan guys five or six times. . . . They started coming to the house. We went to some rallies. After I started meeting these people I was just amazed how normal they were. It drove me crazy, the things I was excluded from [earlier] since I wasn't a member.

Along with their parallels to other accounts of conversion, racist conversion stories also have unique aspects. These usually reflect the secretive and semi-illegal nature of many racist groups as well as their marginality. For example, none of the racist women mention an obligation to evangelize about the specifics of their conversion experiences, as other converts commonly do. Most racist women are interested in bringing other Aryans into the racist movement, but they do not describe their own experiences of transformation when trying to persuade others to join. Thus one woman commented that she recruited fifteen friends into Nazism "by simply telling them the facts about world affairs." A Christian Identity adherent took a similarly impersonal approach to recruiting friends into the movement: "I gave them literature and books to read and talked to them about white history, pride in your race, and related issues."

Furthermore, racist accounts rarely draw on the motifs of self-effacement common in other conversion stories. Racists, unlike former alcoholics who often talk of "hitting bottom," do not describe being forced by circumstance to admit that their life is on the wrong track. Nor does the idea of being forced to admit something about oneself to others, a common motif in the coming-out stories of lesbians and gay men, surface in the talk of racist women. Although they present their former (nonracist) lives as incomplete or bad, they rarely portray those earlier selves as unstable or off-balance, as those describing experiences of religious conversion often do.[31] And they convey little sense of the self-abasement in awe of a greater power that structures accounts of conversion to religion or sobriety. Instead, many racist women tell stories of efforts at self-empowerment through activism, even though, as I discuss below, few conclude that those efforts have in fact succeeded.

Stories of Being a Racist

While stories of becoming a racist situate new racist commitments as rational outcomes of an unfolding self, stories of *being* a racist tell of the present and future racist self. In "becoming" stories, both the conclusion and the major themes are fixed by current identities, but "being" stories are more open. The future, an extrapolation from the present, can take more than one form.

For racist women, these two kinds of stories are quite different. Their accounts of becoming a racist are filled with action, agency, and self-empowerment. They cast life as movement, direction, and change. These tales focused on racial conversion acknowledge previous mistakes and racial blindness; but at their core, they are full of self-satisfaction and zeal. They proclaim that only through racial commitment can an authentic self—a coherent, true identity—be found. Joining a racist group is an accomplishment, a task of self-completion.

In contrast, stories of being a racist—stories of now and the future—are passive and guarded. Although some women, especially those who are very young or in white power skinhead groups, talk of organized racism as a means of empowering themselves, most speak with less assurance and even describe the personal toll of being in racist groups. Their stories of becoming a racist contain a sense of possibility, but their stories of being a racist are defeatist.

That negative tone is surprising, for in the genre of political testimonies—on the left or right—we typically find great excitement. Even contemporary racist activists, whose racist commitments stigmatize them and marginalize them politically, usually appear in published accounts as adventurous or spirited. There can be great personal fulfillment in racist political action; as the social psychologist Raphael Ezekiel comments, "Organizing is the leader's jones. He has to have it. Like every jones, it is his world, his lover, his identity. Without it he is nothing; when engaged, he is God."[32]

Such accounts, however, focus almost entirely on men. The sense of satisfaction widely observed among male racist leaders and evident in the self-aggrandizing autobiographies published in racist propaganda is rarely found among women. These women present racial "enlightenment" in terms of passive resignation at best, and more often with despair—as a burden, an onerous responsibility, an unwanted obligation.[33] They discuss their racial mission with little bluster and almost no swagger. In contrast to the male members of the British National Front studied by Ezekiel, who were eager to impart the fascists' party line to others, the racist activist women I interviewed were reluctant to describe political knowledge as preferable to ignorance. As one Nazi group member told me, "It's painful, it hurts, it's all-consuming when you have the knowledge." Another said flatly, "If I had to do it over again, I wouldn't want to know anything." A member of an Aryan supremacist group commented, "It's hard feeling this duty to alert other people."[34]

Although almost one-half of the women said that they had tried to recruit others into the movement, nearly all were hesitant, even negative, about enlisting immediate family members, especially their own children (whether those children were real or only prospective). As one Nazi survivalist stated, "I won't teach my children to be political . . . I don't want them to have that burden." A Nazi skinhead declared that she did not want her children to be active racists, though her husband did: "It's too much responsibility. I want them to have the knowledge, but I don't want them to have to go through what I have gone through. What maybe I still will go through." An incarcerated white supremacist similarly cited the danger of being a racist, saying that she was trying to make sure that her son did not become involved because "the house would be burned down overnight." A Klanswoman said that she "wouldn't encourage anyone to join—it's just something I did."

Many seemed ambivalent about recruiting outside their own family as well. When I asked one Klanswoman whether she brought her friends to Klan meetings, she told me that she did not, because "they don't like to go out at night." Questioned about whether she recruited among the young people who hung out at her house, another woman said that she did not, because "young people today have no stick-to-it-iveness. If some little thing turns up that just doesn't suit them, they're quitters." Most efforts to recruit were portrayed as casual efforts, such as "sharing literature and pro-white books" or "introducing friends to some people involved with the movement."

Even women who brought their children to racist events could show surprisingly little determination that they should become activist adults.

[I took] them to the dedication of the white race. . . . We dressed the kids up in fatigues and little hats because I didn't have time to make little robes, and we took them and we had them dedicated [to white supremacism. . . . It's my responsibility to train these two [but] they can make their own choice when they come of age.

I hope my children will be involved or at least understand why their father and I are involved but I will not force anything on my children.

I really can't say whether or not my children will join [our Nazi group]. They will be raised National Socialist with racial pride, family values, and morals.

Racist activist women attempt to reconcile this personal reluctance with their ideological commitment to recruit in one of two ways. Some simply hope that racial separation will increase sufficiently that by the time their children are adults, they will be able to live in an all-white world without incurring the costs and risks of racial activism.

I want them to have a strong opinion. If we can get into a community where they can just live their lives and not have to be political activists, I think that would be great.

I wouldn't want them to get political . . . I really believe that it would be better if people . . . had the right to live with other people who were just white people.

Others reason that once taught that nonwhites are different, their children will naturally segregate themselves by race as adults. A midwestern Nazi whose house is festooned with disgusting and violent images of African Americans and Jews spoke disingenuously but revealingly of her children, "I don't teach them hatred of other races, but I do teach them that we are definitely different." Similarly, a white supremacist whose racist husband is serving a prison term for assaulting an African American man described with remarkable vagueness how she educates her daughter about the races: "My daughter understands. She knows she's a special person. . . . It's the little things. When she didn't know what a black kid was, I explained that she's different because of her color, to let her know that she shouldn't be involved with nonwhites. I don't push her to believe any beliefs."

In addition, many women took pains to deny their own racial activism. Even some who were in minor leadership roles claimed that they were not activists, or that they tried not to be "too active," or that they were active only when it was "necessary for survival." As a prominent Aryan supremacist commented when discussing her own affiliation with a violent racist group, "I was in kind of an unaware state [when I joined]." Some described their work as "very limited" or "only helping out." Others denied that their work had an effect outside "its own little boundaries."

There was a sharp contrast between these women's descriptions of their groups and of themselves. Most claimed that their racist group was making great strides, "getting stronger," "attracting new members," or on the brink of "awakening the white race." Such exaggeration of strength is a tactic used by racist groups to intimidate opponents, and these women easily slipped into the propaganda they had been trained to spout. But when they spoke of their own roles in the racist movement, few sounded so heroic; instead, they used passive and even dreamlike language.[35] One Klanswoman said of her time in an earlier group, "I knew what went on but it just seemed like something you'd see in a movie or read in a book."

There are two reasons for this difference in tone. These women, as individuals, feel that they are the victims of unjust public condemnation. A white separatist complained that fear of losing her job made her hide her real feelings about African Americans and Jews. Another said that "people think I'm full of hate." A Nazi protested that she didn't "like the way people view me as a hater." An Aryan supremacist told me, "People look at us as though we are sick, as though we are the problem of society." Seemingly oblivious to her group's efforts to "rid America of blacks and Jews," one woman complained that she "could no longer go to certain stores downtown without people [saying], 'Oh, Nazi-redneck get out of here. You're a Nazi. We don't want you in here.'" Another woman, after detailing her work on behalf of white supremacism, complained that she felt uncomfortable in her church when she heard "people talking, whispering behind our backs" about her Klan allegiance. Others felt that they were stigmatized unfairly because earlier racist groups had such bad reputations. A middle-aged woman, for example, insisted to a friend that "her Klan" was not violent. Her friend, she explained, "was comparing us [the Klan] with the Klan of the 1800s and it's totally different . . . 'cause we have never burnt a cross in anybody's yard, we have never hung anybody." Such comments are consistent with these women's general sense that participating in racism has been costly for them personally, even if it has bolstered a larger racist agenda. Several spoke of the racist movement absorbing too much of their time, leaving too little for their children and family. Others resented the compromises they had made—hiding their activist lives from coworkers and bosses, having to "conform to earn a living," being "blacklisted from any professional positions."

Many women feel that they have been unfairly hurt by others in the movement. They strive to distance themselves from those they see as more extreme, simultaneously claiming, as did one Klanswoman, that their actions are "no different than being in the Girl Scouts" and that "most of the [other] people in the movement have too much hate." In the same vein, a skinhead told me of a woman racist leader who "used to tell me [that] people that had brown hair and brown eyes [like me] were just filth and trash and wasn't worthy of being around. She really scared me." They thus see themselves as victimized by those within their own movement, particularly by certain men. Their descriptions of these men echo the stereotypes of racists held by those in mainstream society; they criticize them as "your Joe Six-pack," as "dumb enough to walk down the street with a swastika on their T-shirt yelling at black people," as "idiots that don't know what they are talking about," or even as "scumbags with fraudulent, unmotivated behavior."

The women's understanding of the politics of their movement also leads them to describe the movement and themselves in very different terms. Rather than burning with ideological passion or a desire to spread racist ideas, they feel hopeless about the "degenerate" society that surrounds them and the possibility of changing it. Male racial activists talk about their empowerment by racial knowledge and racial activism, boasting of their ability to change the world,[36] but for these women, racism is a politics of despair. They see activism solely as a means to protect their children or themselves from a troubled society that they have come to understand in racialized terms, but they give it little chance of success. As a white supremacist said, "I would like my future to be a

little-house-on-the-prairie picture . . . but it will not be like that. I think
we'll be struggling my whole life . . . surrounded by immorality and corruption." These women's activism is defensive, giving them no self-
satisfaction or sense of power. The racist movement promises to fend
off what they see as threatening to engulf them and their families, but
it promises and delivers little to them personally.

The emotional resignation found among these women activists is another indication of how they align their sense of self with the goals of
the racist movement. To the extent that racist politics yields no obvious
and tangible rewards to women activists, they construct their participation in the movement as involuntary, automatic, and unconscious.
Making sense of racial politics by denying personal agency is a common
response of those involved in political causes that are widely condemned;
as the historian Gabriele Rosenthal found in a study of Germans who
witnessed World War II but did not face persecution, such denial serves
to normalize the consequences of involvement.[37] The stories of women
racist activists, however, are not merely self-justifications. They convey
both a feeling of hopelessness in the face of outside social or political
forces and a sense of powerlessness to reconcile the contradiction between what the tellers see as the movement's lofty goals of Aryan supremacy and their actual experiences in the racist movement. Though
all the women racial activists praise those goals, many derive little gratification from the process of working toward racial purity. It is in this
sense that their resignation—their expressions of self-denigration, emotional pain, victimization, and lack of awareness—represents a gendered
response to experiences within male-defined racist politics.

Such feelings make it difficult for the women to create a positive
vision of their personal future in organized racism, despite being optimistic about the future of the movement. Thus, being a racist makes
these women tense and uneasy. Some women talk positively of their life
in racist groups and easily express pride in the racist movement, but
most have great difficulty expressing pride in themselves as racist activists. When asked about her group (Skrewdriver), one white supremacist
skinhead commented, "To me Skrewdriver means pride in my race and
pride in my womanhood."[38] But asked about herself, another skingirl
of about the same age answered: "I'm proud of my [racist group] family and what they've done and how I'm a part of them and what
we're doing as a group. And any personal attributes that I'm particularly proud of, I mean, I'm not, I don't think I have very low self-esteem,

but at the same time, I don't usually go about thinking of what I've done."

The life stories of racist women sketch how they became involved in racist groups. Most entered through a personal contact—sometimes a friend or family member, but as often a mere acquaintance. The ways in which they met a racist activist varied as well. Some meetings were predictable from the people the women knew and the places they frequented, others simply happenstance. Some women described backgrounds that arguably made them receptive to the message of organized racism, while for others, racist activism was an abrupt departure from their earlier lives. Whatever their mode of entry into racist groups, each had to make adjustments to become a racist activist. For most, who had not grown up in racist families, these entailed substantial changes in their self-identities and the definition of their self-interests. They had to come to see themselves as part of a racist movement defending the interests of whites and Aryans.

Is this process of self-adjustment unique to racist women, or does it happen to racist men as well? It is difficult to know because there are no comparable life histories of male racist activists. However, several autobiographical sketches and biographical accounts of male racists hint at the gendered nature of racist activism.[39] Although men and women alike come into organized racism primarily through social networks, racist men, but not women, generally present themselves as agents of their own political enlightenment. Men talk of becoming a racist as the result of an internal process rather than the promptings by others. In "Why I Joined the Nazi Party," his declaration published in the *Stormtrooper,* Karl R. Allen describes his Nazism as an essential aspect of his inborn character: "Nazis are born not made. Nearly every man I've met here at [Nazi Party] National Headquarters has told me, 'I've been a Nazi all my life.' Some of them realized it right away; others waited a while. But all of them know, once they heard the call, that here is the Cause they were born to serve." He attributes his conversion to Nazism to an inner drive, a craving not satisfied in other ways: "Although I always stayed busy, I never felt a sense of 'accomplishment'—of doing something really worthwhile, other than earning money and making a living." But when he heard the words of a right-wing speaker, Allen recalls, it all "made sense"; he embarked on a program of study that led him to conclude that Hitler was right, and he applied for membership in the Nazi Party. Like the women recruits, Allen was converted to Nazism after contact with an individual, but his testimony focuses on the impact of the *ideas* he heard rather than of the speaker himself. The speaker is cast primarily as an instrument through which Allen's inner drive to embrace Nazi philosophy was fulfilled.[40]

Similarly, John Gerhard of the American White Nationalist Party (AWNP), in a piece titled "Leadership to Victory" and published in the party newsletter in the early 1970s, tells his conversion story: "The road which led to my joining the AWNP started with a desire to save my country and race from what seems like inevitable destruction by our Marxist-Jewish enemies." Like some of the racist women, Gerhard recounts a personal quest for racial and political truth. His testimony takes the form of a journey, starting with George Wallace's presidential campaign in 1968; after a series of unsatisfactory memberships in increasingly extreme right-wing groups, he finally reaches his leadership post in the AWNP. In his story, Gerhard is clearly the protagonist. It is his expressed "desire to save my country and race" that sets him on the road to racist activism, and his own determination brings him to his destination.[41]

More recently, the imprisoned white supremacist David Tate also presented himself as a self-motivated searcher for racial truth. He describes parents who were "middle class from upper-middle class families" but claims that as a youth he became "aware of 'racial' differences thanks to the hypocrisy of the system." Pointing with satisfaction to "the rise of the skinheads and increased participation of Aryan youth," Tate notes that in his youth, "there were few of my age who participated actively in the movement. I was a rare exception."[42]

The racist self that men construct differs sharply from the resigned, nearly passive self that racist women present in their stories. Women's talk of bodily harm underscores the sense of vulnerability that justifies their entrance into organized racism, while their desire to safeguard their children from a life in organized racism highlights their sense of dissatisfaction with the life they have found there. Few men reveal similar conflicts: indeed, male racists, or at least male leaders, experience the racist movement as a positive, self-aggrandizing opportunity. For women, becoming a racial activist requires adopting a racist self that is fraught with complications, a self that many ultimately find unsatisfactory. In the next chapter, I turn from discussing the individual racist identities that women come to adopt to examining how women acquire collective racist identities: that is, how they develop a sense of themselves as participants in a larger white racist movement.

2

WHITENESS

Late in the afternoon, after a long interview full of vitriolic attacks on Jews, African Americans, immigrants, and a host of other groups, Susan turned our conversation to her conflicted feelings about being white. A longtime member of a small but highly visible Nazi group on the West Coast, she pondered why she had remained active in the racist movement despite what she regarded as unprovoked assaults by antiracist groups and investigations by the government: "The masses of whites that are so brainwashed have convinced me to stay with the cause and to struggle to reeducate them. Our race is so guilt-ridden and ashamed of its own accomplishments and that is amazing. We [i.e., her group] have received hate mail and a good portion of it claimed to be from whites that said, 'I am white and ashamed,' [and] 'I take no pride in being white,' [and] 'I was born white, not by my choice.'" With scorn tempered by sympathy, Susan described "the masses of whites" as lacking a sense of white pride and racial ability. Their racial quiescence, she noted, was imperiling the race. Against all evidence, Susan saw whites as an endangered race, facing demographic and cultural extinction brought by social institutions that she decried as "blatantly antiwhite": "The masses of white folks have been stripped of their culture, heritage, history, and pride. That is why we do the things that we do—to educate, to instill a sense of pride in these people, to offset the effect of the regular mainstream media which is blatantly antiwhite. Whites are the true endangered species. We are less than 9 percent of the world's population. We are the ones in danger of dying out in one or two generations."

Susan's contorted views of whites are typical of those in organized racist groups. Her ambivalence toward the "masses of white folks" starkly illustrates the contradictory blend of concern and antipathy that underlies the peculiar ideas about whiteness held by racist activists. To become a white racist, it is necessary to identify with whites as a racial collectivity. Nevertheless, organized racists, like other marginalized and highly stigmatized groups, come to disdain and even loathe outsiders—including the majority of whites.

To white supremacist activists, other whites at best are racially apathetic, at worst embrace racial tolerance. Most regard whites not in their movement as holding a problematic mix of admirable and deplorable beliefs. For example, when a middle-aged woman told me of her personal racial genealogy, her account of how pride and respect for her European background prompted her to join the Klan—her story's ostensible theme—was complicated by anger at the perceived rigidity, sexism, and "political correctness" of her racial ancestors and contemporaries. "As a woman, as a descendant of Nordic-Teutonic tribes,[1] as an above-average person," she explained, "first I was brought up by my paternal grandmother's mid-Victorian bylaws, as fed to her daughter-in-law, my mother. Then by later immigrants' children such as my college housemates and in-laws. Then in a male-dominated society. And presently by a politically correct regime wherein truth may not be told if it denigrates another race."

Comments like these raise the question of how racist activists understand and use ideas about whiteness. What moves someone beyond the construction of an individual racist self to a *collective* racial identity?[2] In particular, how is the self constructed as an actor in a racist movement—as a *white racist activist?* Among the women I interviewed, that collective identity rests on two foundations: their identification with a larger racial community of whites and their identification with efforts to implement white racial agendas. These two bases—white and activist—make their identity complex and often contradictory. They must accept whiteness as a unifying racial identity to which political commitment is possible, even when the boundaries of whiteness as a racial category are indistinct and perplexing. They also must believe in the efficacy of a racist activism that both depends on and sharpens the contrast between whites who are committed to action on behalf of racial preservation and those who are racial free riders or even disloyal to a white agenda. For racist activists, other whites are simultaneously allies and the most threatening traitors.

IDENTIFYING AS WHITE

Toni Morrison writes of a character in an Ernest Hemingway novel: "Eddy is white, and we know he is because nobody says so."[3] That whiteness goes unremarked by its possessors is one of the most striking conclusions of scholarship in the emerging field of "white studies." In a white-dominated society, whiteness is invisible. Race is something that adheres to others as a mark of otherness, a stigma of difference. It is not perceived by those sheltered under the cloak of privilege that masks its own existence.

The widespread equation of racial identity with culture in modern U.S. society means that majority culture, like majority race, is unmarked. If minority culture is labeled as distinctive or exotic—the cultural "other" defined by "ethnic" food, dance, and clothing—then white culture is normative and thus unseen. For this reason, those who identify as whites can see themselves as lacking any racial culture. In the innovative ethnography of whiteness by the sociologist Ruth Frankenberg, a woman—whose "cultural positioning seemed to her impossible to grasp, shapeless and unnameable"—talks of being in a "cultural void."[4]

Lacking an explicit sense of white culture or even of whiteness, majority populations rarely are aware of the racial politics that benefit them. Political agendas that favor whites, especially middle-class whites, are seldom acknowledged as racial in their intent or consequences. They are presented as defending goods that are ostensibly nonracial, such as quality schools, property values, equal access to employment, or neighborhood safety. Whiteness is unmarked because of the pervasive nature of white domination. Its very invisibility, in turn, thwarts challenges to white racial privilege.

Unlike most whites, members of organized racist groups have to be highly conscious of being white. For them, whiteness is a central and conscious aspect of identity, shaping how they see the world and how they choose to act toward others. Whiteness is a central topic of conversation in racist groups and a focus of their propaganda. Racist activists see whiteness as highly remarkable—and they often remark on it. Rather than being a peripheral or unnoticed feature of the social landscape, it is for them a central organizing principle of social and political life.

The subject of white racial identity is treated in nearly every publication of the racist movement. Christian Identity groups, in particular, place great emphasis on promoting a sense of racial distinctiveness and superiority among whites, condemning as "whoredom" all forms of intercultural exchange, integration, and marriage or dating. In her column "For Women Only," which appears in the Christian Identity newsletter *Scriptures for America,* Cheri Peters, wife of CI leader Pete Peters, recalls how her grandmother "stressed the importance of *white* skin." In explaining her difficulty in understanding why white girls desired to look like Mexicans, Cheri cites her grandmother's admonition against tanning: "She told me to be proud of my white skin. . . . In today's society my grandmother would be what is called a 'racist.' If only we had more 'racist' grandmothers today."[5]

The visibility of whiteness also is heightened for racist activists because they see it as a marker of racial *victimization* rather than racial dominance. The racial self-consciousness of white supremacists grows out of the notion that whites have endured oppression in the past and present. Examples of such purported discrimination against whites are legion in racist propaganda and in the talk of white racist activists. A white power skingirl complained to me that "whites aren't allowed a 'white man's America' or white scholarship fund. We are not granted permission for a white history month." Her solution? "To execute, to do away with both Jews and government." A member of a militant Christian Identity compound was less specific but no less vehement, telling me that "white Christian people are persecuted for being white, persecuted for believing that God created them different, created them superior." Even slavery is incorporated into the litany of historical atrocities suffered by whites. As an older neo-Nazi woman put it: "There was white slaves. Way before there was black slaves. So they [blacks] are not the only ones that did without. . . . White people from Nordics and Vikings came over on their ships. The white people went through a lot of hell to exist to this day."

Boundaries of Whiteness

The ideas that racist activists share about whiteness are more conscious, elaborated, and tightly connected to political action than those of mainstream whites, but they also reflect the views of whiteness dominant in mainstream culture. Whiteness is generally (and paradoxically) defined more precisely by who is *excluded* than who is *included*. Whites are those who are *not nonwhite*: those who are not racially marked, those who are not clustered together to form a category of racial minority. Such reasoning is seen in the words of a very young Nazi who claimed her identity of whiteness only gingerly, embracing membership in the race primarily as a means of asserting dominance over others: "I don't like most white people, but I choose white people over niggers, spics, chinks, japs, vietnamese, wops, whatever."[6]

Scholars in the new field of white studies find that whiteness is defined by its boundaries. In her ethnography of white ethnic communities in the United States, the anthropologist Micaela di Leonardo argues that white ethnics locate themselves racially by contrasting themselves against those they perceive as undesirable racial extremes—the bloodless modernity that they associate with elite white culture, on the one hand, and the primitive wildness that they regard as emblematic of African American culture, on the other. In a similar vein, Frankenberg concludes from her interviews focused on growing up white in America that "whiteness can by definition have no meaning: as a normative space it is constructed precisely by the way in which it positions others at its borders. . . . Whiteness is in this sense fundamentally a relational category."[7]

In determining whiteness, borders are more significant than internal commonality. Over time whiteness has been constructed, in the words of the legal theorist Cheryl Harris, as "an exclusive club whose membership was closely and grudgingly guarded."[8] If we view whiteness as defined by its borders, we can see clearly how ideas about race are spatial, how social space is divided along racial lines. The importance of space can be discerned in the language of most whites, but it is particularly evident in descriptions by racist activist women of their efforts to enforce white privileges. For example, one Klanswoman told me a story of racial contestation over space involving a new woman minister in her church: "The first thing that happened was she went to the colored section and she started bringing the colored into the church. Well, there's no objection if you're going into missionary work. But she brought them here into the church. I stopped going. I object to them coming into my community. They can have their own. Otherwise no."

Racist groups support not only racial separation but also absolute racial hierarchies of domination and subordination, superiority and inferiority. They seek a division of racial space that is vertical as well as horizontal, thereby ranking as well as distinguishing among racial groups. A white supremacist boasted of the community where she grew up in the deep South: "There's not a black or Hispanic. There's really not. They're not allowed there. They get harassed to the point where they're leaving. It is racist. I mean extreme racist."

Contradictions of Whiteness

Although white racist activists must adopt a political identity of whiteness, the flimsy definition of whiteness in modern culture poses special challenges for them. In both mainstream and white supremacist discourse, to be white is to be distinct from those marked as nonwhite,[9] yet the placement of the distinguishing line has varied significantly in different times and places. Nineteenth-century Irish immigrants to the United States, in the words of the historian Noel Ignatiev, "became white" as a result of prolonged racial and political struggle; Jewish immigrants followed a similar historical trajectory, though with only partial success. In contrast, for Mexican Americans, at least in western states, the likelihood of being included in the racial category of "white" decreased through the twentieth century.[10] These historical outcomes suggest that whiteness is a racial identity in flux, a racial category always in danger of challenge and modification. Oddly, whiteness is at once intensely significant and ultimately meaningless.[11] In her scholarship, Harris points to the lack of any "inherent unifying characteristic" in whiteness, an absence that leaves its boundaries representational, political, and fluid.[12] Like the boundaries of emerging nation-states,[13] the borders of race can be indistinct, difficult to police, and contested.

The fluidity of race is acknowledged differently among white supremacist groups. Traditionally, racist groups in the United States have embraced xenophobia, nationalism, and viciously anti-immigrant political agendas. For them, whiteness has rested on national origin as well as skin color. In recent years, however, a number of organized racists have come to support the idea (still resisted by many) of a transnational racism or Pan-Aryanism based on international commonalities of whiteness, anti-Semitism, or Aryan heritage.[14] In this new conception, whiteness can transcend national borders but still be fixed as "Aryan." Racist activists also differ over how broadly the idea of whiteness can be stretched within the United States. The propaganda of racist groups presents whites and nonwhites, Aryans and Jews, as diametrically opposite and clearly defined groups. In private conversations and in my interviews, however, racist activists often struggle with such sharp delineations. For many, distinguishing the borders between whites and American Indians and between whites and Jews is especially problematic.

Surprisingly, some racist activist women regard American Indian ancestry to be authentically white, even though contemporary American Indians are maligned and victimized by racist group members. This curious notion reflects a belief in American Indians as "noble savages"—primitive but pure—that augments claims about the long victimization of whites.[15] If Indians are "really white," and if Indians collectively have been historically victimized, then members of the white race have an additional set of racial grievances. As one white supremacist related:

I'm fucked anyway because I'm a minority. We whites are a minority. I was denied my Indian heritage and I did grow up as a white person. Denied by my father. I wish I had been raised as a Cherokee. . . . [The] reason for my white supremacy [is] because, okay, whoever brought the niggers were assholes, because this was Indian territory. This was their country. White man took it over. And I'm from Indians, so it pisses me off.

The relationship between Jews and racist whites, though more overtly confrontational, is similarly fraught with ambiguities. As the next chapter details, Jews are almost uniformly perceived by organized white supremacism today as the central enemy. Virtually all racist group propaganda grossly caricatures Jews as a victimizing group immutably in battle with Aryans. Individual white supremacists concur: without exception, every racist woman I interviewed took pains to voice her hatred and fear of Jews even when answering unrelated questions.

Yet many racist women activists find it a struggle to place Jews, who usually appear white, in a racial schema based primarily on the dichotomy between white and nonwhite. In this regard, Nazi ideologies fit awkwardly onto the rigid templates of race that underlie white supremacist ideologies in the United States. In written racist propaganda, these tensions are obscured by the virulent descriptions of Jews as a group apart, so treacherous as to be nearly nonhuman. But the private talk of racist activists makes more obvious that categorizing Jews is a problem. Some women claim that unstated physical similarities between Jews and whites uniquely position Jews to be racial spies or to enter into sexual relationships with Aryan whites. Others assert that Jewishness is something chosen, not given: it is a cultural pattern, a way of life, rather than a racial category. As one skingirl declared: "Jewishness is not a race and never [has] been a race. That's, a lot of people don't understand that. They follow the Jewish way of life. That's what it is. It's not racial."

In either case, Jews are seen by white supremacists as particularly loathsome precisely because their elusive racial designation gives them unwarranted access to whites. Lorraine, a neo-Nazi, contrasts what she sees as the mutable characteristics of Jews with the stable appearance of African Americans. Jews, she argues, can be observed "going Jewish," but blacks remain black: "There's a few Jews that are what they call 'Jew power' but very few, because Jews will like to mix. Jews especially like to go after the red hair and blue eyes. Why, I don't know, but this is very true. But if you see a Jewish person that's going Jewish, they look Jewish. They have the nose, they have the ears, they have the mouth."

The ambiguities of racial definition and boundary in the white supremacist movement coexist with a strong emphasis on racial commonality and racial loyalty. Members perceive the need to create and enforce racist unity in the face of splintered and contested ideas about whiteness and race.

IDENTIFYING WITH RACIST AGENDAS

Whiteness, which for most whites seems inconsequential or wholly invisible, is both embraced and regarded as highly significant by organized racists. For them, whiteness defines a community that, at least potentially, is unified and capable of being mobilized in the service of racial agendas. Yet the centrality of a common racial agenda to the white supremacist movement does not make it unproblematic for racist activists.

To accept the mobilizing potential of whiteness means envisioning whites as a racial community, much like the modern nation insofar as it is, as the historian Benedict Anderson suggests, "an imagined political community." Though nationalism is usually understood as "the awakening of nations to self-consciousness," Anderson characterizes it as the invention of nations "where they do not exist." So too is racist activism based on an imagined community of whites, on an ability to "visualize in a general way the existence of thousands and thousands like themselves."[16]

Racist activists deliberately shape an imagined racial community of whiteness in myriad ways. One involves violent confrontation with those marked as "nonwhite." As I explore further in chapter 5, many racist activists believe that force can create a unitary, self-interested community of whiteness. They insist that a collectively accepted sense of white racial power can be generated through in-your-face aggression, the violent thrust of racist cultural spectacle, and terroristic acts.[17] In a more subdued fashion, racist activists also seek to "imagine" into existence a community of self-conscious whites by creating white culture's lineage. "Naming one's race," the philosopher David Theo Goldberg notes, presupposes a racial "self-recognition" in a racial lineage.[18] Racist groups distribute flyers depicting the Christian nativity scene with Ku Klux Klan and Nazi members taking the place of shepherds and kings as witnesses to the birth of Christ and as heirs to the Christian vision. Such efforts aim to construct a white racist history, filling the void that racist activists see in mainstream white culture.[19]

Many racist women recount their personal history within a larger history of the white race. For some, naming racial lineage is a means of claiming a more honorable or glorious racial family tree. As an avid follower of National Socialism told me, "The word 'Aryan' means 'noble.' Therefore to be Aryan means to be noble. This is not something that is easy to do in current times." Other women make their claims of white culture more defensively. They recoil at what they see as efforts to undermine white history and tradition. A Klanswoman recalled her horror at discovering that her son was being taught the contributions of African American leaders to U.S. history: "I was outraged. Me and my mom went down to the school and we talked to them [and I said] 'I don't care to learn both sides.' . . . I'm upset that [my son] knows black history and he still doesn't know his American history."

Racial Loyalty

As they strive for racial community, some white supremacist activists come to rely on *strategic* definitions of whiteness. In contrast to mainstream whites, who tend to establish what the philosopher Marilyn Frye terms a "generously inclusive" definition of whiteness that embraces everyone not obviously nonwhite,[20] racist activists espouse a more restricted and hierarchical notion of whiteness. They reject what Frankenberg labels the "production of a white self innocent of racism" in favor of a white identity based on explicit loyalty to race and racism. Many racist women activists, to varying degrees, thus see race as unstable, a product of political commitment as much as biology. Such strategic definitions are especially striking because they contrast sharply with racist propaganda that portrays race as fixed and biological.[21] Research based solely on racist propaganda and public speeches necessarily overlooks this clash of views.

Consider the statement of Molly, a skinhead from a western state. In a rambling discussion, she referred to racial characteristics as arising from both biology ("racial blood") and society ("environment"):

If you take a person of pure racial blood, that person is likely to be very healthy, very strong, have a good personality and outlook on life, if they are in their natural environment. By natural environment I simply mean any environment that is compatible to the one their race has been in for the many thousands of years that it has been around. If you put that same person into an alien environment, they become distrustful and in the lower evolved [races] they can become very violent.

Some racist activists embrace a twisted version of the idea, now a scholarly commonplace, that race is a social construction rather than a biological given, that the definition and boundaries of race are produced by social forces rather than by skin color or genetics.[22] Such a logic is evident in a number of interviews in which racist women sought to distinguish someone's *true* racial identity from his or her superficial racial markings. They described relying on a person's actions to define race at least as much as on intransigent characteristics such as skin color or physical features.

The narrative of Virginia, a southern neo-Nazi, provided the starkest example of this construction of race. When she described her best friend, an African American man, she explained that because he was a confidant, he was "really white." People who are "on your side" are necessarily white, Aryan, or Christian—regardless of their appearance. Having an interracial friendship thus did not disturb her racist identity: she assigned race on the basis of loyalty, not skin color.

My best friend was black. He says, "I'm not a nigger. I hate niggers." He ended up being like my brother, my best friend, you know, everything. We were like this. [She put her fingers together.] . . . He wouldn't even speak to his own family because he hated niggers. He dressed like us, talked like us, walked like us, hung out with us,

*listened to our music, everything. . . . [He said,] "God played a dirty
joke on me and put me in a black wet suit, but I'm totally, I'm all
white inside." . . . He was really white.*

In an even stranger twist, her African American friend was killed because
of his color: two white men "out partying" gave him a ride from a gas
station and then ran him over with their car after he asked to be let out.

*They let him out of the car. They drove on and then [one white man]
turned to his partner and he was like, "Hey, fuck that shit." And
he turned around. And he went really purposely. . . . He full throttled
the fucking pedal. He [i.e., her friend] got killed because of the fact
that he was black. . . . I mean, he was really cool. And he was nineteen
when he got killed and I was, like, I was devastated.*

Conversely, for some racists, those who wrong you must be nonwhite, non-Aryan, or Jewish. This belief fuels the incessant search for
white "race traitors"—that is, white-appearing persons who act to sub-
vert white racist agendas. A telephone "hate line" aimed at Aryan
women who "have abandoned the last of the Aryan heathen warriors
in their darkest hour of need" is typical of the venomous sentiment
directed toward those deemed to be race traitors:

*Whatever the case or cause may be, may you die a slow and painful
death. . . . You bastards of the Aryans have chosen the side of the
enemy only because you fear losing with your own race.*
   *You're also in favor of the Zionist overlords and their lackeys,
therefore you deem it necessary to fight against your own kind.*
   *Do you have anything to offer your race, and earth, white women?
Or are you a cowardly wench that seeks a heinous life of ease?
Make your decision. We have. We know the odds against us are very
great, but we will die on our feet before we live on our knees.*[23]

Similarly, a white power skinhead girl writing in a racist newsletter
decries the "non-White loving baldies who call themselves skinheads
[and] would swear 'till death that they are White warriors, yet their
actions are truly contradictory."[24] In a pamphlet titled *White Genocide
Manifesto*, published by his "14 Word Press," the imprisoned white
supremacist leader David Lane pointedly cautions:

*Let those who commit treason with the Zionist destroyer, or sit on the
fence, be aware. If we are successful in our goal, expressed in the 14
WORDS: "We must secure the existence of our people and a future for*

White children" *then your treachery will be appropriately rewarded.*
If not, and the White race goes the way of the dinosaurs, then the
last generation of White children, including yours, *will pay for your*
vile complicity at the hands of the colored races who will inherit
the world.[25]

Even Christianity can be perceived by some racist activists as traitor-
ous to whites. Although some women say that their racism reflects true
Christianity, others decry most organized religion. They complain, var-
iously,

Christianity is a slave religion that worships the Jew.

The dominant religion in the once-white countries in almost all of its
various cults and divisions is determinedly pushing race mixing and
the brotherhood of universal mankind. You cannot take back a religion,
if indeed it ever was ours, from a billion nonwhite and brain-dead
race traitors.

Judeo-Christians and humanists are agents of the destruction of the
white race and Western civilization. They are all now discriminated
against by the Jewish overlords due to the ancient hatred of Western
civilization from the conquests and occupations of ancient Palestine by
the ancient Greeks and Romans.

This concern with race traitors created problems in my encounters
with racist women. Although every woman I contacted for interviews
assumed that I had white skin,[26] many were less sure about my racial
loyalty and thus less ready to trust that I was "really white." One of
these suspicious women was Emily, a leader of a white power skinhead
group. Throughout the interview, Emily's language was full of racial
expletives and obscenities. Only with difficulty could I keep her focused
on her life history. When I began my standard cautionary speech about
the ideological gulf between us, Emily cut me off. She repeatedly hurled
racial challenges at me and ignored my efforts to answer. When, for
example, I asked about groups with which she had been associated, she
replied: "White supremacy, neo-Nazi, the belief in anarchy. I can't stand
Jews. Are you a Jew? I can't stand Jews because they're the ones that
said 'Crucify Jesus,' okay? I don't believe in government because it's
mostly ruled by the fucking Jews anyway." Emily's demand *"Are you a*
Jew?" is bracketed between statements of her antipathy toward what
she fears I might secretly be: *"I can't stand Jews."* Yet she does not wait

for an answer. If people can adopt and change racial allegiances, racial identities, and even racial categories through their actions and beliefs, no verbal response can suffice. The truth can be revealed only through my actions toward her and others like her.

Emily's disdain for race traitors emerged again when she explained why she agreed to let me interview her for this research while a white supremacist friend, Karen, declined. "I think it's really fucked up that Karen would tell all her shit about white supremacy and all the things that go along with it, yet when me and her were sitting in front of . . . a black lady Karen stands up [and says], 'I'm not saying shit about my Aryan beliefs.' And walked out." Emily viewed both Karen and me as not white because of our cowardice about expressing white ideas in front of an African American: "At least I ain't ashamed. . . . I'll tell them [African Americans] about what I think, you know. I'm the only one that is white [and] open about it And it pisses me off about you. The two of you, deep down, you suck up to niggers."

Thus, the notion of whiteness—presented as an undifferentiated category of racial identification and loyalty in the propaganda of most racist groups—is contradictory and internally stratified in the minds of individual racist activist women. A Nazi woman seized on the idea of "tribe" to describe how there could be such variability among a single race of whites: "I see myself as a kind of Aryan tribalist. One tribe can vary a lot from the next."

Racial Responsibility

Becoming a white racist activist involves more than adopting a particular definition and collective identity of whiteness. It also requires belief in the necessity of taking action on behalf of the white race, the adoption of a political identity as an *activist*. To create racial and organizational allegiance, racist groups deliberately set out to instill this aspect of collective identity in new recruits.[27] Women in racist groups commonly express their activist conviction as a principle of "taking responsibility" for the white race. One neo-Nazi woman framed the idea of racial responsibility in vague but nonetheless menacing terms: "I think that you can't really blame other people for the predicament you're in. The white people in the United States need to take responsibility for their action and if there are people who are troubling them, they *can take care of them,* it's not beyond their power."

If loyalty to race forms the boundaries of whiteness, then those who accept the mantle of racial responsibility display a higher form of racial consciousness. When women discussed levels of hierarchy within their racist groups, several commented that elite positions, such as those held by self-designated "storm troopers" or within "revolutionary underground units," belonged to those who were "most conscious of being white people" or who were most aware "of the need to have a movement on behalf of the white race." A middle-aged Klanswoman recalled that her father "was part of [a racist group] for many years. It was an elite group. Just a very few were allowed [in]. Others had to be part of an auxiliary." Such higher-level activists are, as an older skinhead put it, "people with definite ideas rather than wishy-washy ideas. People who have the same values that I have." Although some women deny that they have any power in the racist movement, others place themselves, ideologically at least, within this racial elite. A neo-Nazi claimed that she was constantly treated unjustly because of her white skin, but "I don't cry about it. I take revenge." A Klanswoman characterized the Klan movement as "a struggle in which only the strongest [i.e., like herself] can survive."

Those who are disloyal to whiteness—that is, those who openly work against the interests of the white race—are considered not white. But even among those regarded as white, there are some who shirk their racial responsibility, who do not act in accordance with their whiteness. In the written propaganda of the racist movement they are "the ill-informed, degenerate brainwashed section of the Aryan race, which is a considerable amount, [who] will shut their windows, lock their doors, and turn on the Cosby show while their kids are doing their part by reading books such as *The Diary of Anne Frank*. But then whose fault is that the Aryan race is the only race who's ashamed of their ancestry?"[28] In interviews, racist women portray them as "whites that have been stripped of their culture, heritage, history and pride."

The movement is growing stronger . . . it is gaining more respect because we ourselves are weeding out the useless and weak. Let them depend on someone else to protect them.

We're trying to wake people up. We're trying to make people realize who they are and the place that they need to take in their society. The biggest problem is that a lot of them don't want to be woken up.

Even worse are those who are "racially aware" but choose not to act on behalf of the white race. Many racist women disparaged such whites:

The individuals that talk a good line, but don't do anything. They want to complain about the government or the new world order or minorities, et cetera, but try to get them to contribute a few bucks or to put out [racist group] business cards or flyers and they will always have an excuse not to. Recently, I had an older man tell me, "I'm too goddamned old to get involved." I said, "No. That is a lot of crap. What you mean is that you are too old to be white." It is the b.s.'ers and the hopeless kosher conservatives [closeted anti-Semites] that bug me most.

The rich old conservative farts won't give up their money [to racist groups]. Because the only thing they are interested in conserving is their money, not their race.

The life story of Doris, an activist in a small underground Nazi group, illustrates how other whites are gauged by the yardstick of racial responsibility. Doris was involved with a group whose main ideological principle was Aryan solidarity, which members used to argue for the exclusion of non-Aryan immigrants from the United States. Her group's emphasis on a social, spiritual, and intellectual hierarchy among and within races—with activist Aryans regarded as the highest stage of human evolution—is reflected in Doris's judgment of white society.

Early in the interview, Doris urged me to differentiate between her group and others in the racist movement. Despite her group's explicit embrace of Nazism and Holocaust denial, Doris insisted that they were "less focused on hate" than other white supremacist groups: "The other ones are vicious and they are not philosophical at all." Doris's underlying belief in a gradation among whites extended even to the white supremacist movement, and she believed that the followers of her own group were among the most intellectually sophisticated and highly evolved. Far from glorifying the racist movement, as the literature of her group does, Doris had a very negative opinion of most racist activists: "I think most of the people who call themselves part of the movement are people who have been attracted to a stereotype, what they think it means. . . . They just act like white trash."

Doris's views of racial responsibility also affected the dynamics of her interview. Not long into our conversation, she interrupted herself and commented: "I'm just assuming you're my [kind of] white. I could be wrong here." When I responded with a quizzical look, she continued, "It [whiteness] covers a lot of territory, you know. There's all kinds." Later, Doris tried to assess my commitment to her kind of whiteness by discussing an acquaintance, a woman she described as having "had bad experiences with minorities" but being nonetheless unwilling to do anything about it. She characterized this woman as white but—because of her reluctance to act on behalf of white people—almost a traitor to whiteness, and Doris pointedly drew the connection to what she regarded as my ambiguous racial position. "White people who would never make a stand over any issue like race," she continued, "are too afraid to have anyone call them a racist or get any bad publicity [even though] they do agree." Again, the issue of whether I was a "race traitor" or a "race loyalist" hung over the interview, marking another possible gulf between us.

One obvious tactic used by racist groups attempting to nurture ideals of racial responsibility is to create what one scholar describes as "a cult of heroes and martyrs."[29] White supremacist propaganda and internal documents routinely recite the names and biographical details of racist leaders. Moreover, white supremacist groups (with perhaps increasing frequency in recent years) time events and even terroristic acts to coincide with anniversaries of significant racist martyrs and heroes. Hitler's birthday (April 20), the anniversary of the violent conflict between the white separatist Randy Weaver and federal agents in Ruby Ridge, Idaho (August 21–22), and the date of the bombing of the federal government office building in Oklahoma City (April 19) all have become occasions for commemoration and violence.

Despite this emphasis on heroes and martyrs, women racists express little interest in them. One prominent women's neo-Nazi group circulates what they call an "Aryan Martyr's Map," which identifies where white supremacists died in battles with law enforcement officials, sanctified as places where "great men and women . . . gave their energy and their lives for the folks."[30] But most women talk about notions of heroism and martyrdom abstractly, if at all, perhaps because honor and recognition in organized racism are reserved almost exclusively for men.[31] Racist men in the movement's rank and file compare themselves to white supremacist leaders, as "following in the path that Hitler set out" or as "carrying on the work that [an imprisoned member of a racist underground group] is not able to." In contrast, racist women do not refer spontaneously to racial heroes outside of immediate family and comrades. They cited prominent figures only after I specifically asked them to identify people whom they saw as heroes. The most frequently named was Adolf Hitler—not surprisingly, given the prominence of Hitler books, pamphlets, and memorabilia in organized racist groups. It is instructive, however, that Hitler alone was consistently named correctly. The second most commonly mentioned hero was Hitler's deputy Rudolf Hess, although he was often referred to as Adolf Hess, Rudolf Hessian, or some other misnomer. Third was the American Nazi George Lincoln Rockwell, who was also called George Lincoln and Lincoln Rockwell. The only woman's name put forth (by two women) was that of Kathy Ainsworth, a schoolteacher and Klan member arrested for the 1968 bombing of a synagogue in Meridian, Mississippi, and later slain in a gunfight with authorities.[32]

Racist women tend to discuss racial responsibility in terms of principles rather than individual racist heroes.[33] In a perverse way, they assert a racial "morality," based on faith in whiteness and loyalty to racist agendas rather than faith in God and commitment to mainstream religion. One explained, "My race is my religion to me. My race is first and foremost. In that sense, I guess I'm extremely religious. Christianity is a big lie." Some of the women I interviewed found validation in their perceived adherence to racist "morality." It affirms that they are doing the right thing, that their life has meaning. By conveying a sense of belonging to a collective struggle, it helps counter the feelings of resignation and despair that they experience as individuals. As discussed in chapter 1, many racist women express pride only in their groups, not in themselves, but some point to their racist activism as evidence of their personal worth. An East Coast skingirl told me that having "high morals" helped her recruit more people into organized white supremacism: "I'm proud of the fact that I'm a skinhead with a goal and high morals. I'm proud of being a part of what I feel so strongly about. With my education and morals, I can get people to talk about the movement and open their eyes without them dismissing me as an uneducated, nothing-going-for hick. I'm determined with a purpose and goal." A neo-Nazi woman similarly argued that her exemplary character would set a "good example" for others: "I am responsible in everything I do. I set goals for my life and can reach them. I am active in the pro-white movement without being a hypocrite. I practice what I preach and set a good example. I am preparing myself and my family for the future constantly."

Other women said that working on behalf of the white race gave them the sense that they were contributing to the world, that they were on the correct moral path. A Klanswoman commented: "I am proud of my lovely children. I enjoy my work. And I am proud that I am doing my part for my race." A racist skingirl claimed, "I am proud of my loyalty to my race because I could have race-mixed when I was younger and lots of black men wanted to date me, but after seeing what happened to my girlfriends I knew that it was wrong to date outside of my race." And a Christian Identity adherent told me: "I'm proud that I'm a white female who realizes what is happening to my people. I'm proud that I completed my education and will continue to educate myself. . . . I'm proud of the way I live my life and will continue to do so because it gives me strength and self-pride."

The historian Glenda Gilmore reminds us that political rhetoric "can license people to do evil in the name of good."[34] Certainly, finding morality in the service of racism is appalling; the claim falls far outside any reasonable standard of moral conduct. But it is important to recognize how and why racist women make such claims. The sense of moral worthiness that these women locate in the racist movement gives them a fervor for racist politics that helps compensate for the problems they experience in organized racism. Much like many women in very different social movements, racist women report finding more satisfaction in feeling selflessly engaged in a struggle for what they see as right than in the specific practical details of activism.

As they become part of the racist movement, women develop a collective racist identity that requires them to identify self-consciously as white, making explicit a racial identity that most whites take for granted. Unlike mainstream whites, racist activists are forced to acknowledge how fluid and imprecise the idea of "whiteness" can be. Jews and American Indians pose particular problems, being neither clearly "white" nor clearly "not-white." Furthermore, racist activists are confronted with the reality that many whites, however defined, fail to support racist agendas. At best, they defend their racial position only casually; at worst, they are active race traitors. In contrast, racial activists must be racially loyal and racially responsible, ready to take personal risks to defend the white race. Faced with these complexities, racist activists define true whites by their actions. Those who act on behalf of the white race as a whole—and those who are steadfast personal friends—are white.

Racist men enjoy plenty of heroic images to cement their identities as racist activists—male racial warriors are stock figures of racist propaganda and there is a thriving cult of male racial martyrs. But women find the identity of "racist activist" more complicated. The racist movement provides them little glory or recognition. Instead, these women measure themselves against what they construct as a racialized moral standard. They claim a measure of personal accomplishment when they work for the greater good of all whites. As we have seen, this sense of worthiness does not fully counter their disillusionment within the racist movement, yet it supplies one reason that women remain in racist groups. A second, external reason—the fear and loathing of racist enemies—is explored in the next chapter.

3

ENEMIES

The idea of an *enemy* is the foundation of white supremacism. Blistering attacks on immigrants, Jews, African Americans, and other groups supply the core of organized racist propaganda and the most common topic of racist talk. Racist activists compete in person and in print to mount the most vicious verbal attacks on minority groups. The stories of racist women are full of invectives against their enemies:

The Jews, they have been kicked out of nearly every country they have ever been in for crimes against the people of those countries and made up the Holocaust for their own financial gain.

I remember my first experience with a black. He spit in my playmate's hair. It never got any better, only worse.

I am tired of working and my hard-earned tax dollars going to the very ones that hate me. . . . I am sick and tired of the Jew-controlled government teaching my child what they want him to believe. . . .
I am tired of having to look at disgusting homosexuals every time I leave my home. I am tired of seeing my white brothers go to prisons for standing up for their rights. I am tired of the police and courts being afraid of these so-called minorities.

A Jew is permitted to rape, cheat, and perjure himself; but he must take care that he is not found out, so that Israel might not suffer.

Jews are just a real evil thing in society and they're really trying consciously, deliberately to destroy us.

By graphically describing the fates that they hope (or intend) minority groups to suffer, racist activists flaunt their racism. One white supremacist woman told me, "We should rid our land of the Jews"; another said that "we just need to go back to the days of slavery when niggers were put in their place, where they should have stayed." One summarized her feelings, "Most blacks should be put into prison." White supremacist tattoos carry the same message, declaring "Delenda est Judaica" ("The Jews must be destroyed") and "RaHoWa" ("racial holy war").[1]

Discussions of enemies pervade all racist groups. The idea of an enemy forges bonds of common hatred among members who might otherwise find little in common. At a Klan rally, young skinhead men covered with swastika tattoos sit next to middle-aged Klanswomen cradling small children and chat amicably about the dangers of hidden Jews in government and the growing threat posed by Hispanic immigrants. Collective vitriol against enemies can be intricately choreographed, as racist leaders escalate the rhetoric calling for violence, even death, to be meted out to enemy groups. But the talk of enemies also can be chillingly casual, functioning as an incidental point of interpersonal connection much as the weather does for strangers at a cocktail party.

When racist activists recite their litany of enemies, the scope of the category, acerbic language, and broad claims of enemy power and infiltration make the list seem ludicrous. In a digression from her life story, one Klanswoman offered a diatribe that is unusually compact but typifies the thinking of virtually all racist women:

The white race is responsible for many reasons. First, we did not resettle the freed slaves back in Africa as Lincoln wanted. Second, we allowed foreigners to leech off our people and become burdensome citizens. Third, we allowed the Jew to encourage miscegenation between us and nonwhites so as to prove that we are not racist. Fourth, we allowed Zionists to own the Federal Reserve bank and charge usury, which is outlawed in the Bible. Fifth, we allowed foreigners a place in our government and our men let themselves accept political bribes to sell our people out. Sixth, we trusted the Jew with the care of our government and media.

ORGANIZING HATE

The racist movement rests on the principle that certain groups are enemies and must be combated. Yet my interviews suggest that most women
come into racist groups with more or less mainstream racist ideas about
minorities. Only after becoming associated with white supremacist
groups do they learn "the truth" about racial enemies. In racist groups,
they learn to transform the beliefs that the anthropologist Philomena
Essed calls *everyday racism*[2] into an overarching activist ideology that I
term *extraordinary racism.*

Everyday racism, which reflects negative, stereotyped views of minority groups, lacks any systematic explanatory force. It is pernicious
but unremarkable among whites in a racist society. In racist groups,
however, everyday racism is intensified, made explicit, and mobilized
against specific enemies. It is molded into extraordinary racism, an ideology that interprets and gives meaning to a wide variety of phenomena
that seem unconnected to race, ranging from the global economy and
the growth of media monopolies to more immediate personal issues such
as the quality of family life, city services, and medical care.[3]

Racist groups teach members to think about race comprehensively,
to fit their ideas about enemies into broad interpretive schemas.[4] The
attributes and intentions of Jews and racial minorities, especially African
Americans, are the main focus of extraordinary racism. Sexual minorities are loathed and targeted for assault, but they are rarely seen as
central or powerful antagonists. They are viewed as disgusting rather
than dangerous, the consequence and not the cause of social degeneracy.
As a publication of one white supremacist group declares, "The homosexual population is quite small and not the major threat to Aryan
survival. The [mainstream] right-wing is obsessed with this subject and
devotes too much time and money on the subject. . . . The best that Aryan heterosexual society can do is to limit the collective influence and
keep the closet door shut."[5] In contrast, extraordinary racism proclaims
that nonwhites and Jews control the world, engaged in unremitting
struggles for dominance that increasingly dispossess whites and Aryans.
Its comprehensive explanatory grid makes extraordinary racism almost
impervious to the counterarguments or calls for racial tolerance used to
fight everyday racism. The difference between everyday and extraordinary racism is the difference between being prejudiced against Jews and
believing that there is a Jewish conspiracy that determines the fate of

individual Aryans, or between thinking that African Americans are inferior to whites and seeing African Americans as an imminent threat to the white race.

The struggle between Aryans and their enemies can be depicted in simple terms—with a focus, for example, on the numerical and political threat that population growth among nonwhites poses to the white race. Or it can be cast as a complex theory, like the crypto-theology of Christian Identity that locates the origin of racial strife in the two seedlines of Adam and Satan. In any case, the schema creates a sense of immediate threat that necessitates defensive action. A white supremacist group appeals to Aryan women by declaring, "The times that we are now living in seems to be of complete and utter chaos, and that is good. The more commotion the Blacks and Jews create, the harder it will be for the average white man and woman to tolerate it."[6] Their newspaper elaborates the claim:

Victory means a secure and exclusively White country. . . . To achieve a great and difficult goal requires several things. First we must identify, name, and hallow the goal. Second we must resolve to achieve that goal, no matter what the cost. In this case that implies disciplined fanaticism, meaning total commitment, combined with reason and judgment. Thirdly, we must have a plan of action. This plan of action must take into account the successes and failures of the past, and the tactics of the enemy.[7]

Recruits to racist groups arrive at their new understandings of the racial order—the ideology of extraordinary racism—via deliberate indoctrination by leaders, casual talk with other members, and written propaganda.[8] A few of the women I interviewed, generally those from racist families, reported reading racist literature or hearing racist speeches before they became associated with racist groups, but for most, exposure came only after that association.

Perhaps the least effective method of teaching racism is through formal speeches by group leaders. At a neo-Nazi gathering I attended, most people paid only sporadic attention to long, boring speeches by the group's self-proclaimed leaders. Even a livelier (at least to me) presentation by two younger members, a husband-and-wife team, on how to assess the psychological profiles of potential recruits and adjust recruiting efforts accordingly, had no more success in sustaining the interest of the audience, many of whom left early or spent time conspicuously reading the newspaper. Speeches belabored the supposed evil nature and

intentions of Jews, African Americans, and others, but much more animated discussions of racial enemies occurred in informal conversations
held in the food line, in the queue for bathrooms, or in small groups
clustered at the outskirts of the tent where speeches were given.

Members of racist groups also learn about enemies through written
propaganda. Every woman I interviewed spoke of regularly receiving
racist propaganda in several standard forms, including newsletters, au-
diotapes of speeches, videotapes, white power music cassettes and CDs,
and magazines or 'zines. Some received large amounts of such material,
acquiring personal libraries of hate material that surpass those of researchers and libraries. But despite these impressive collections, few of
the women seemed to spend much time thinking about their contents.
A skingirl who assured me that her reading of racist material included
"anything I come across, every day if I can" nonetheless could not explain skinhead or neo-Nazi ideas in more than the most cursory fashion;
just as unsuccessful was a skinhead who described herself as receiving
"hundreds of newspapers, magazines, flyers, stickers, books, et cetera
[that I] read at least four times a week since I was fourteen and first got
involved." Only rarely could an interviewee say what she objected to
about African Americans, Jews, or other enemy groups without lapsing
into the pat phrases of racist groups or describing some personal affront.
Almost none could fashion more than a sentence or two in her own
words to explain her group's carefully documented beliefs.

The rhetoric of almost all written racist propaganda certainly presents
a formidable obstacle to any but the most dedicated reader. Books,
newsletters, newspapers, and magazines published by most racist groups
are written in an impenetrable style. Long blocks of text justifying the
group's positions are broken occasionally by crude cartoons or caricatures of enemies, mixed with references to obscure internecine battles
among racist leaders. Exceptions to the dreary nature of racist written
propaganda are the publications of some neo-Nazis and skinheads who
favor bold, aggressive graphics, shocking photographs and drawings,
screaming headlines, and relatively little text. These are provocative,
though not particularly informative.

Cable television, once regarded by racist groups as the medium of
choice for recruitment because it reaches casual viewers in the privacy
of their homes, likewise is limited in its effectiveness as much by its
dismal production quality as by legal and political challenges to racist
access to public airways (important as these are). Almost all the women
I talked with were aware of racist TV shows, carried from time to time

on a hodgepodge of local cable access channels. Yet though these women claimed that they watch the shows "weekly" or "whenever one is on and I know about it," or that they collect tapes of the broadcasts, only two were able to name the featured guests or the topic of more than a single broadcast. The soporific nature of these shows, which usually follow a talking heads format that enables the host to talk about himself at great length, must be partly responsible. A Klanswoman told me that one of them "is the damn silliest thing ever and [its host] is a total buffoon."

Computer bulletin boards, chat rooms, and Internet websites are becoming increasingly popular ways to distribute racist propaganda. Many feature arresting visuals, well-written text, and hypertext links to racist documents and other hate sites. These can link racist groups from different parts of the globe effectively while making it impossible to trace any single agent. They are also ephemeral media for disseminating racist ideas, thereby appealing to those who might be reluctant to have racist propaganda visible in their homes.

CONSTRUCTING DIFFERENT ENEMIES

The ideology of extraordinary racism is based on the idea of racial enemies. Yet there are stark differences in how racist groups construct hatred of racial minorities and of Jews, as I detail below. Hatred of racial minorities tends to be concrete and personal. Almost all the women I interviewed could point to negative encounters with African Americans or other racial minorities, although these childhood playground taunts, verbal insults, and failures to get a job may often have been perceived as exemplifying racial hostility only in retrospect. In contrast, their hatred of Jews was highly abstract. One reporter wrote of the mostly young and well-educated members of a terrorist group in the Northwest that none "had ever had a personal confrontation with Jews."[9] In my interviews, too, most women were hard-pressed even to name a single Jew, though I broadened my questions to include historical figures or anyone in a public position. Several then mentioned "Rothschild" but were unable to provide any details about the family or its members. One proffered "Greenberg" and another "Alan Greenstein," botched efforts at naming Alan Greenspan, the chairman of the Federal Reserve System. But their failure did not seem to bother them: their anti-Semitism was rooted in a belief in invisible Jewish conspiracies that requires no specific or personal referent. Indeed, some pointed to their inability to name names as proof of that hidden conspiracy's effectiveness. As is true of any conspiratorial worldview, the absence of confirming evidence only strengthened the conviction of those holding it.

In addition, racial minorities and Jews were said to pose different problems. Building on racist sentiments that are widely shared among whites, racist groups declare that racial minorities—especially African Americans—present an immediate, visible danger to whites by menacing white bodies and property through crime and moral license and by gaining unfair advantage in employment and other social services. These claims are bolstered by specific references to the personal harm suffered by racist activists or their families or friends from racial minorities. Jews are also described as threatening whites, but in language that is more abstract and obsessive. Racist groups today have only a thin base of popular anti-Semitism on which to draw; they therefore paint Jews as mythically and irredeemably evil, but provide little support for their claims from the lives of racist activists. Jews are said to control world history, dominating all others through an unseen conspiracy. The sociologist David Smith describes this anti-Semitism as the "radical belief that the Jews form a surreal group with demonological traits."[10]

Racial Minorities as Enemies

Because many whites have racist beliefs, the racist movement can construct an ideology of extraordinary racism by using themes from everyday racism. One such theme is racial difference. Since the nineteenth century, race has marked the boundary between respectability and moral license, normality and abnormality, and disease and health.[11] As the literary theorist Henry Louis Gates Jr. observes about contemporary U.S. society, "race has become a trope of ultimate, irreducible differences between cultures, linguistic groups, or adherents of specific belief systems."[12] Beginning with the everyday racist assumption that whites are civilized but nonwhites are primitive—seen as being in what the theorist Paul Gilroy refers to as a state of "irrational disorder" or "human nature uncorrupted by the decadence of the civilizing process"—it is not difficult for racist groups to elaborate a racial trope that positions racial minorities as fundamentally different and inherently inferior.[13] Such sentiments were frequently voiced in my interviews with racist women. As a white supremacist skingirl declared, "Everyone that's not white, they're mud races."

A second theme is the threat posed by racial minorities. Racist groups elaborate and systematize existing everyday white beliefs that African Americans, Hispanics, and other people of color harm the security or privileges of whites.[14] When racist activist women speak of racial minorities as threatening their safety, moral rectitude, or property, they sound very much like mainstream racist whites. One skinhead deplored that when she was "living in the city I was really constantly gonna have to look behind my back [to] make sure that I wasn't gonna get robbed again [since] they had already robbed me once." To her, the future seemed no better: "I don't dare try to better myself here because they'll just come and rob me again. One day they're gonna rob me and rape me." Another woman expressed similar fears for her children: "I would like to be able to send my children to school and not have to worry about them coming home with a black eye, split lip, or broken arm from fighting the gangs. I don't want to get a call from some pawn of the government police telling me there has been a gang fight and my children were injured or killed." Themes of racial threat are also common in written racist propaganda. African American men, in particular, are caricatured as criminals—drug dealers, thieves, and muggers—and as the sexual predators of white women and girls in almost every publication distributed by a racist group.[15]

The threat posed by racial minorities is economic as well as physical. In language similar to that used by some conservative politicians, racist groups depict hordes of nonwhite immigrants or welfare recipients as overwhelming the resources of the U.S. economy and taking tax money, jobs, housing, and resources that rightfully belong to whites. A Klanswoman told me, "I have seen the disappearance of Caucasians from TV in medical, government [and] entrepreneurial walks of life. News anchors followed. Increasingly there were Africans, Asians, American Indian, et cetera spokesmen for a nation that my ancestors had developed and dominated. I did not want or need other races to feed me my daily dose of information and advice."

Members of racial minorities are seen as threatening white prosperity with their ability to turn the tables, to change from victims into victimizers. The logic behind this fear, expressed in some way by almost all those I interviewed, is curious. One woman told me that African Americans exploited slavery to gain unfair advantage over whites: "Blacks think the white man owes them. We don't owe [them] shit. Their own tribal chiefs sold them." This transformation also appears in descriptions of African Americans using racism to their benefit: "If a white person and a black person get into a fight, whether or not it's racially motivated, someone will try and make it into [that] the white person is racist. It's the white person's fault."

Using similarly twisted logic, racist activists even use a defense of racial equality to disparage racial minorities, drawing on ideas of equal opportunity whose general acceptance was won through efforts of progressive groups lasting more than a century.[16] Like mainstream conservatives, members of racist groups oppose affirmative action programs as denying equal opportunity. A Klanswoman told me, "It's always the KKK, the KKK this, and the KKK that, but the NAACP is always pushing something. The job market, they have so many minorities for this. And you've got your United Negro College Fund. You don't hear about a United White Persons College Fund or anything like that." Her argument resembles that of David Duke, the former Klan and neo-Nazi leader and perennial candidate for elected office in Louisiana who founded the perversely titled National Association for the Advancement of White People (NAAWP). Similarly, a woman from a Klan in the central states disguised her belief in the inferiority of African Americans by emphasizing that racially separate systems would promote equal opportunity: "I think it is in the best interests of all people to separate out. Let's take the blacks as an example. We whites can't oppress them if they have their own land, their own government, police forces, judges, and so on. They would rise or fall on their own merit."

Racist groups can be dangerously disingenuous in the solutions they proclaim to white problems with African Americans. Some insist publicly that they advocate only racial separation, not supremacism.[17] One neo-Nazi woman told me that she could make common cause with African American leaders like Louis Farrakhan who advocate racial separation and distrust Jews,[18] explaining, "I can get along with black power. 'Cause they're believing the same way I do. I just don't think God wants us to be all mixed up in one bowl." But such statements must be considered in a larger context of claims and actions. For example, a Christian Identity woman said she had no ill will toward other races, insisting only that "we cannot share gods, religion, or holy books with another race. Just as we cannot share countries, flags, music, sports, education, technology, territory, or anything else with another race. It destroys the senses of exclusivity, uniqueness, and value necessary to racial survival." Yet despite her seemingly neutral words, she was under investigation for an assault on a group of African Americans. Similarly, a young woman who related what appeared to be an innocuous life dream—"I would like to live in an all-Aryan homeland on this continent. I hope I do live to see it. That is without a doubt my greatest wish for the future"—admitted later in the interview that she had served time for an attack on a racially mixed couple. In perhaps the most striking example of how racial supremacism can initially be disguised behind calls for separation, a woman who initially told me that she simply supported "the need to segregate" later declared that she would like "to, like, get one state, put all the niggers under the age of three in this state. Raise them up as slaves. Send all the parents on boats. Send them out halfway in the middle of the ocean and blow them up."

These statements by racist activists are frightening and seem far removed from the racist banter of ordinary whites. But the practices and ideas of everyday racism make it fairly easy for racist groups to convince recruits that extraordinary racist ideologies are valid. They accomplish this in two ways: by teaching recruits to generalize from personal experiences to abstract general principles and by teaching them to reconsider personal experiences in light of abstract principles.

From Experience to Principle In my interviews, most racist women activists described their fear of racial minorities in terms that were more pragmatic than ideological. They claimed not that they joined racist groups to protect the white race in general but that they were motivated by personal concerns. It was in racist groups that they came to understand their own problems better and to realize the threat that faced whites. A Klanswoman told me that she felt helpless when her town's schools were integrated: "*They* came to the schools, then lunch money was taken away. Parents and principals couldn't do anything. Then they carried guns and children and teachers got afraid. Parents couldn't get relief from the school or sheriff so they called in the Klan and they called in the skinheads."

Jody, a skinhead from the Northwest, told me a story that similarly centered on the inability of the authorities to provide relief; here the victim was her best friend, who had been raped by a group of men. Underscoring the elasticity with which many racists apply racial classifications, she first described the men as from India but in a later telling presented them as African American. They were against "people-like-her"; therefore, they must have been black: "[My friend] tried to charge them but police didn't do anything. Two of them were charged and went to jail. . . . We met up with the skinheads and they had heard about her experience. They did what no one else would do. They protected her.

No black man will ever lay a finger on any white woman as long as there are people like the skinheads who will fight." To convey her vulnerability before joining the racist movement and her power after joining, Jody shuffles her account to fit this larger scheme of cause and effect. Though she first insists that the police did nothing, she then adds that they jailed two of the rapists. The police are powerless, the skinheads all-powerful. They can protect her friend and, by implication, safeguard all white women against all nonwhite men.

These themes of peril and protection are common in stories of how personal experience informs political lessons. A Nazi woman saw her future as "a struggle to survive in an increasingly antiwhite nation," confiding that "if the [racial] war does not break out within the next ten years, I'm afraid my children will be exterminated by the enemies of our race." More prosaically, as one Klanswoman told me, "it's hard to make house payments . . . the future is getting rougher, more criminals, very dangerous." Another Klanswoman said she sought a future with "a lot less violence, a lot less murders, you know, just a more stable, definitely more stable than it is today, and I'd definitely like to see the drug problem hit a rock bottom."

The propaganda issued by racist groups puts the jeopardy posed by racial minorities in abstract terms, warning of "race suicide," "race mixing," and "race war." But women were more likely to talk about concrete worries affecting their *own* children and families, not about the future of the white race. The women often explained their activism as a necessary sacrifice for the future of their children. An Aryan separatist claimed that she joined her group after "thinking of all my family and how much I cared about them . . . my children and how I wanted them to have a nice place to grow up." Another, childless, said she was motivated by a concern for her cousin: "I don't want her to grow up in a life where she's got to battle for something she's good at because of a minority." Even when one white power activist discussed the idea of racial threat more abstractly, she still viewed it through the prism of her children and family life: "When you just give your children over to be taught things that you do not believe you're just asking for family trouble and eventually it leads to national trouble, which you can see when the communists came over and infiltrated in the early 1900s in churches and universities. It just slowly crept into all of our schools."

Men who are racist leaders and women who are racist group members espouse similar goals in very different ways. When one Klanswoman expressed her opposition to interracial marriage, for example, her considerations were personal and practical. To her, a mixed-race baby was a problem not because it violated racial principle—threatening the integrity of the white race, the abstract ideal held out by male Klan leaders—but because it would damage family support networks: "You're giving up your family to [have an interracial baby] and then all of a sudden you get to feeling, 'Well where's this getting me? How am I going to survive? I used to go to my father and my mother and talk to them about various things. Now I don't have them.'"

Attention to pragmatic issues gives an immediacy to issues of race. At the same time, it obscures the arbitrariness of racist ideas by making them appear to arise naturally from personal experiences rather than derive from the ideologies of racist groups.[19] General solutions appear to emerge seamlessly from personal woes; for example, a Klanswoman's tale of her failed job searches concluded with her determination "to encourage white productive people to come together and form a union against their adversaries." The data do not exist to conclusively determine whether such magnification of personal issues into overarching beliefs is more likely to be found among racist women than men, but the words of racist men rarely include such detailed attention to the experiences of daily life.

From Principle to Experience Racist groups also teach members how to apply abstract notions to personal experiences. Kay, a member of a southern Klan, complained that she could barely make ends meet as a welfare recipient with a husband in jail and a child at home. Silent about the irony of receiving welfare from the federal government that racist groups teach their members to hate, she mostly worried that her race would exclude her from federal programs. "A lot of hungry white people in America," she complained, "can't get food stamps or whatever they need, government assistance, because the niggers here are fucking each other like rabbits. . . . Instead of getting jobs, they're out there selling crack to the white people, trying to kill us off." Embedded in her short statement are manifold ways that blacks cause her misery. Their needs threaten to monopolize government largess that would otherwise benefit economically precarious whites like herself. Growth in the African American population will increase this threat in the future. African Americans sell drugs in order to wipe out white communities, and families like hers—headed by mothers who are struggling financially to raise children alone—are particular targets. Such ideas do not seem original with Kay; a racist woman activist on the other side of the country complained in much the same terms, "All these people are coming over and taking over our country, getting our money, looking to use our people. Overpopulating us and trying to kill us with their drugs."

Racist groups encourage their adherents to use general principles to explain specific incidents in daily life. As she shared a story about trouble in her son's school, a Klanswoman was reminded by her friend that "the minorities' lack of intelligence holds back most white kids in school." After accepting the principle that nonwhites are threatening the survival of whites, one can easily find anecdotes that seem to illustrate the encroachment of racial minorities on the prerogatives of whites. Thus, almost all the women cited numerous incidents that, they argued, showed African Americans, other persons of color, or nonwhite immigrants threatening their financial or physical security or that of family members. Indeed, in the racist women's stories, members of racial minorities are most often linked to memories of fear, vulnerability, and anger. When they recall being jostled by children in elementary school, being threatened by groups of fellow students in high school, failing to get a desired job, or worrying about their safety on the street, the women recount incidents in which specific members of racial minorities are the protagonists.

Racial affronts loom large in stories of lives that are structured by racism. Even if the details of each episode are accurate, they are interpreted and given significance in accordance with the women's current immersion in organized racism. Incidents involving other races are seen as racial, or not, depending on a woman's overall beliefs. Episodes that would seem unremarkable to one person appear highly important to another; a listener may thus find shockingly trivial the incidents that are later recalled with great venom. One Klanswoman presented a story of sharing a seat on her school bus with a purportedly overweight African American girl to explain what convinced her that her racist practices were righteous. For another woman, her cousin's inability to secure a job in a pizza parlor was confirmation that "something needed to be done" about African Americans. Incidents are strung together to make a story that justifies racist rage. Racist beliefs influence what is recalled and its status as a racial incident. In turn, these remembered racial incidents seem to confirm racist beliefs. Thus memories justify the very practices that give them shape and make them memorable.

Jews as Enemies

Racist groups see Jews and racial minorities very differently. Pondering the roots of her obsessive hatred of Jews, one woman recalled a process of gradual revelation: "Over time, I just got interested. It brought to my mind what I hadn't thought about before." Although U.S. society continues to be intensely Christian-centric, this bias now is most evident in the tendency to ignore beliefs and practices that are not Christian. Overt anti-Semitism, though not unknown, is less common. Indeed, few women I interviewed had heard openly anti-Semitic statements before they discovered organized racism. People who join racist groups usually already feel antipathy toward African Americans and other racial minorities. But they need to be taught to hate Jews.[20]

The anti-Semitism of organized racism is conspiratorial, requiring that followers suspend ordinary logic. Its premise instead is that things are not what they seem and that different standards of "truth" and "evidence" are required. While racism against racial minority groups is a distorted but recognizable version of general notions of race among whites, the anti-Semitism of racist groups flouts conventional thinking, teaching that the truth is deliberately hidden behind a veil of illusion. In addition, it is extremely wide-ranging, claiming to explain phenomena— the economy, government, media, and international affairs—that the uninitiated would see as unrelated to religion, ethnicity, or race. Even personal events, such as a boyfriend's lost job, a miscarriage, or a husband's imprisonment, are taken as evidence of the Jewish conspiracy controlling everyday life.

Conspiratorial thinking ensures that the racist belief in the unreliability of overt markings of race, religion, or ethnicity will lead to perceptions of evil intent. African Americans can become white by demonstrating racial loyalty, but Jews can deliberately change their racial characteristics to trap unsuspecting Aryans. A Nazi woman claimed she had a special power to find "treacherous Jews" regardless of their attempts to disguise themselves: "When I realized he [a deceitful lover who claimed to be Christian] was doing these things, my left arm . . . turned blue from the tips to the elbow. It just actually turned blue. When he left and I sort of got away from him, it turned white again."

The learning of anti-Semitism is not unique either to women or to American racist activists, as is evident in the alarming account by Ingo Hasselbach, a German former neo-Nazi, of how he taught anti-Semitism to new recruits:

*We often didn't get into the Jewish question at first because it was too
complex and explosive. Recruits had to build up to anti-Semitism.
. . . [Y]ou could start with anti-Semitism, when you were sure that
some basis for hating "inferior races" was there, which made it easier
to absorb the idea of a person so inferior that his very existence
threatened to negate your own. . . . And you could watch a 14-year-
old quickly develop a total feeling of injustice. This could have been
someone who'd never thought about the Jews before, and in a way that
was even better, because he'd had no time to develop perspective or
counterarguments. What you wanted was a fresh tablet upon which to
write.*[21]

Racist women similarly indicate that their anti-Semitism began with
contacts with confirmed anti-Semites. One woman, for example, explained, "I was friends with [Annabel, a racist activist] and [she] started
bringing up things that just made sense. The Jew being the dollar, the
Jew behind the TV, the Jew is behind the products that you buy at the
grocery store."

This message is reinforced in racist group propaganda. In speeches,
flyers, magazines and 'zines, song lyrics, and videos, the members, aspiring members, and potential recruits of racist groups are bombarded
with messages hinting that Jews control the world to further their own
evil interests, messages meant to lay the foundation for later revelations
of Jewish conspiracies. Jewish men are depicted as wealthy owners ex-
ploiting Aryan workers and controlling the government and economy.
As a Klanswoman commented, "American bankers and big business
[have] sold out for [Jewish] money." Earlier stereotypes of Jews as communists and communist sympathizers generally disappeared with the
breakup of the Soviet Union; but they continue to appear as figures of
moral evil, particularly as sexual harassers and sleazy abortionists who
victimize Aryan women. That the Jews being stereotyped are in fact
Jewish men is clear from the rarity with which Jewish women appear in
white supremacist propaganda, showing up only occasionally as nurses
at abortion clinics, man-hating feminists, supporters of African American criminality and indolence, or, very rarely, seducers of Aryan men.

Like carnival hucksters who promise ever more thrilling or titillating
sights, racist leaders suggest that there are more deeply hidden secrets
about Jews to be revealed to those deemed worthy of the knowledge.
Those who accept the first premises of anti-Semitism are judged suitable
to know more. As they accept that Jewish control of politicians, schools,

media, corporations, and banks has created what racist groups term a
"Zionist-occupied government" (ZOG), they are exposed to more veiled
"truths" about Jews, learning the intricacies of Jewish conspiracies.[22]
What they learn is that Jews are omnipotent but hidden from the public
eye. Jewish control is absolute. "They" (the unknown group of Jewish
conspirators) can do anything. They can grant, and revoke, all privileges
of daily life. My interviews elicited many statements suggesting the awesome, incomprehensible, and disembodied power of the conspirators,
including "they took my husband away from me," "we are not granted
permission for a white history month," and "if we don't succeed in
waking our people up, we will be annihilated." The historian Glenda
Gilmore describes how enemies can be endowed with "a mythical
force."[23] In her analysis, those enemies were blacks; here, the wielders
of this tremendous power are Jews.

Conspiracy theory connects disparate historical occurrences by a
form of "reasoning" that seems to provide a comprehensive rationale
for them all. A "hate line" telephone message warns that "controlling
the United States . . . has been a strategy of Jews for much longer than
we give them credit for. After all, who was it the United States was
sending over to Germany in World War II to fight against their own
brothers and sisters? Come on, Aryans."[24] A midwestern Nazi woman
called Jews "the people that have been in control, especially very strong
since the end of the Civil War, very strong. So they was part of the Civil
War. They was part of the French Revolution, the same groups. They
made the French Revolution. And it just goes so far back." Underlying
all conspiracy theories is the belief that there is a singular "truth"—a
complete and accurate interpretation of society, history, and politics—
that has been systematically hidden from most people.[25] Racist activists
see government bureaucrats, television producers, book publishers, and
school officials as powerful conspirators, all working together to prevent
the common person from understanding the truth. One Nazi woman
told me, "It's not just the media, but [it's] the powers that control television and radio, who control the schools and get into the children's
minds when they're young." A sister of one of the leaders of a racist
terrorist group in the 1980s recalled that her brother "never had a thing
against Jews until he began studying history."[26]

For those who believe in conspiracies, nothing is as it seems: the
events both of history and of everyday life are always disguised.[27] Conspiracies infect every experience, rendering ordinary perceptions and interpretations useless and misleading. A Klanswoman recounted that her

group "gave me the last piece of the puzzle, so to speak, to make sense of it all. They gave me the information that I didn't get anywhere else." What formerly appeared to be random is now seen to result from deliberate actions. Another commented that "when I opened my eyes, [I] became aware of just how brainwashed white people have become." Those who persist in believing the obvious are laboring under a misunderstanding. Another Klanswoman told me, "I spent time with [an activist]. I was shocked at the vast array of disinformation. . . . The deeper I dug the more lies I uncovered."[28] A neo-Nazi woman explained: "Being part of the movement is realizing that what you hear on the television and everything is not the true story. They don't tell you all the persecution that's happening to people who want to separate [racially] today. We just hear little snippets of it. Learning it has helped me have more of a commitment to want to separate." These women believe that they must act to pierce the veil of confusion. Like advocates of other marginal political causes, they are driven to document their claims. Individuals like themselves, they insist, must "research to find out the truth about issues suppressed by the media, what you don't learn in school." Or as a Nazi from Georgia put it, you must "teach [your children] the *truth* about things you won't read about in history books or see in the news."

Conspiratorial thinking assigns meaning and identity to believers. It reduces a complex world to simple categories of "us" and "them": no one falls in between. Moreover, it refuses to recognize differences among those identified as "them"; all Jews, or African Americans, or government officials are interchangeable and unified in their agendas. At the same time, it simplifies and unifies the group identified as "us," thus validating believers in their beliefs. As a southern woman commented, "In the Klan I found others that felt the way I felt." It creates a sense of commonality and community that spans great distances and transcends borders. In the words of a skinhead, it reveals "the unity between all, even in other states and overseas." A conspiracy that forces "us" to be unified and active gives life renewed purpose and direction. Being in the movement, a western woman claimed, meant that her "life changed forever." Another insisted that the racial movement has made her "responsible and drug-free"; yet another told me that "the pro-white movement has given me hope for a future."

Anti-Semitic conspiratorial thought pushes activists toward violent anti-Semitism by suggesting how "we" (the ordinary people, the non-conspirators) can challenge and even usurp the authority of the currently

powerful "them." A "dial-a-Nazi" phone line proclaims its "dedica-
t[ion] to the establishment of a national-socialist state for the repatri-
otization of the inferior races. And most importantly, elimination of the
tyranny that our ancient enemy the evil Jew has inflicted upon us. That's
right, we're anti-Semitic and proud of it."[29] In my interviews, nearly all
the women made brutal threats against Jews, with calls to "exterminate
them" or to "rid our land of the Jews and isolate them in a country of
their own." This verbal barrage is having tangible effects, as can be seen
in the increasing number of attacks on definably Jewish institutions—
synagogues, temples, Jewish children's camps, and Jewish cemeteries—
in recent years.

Though Jewish communities are terrorized by the desecration of
places of burial and worship, individual Jews are assaulted less often
than might be expected, given their intense demonization in organized
racism. Three factors may account for the relative scarcity of personal
attacks. First, racist activists find individual Jews hard to identify, both
because Jews and Aryans (unlike African Americans and Aryans) often
look similar and because they believe that Jews are generally disguised
or invisible. Second, to racist activists, Jews are an abstract enemy, so
their demise can be similarly abstract. As David Smith argues, anti-
Semitism can "flourish while Jews are left comparatively undisturbed,"
because Jews are "imaginary enemies, who can be fantastically annihilated."[30] Third, the anti-Semitism of modern racist groups is focused
intensely at government institutions, which are viewed as "Zionist-
occupied." Many white supremacist activists long for racial dictator-
ship. They see democratic government as tainted by its association with
Jewish conspirators and declare, "Democracy doesn't work; history
shows that." Antigovernment sentiments are often expressed in conspiratorial terms; thus one woman feared that the confrontation between
federal authorities and Randy Weaver, a white supremacist from Idaho,
might foreshadow her own fate. "The Weavers," she said, "they decided
to go move in a cabin, secluded all by themselves, just to get away, and
they're the number one target of the government . . . I wouldn't want to
move to an Aryan Nations or something right now because I think you
would be a prime target for government [assault]."

The sense that organized racists are, or will soon be, at war with the
government repeatedly surfaces in women's narratives. They speak of it
in justifying the most extreme survivalist preparations, such as assem-
bling large amounts of armaments and moving to remote locations. As
one woman put it: "I never heard from anybody that I know that going

to war with the government's going to be fun and profitable or anything. . . . Everybody is basically very afraid of that prospect and I think people prepare for it because there have been enough signs that people's civil liberties have been infringed in their home, which is supposed to be the place you have." Such a war also justifies violent actions against government institutions and personnel—including the bombing of the Oklahoma City federal building, which occurred midway through my interviews and which many of the women saw as provoked by the government: "A lot of people feel that way. I think it's going to happen again and again and again."

Christian Identity women express this theme in biblical terms. Thus a shut-in from the West equated the struggle of the racist movement to that of the biblical Israelites: "The account in the Bible where the Israelites were fighting a very difficult battle; the 'odds' were against them, they were outnumbered and God told Moses to hold his hands up."[31] Women from groups that lack a religious slant are more likely to use secular metaphors of war when describing the coming battle with the federal government and the emerging "one-world order":

I think our future will be much like what you read about in The Turner Diaries[32] — *an extremely oppressive new world order regime which will take over the U.S. I think freedom of speech and press will be totally gone within five years. I see the government trying to confiscate all weapons. I think that will happen in five years also, possibly sooner. The government can't really do all they want until they disarm the American people. Once that happens, the shit will hit the proverbial fan.*

The Jewish conspiracy taught by organized racism includes three elements: that Jews have distorted modern history, that the Jewish agenda is a "one-world" government, and that Jews manipulate racial strife. On these foundational blocks, the racist movement builds its *extraordinary* ideology of anti-Semitism.

Distortion of History Perhaps the most bizarre aspect of anti-Semitic conspiratorial thinking, and the most outrageous, is the denial that massive numbers of Jews were murdered during World War II. Although their exact argument varies, Holocaust deniers generally dismiss the claim that six million Jews died (supplying instead a significantly lower number), charge that most Jewish deaths were the result of ordinary hardships of war rather than Nazi policies of extermination, and insist that

Jews have distorted history to garner world sympathy and financial support for the state of Israel.[33]

A particularly striking example of the horrific logic of Holocaust denial is found in *The True History of "The Holocaust,"* an anonymous, undated book prepared by the Historical Review Press and distributed by a Klan group. Created to explain what its adherents refer to as the "revisionist historical" position on the Jewish Holocaust, the book claims to proffer new evidence that the Nazis and their allies killed far fewer European Jews than standard estimates suggest. This "evidence" is a jumble of historical hyperbole, distortion, and omission, but the book insists that its conclusions are solidly grounded in scientific fact and discovery. *True History* tries to refute conventional interpretations of World War II by providing "British, Canadian and American churches and schools" with "irrefutable evidence that the allegation that 6 million Jews died during the Second World War, as a direct result of official German policy of extermination, is utterly unfounded. . . . In terms of political blackmail, however, the allegation . . . has much more far-reaching implications for the people of Britain and Europe than simply the advantages it has gained for the Jewish nation."[34]

In recent years, Holocaust denial has become a propaganda mainstay of organized racism. It is promulgated by racist groups and by organizations like the Institute for Historical Review (IHR), which publishes the scientific-looking *Journal of Historical Review*. Such groups focus on various technical aspects of the Holocaust, such as the nature of the gas used in concentration camps or the exact capacity of railroad cars used to transport Jewish prisoners to the camps. They also sponsor speakers who attempt to gain access to college classrooms or lecture halls to dispute the validity of official accounts of World War II.[35]

The extent to which such propagandistic images of the Holocaust are accepted by members of racist groups is unclear. Most women I interviewed did express some reservations about standard accounts of World War II and many interjected, as their own ideas, pat comments about the Holocaust that can be found almost verbatim in white supremacist propaganda; for example, one told me, "The Jews have been kicked out of nearly every country they have ever been in for crimes against the people of those countries and made up the Holocaust for their own financial gain." But many found it difficult to justify their dismissal of standard Holocaust history. When asked her to explain her Nazi group's (and presumably her) opinion of the Holocaust, Margaret provided a typically convoluted response:

We kind of believe that, we don't kind of believe, we believe that the six million figure is greatly exaggerated and a lot of other things about the Holocaust that people accept as fact in fact were really war propaganda. . . . You know, I'm not comfortable with doing it like, you know, I don't know what it has to do with it. If it has to do with history, it has to do with history but I hate to see a political agenda in this particular issue because it doesn't really have a place in there. All these emotions, on both sides, you know, all this emotional crap issue. It should be an objective thing, like, you know, a scholarly thing.

This oddly backtracking and unfocused answer from an otherwise highly articulate woman illustrates the characteristically shallow understanding of racist ideology displayed by even committed believers. It also points to problems in the ideology of Holocaust denial. For white supremacists, the Jewish Holocaust must be denied, but its reality is also desired. Raphael Ezekiel points out that the racist activists he interviewed talked incessantly about the Holocaust to assure themselves that the aims of Nazis can be realized.[36] A belief in Jewish extermination can be empowering to anti-Semitic activists even as claims about Jewish manipulation of history require that that extermination be denied. In the thinking of some racist women, if the genocide of Jews was a good thing, why minimize its extent?

These conflicting agendas make racist narratives on the topic of World War II labyrinthine and nearly impossible to follow. One white supremacist woman told me first that Jews exaggerated the Holocaust and, a few minutes later, that the loss of Jewish lives in World War II was larger than conventionally reported. Similarly, a skinhead provided a self-contradictory description of going to hear one of the country's most notorious Holocaust deniers. She initially seemed to accept the speaker's premise that gassing did not occur in the Nazi death camp at Auschwitz; later she suggested that it might have happened but wouldn't have been "the worst thing to do." As she described it: "He made a video at Auschwitz where he sat down and interviewed a few of the people . . . and [he] got conflicting answers to some penetrating questions, so that was very interesting. He basically gave really good evidence in his video that gassing did not take place in Auschwitz, but you have to consider starvation, typhus, mistreatment, medical experiments, and all the rest of it. I wouldn't say that gassing would be the worst thing to do to a person really."

"One-World" Government The anti-Semitic ideology learned in white supremacist groups is also built on the premise that Jews control the United States with the aim of enacting a worldwide Jewish system of economic, political, and ideological control, known among racists as a "one [or new] world order."[37] A skinhead from the Rocky Mountains commented that "the Jew 'new world order' is the worst thing ever, especially for the white race and also for every single individual in the world—besides the government and Jews." Ku Klux Klan members, Aryan supremacists, and neo-Nazis all embrace the idea that internationalism looms on the immediate horizon and that Jewish interests dominate the push for an international government. Groups like the Ku Klux Klans that have historically stressed xenophobic, anti-immigrant, and nationalistic themes emphasize the threat that a "one-world" government would pose to U.S. national interests. Aryan supremacists accentuate what they see as Jewish control of international relations. All concur that a cabal of very wealthy Jews is controlling the United States through the United Nations. One woman told me that in "the new world order that the government is arranging, America will be reduced to a pathetic state of subservience to the powers that be. Nothing can be done at this point because they will have taken our arms [by] convincing us that it would make the country safer, and we will have coded identity cards that we will need in order to buy food or anything else. All of the UN prison camps that they are setting up all over the U.S. will be used to isolate any offenders."

The anti-Semitic ideas pervasive in racist groups are often expressed incoherently by individual racist activists. One woman, who identified Masons as secretly Jews, asserted, "Jews have the most control. All the presidents except one were Masons which is a Zionist-Jewish religion, who believe that they will take over the world, the 'new world order.' " With more logic, if no more accuracy, a neo-Nazi skinhead stated, "Jews represent only 1.5 percent of the U.S. population yet at least half of all appointees to positions in the government have been Jews. The list of people in control of the government, banking, media, and entertainment reads like a synagogue roster. Their agenda is to bring in the new world order, with most of it being their people in control of things whether in front of or behind the scene."

As with Holocaust denial, the idea that Jewish forces are promoting a one-world order is riddled with contradictions. Most obvious is the mismatch between the racist movement's fear that the current American system will be undermined by Jewish forces of internationalism and its

violent opposition to what they regard as today's American Zionist-
occupied government. Similarly, far-right conspiratorial theorists insisted that the year 2000 would be catastrophic while simultaneously
attributing fears of the year 2000 (which they termed "the Y2K craze")
to a ZOG plot to confuse and thereby dominate the masses.[38] One
woman expressed these confusions succinctly: "The government is controlled by Jews, until it doesn't really matter."

A particularly vexing contradiction for racist activists involves the
media.[39] On the one hand, racist activists concur that the media are
controlled by Jews and promote an international agenda. In the words
of a Klanswoman: "[The one-world order] started in a very clever way
through the media. . . . It's really disgusting what they show anymore:
[in] the Jordache Jeans commercial, they show a black and white almost
in pornography. This Jordache Jeans, they are [a company owned by]
three immigrant Jews. It's just every time something was in the negative
to Western civilization, basically there was always somewhere a Jewish
person behind it." Most are also convinced that mainstream media target the racist movement for criticism or ridicule:

*The more I learned, the more convinced I became that the media has a
blackout on the pro-white movement which is only slowly lifting at
this time.*

*[Before joining] I had always believed the media's lies about racism
being a bad thing and a belief espoused by idiots with no education or
intelligence.*

On the other hand, even ZOG-controlled media can provide a forum
for racist propaganda. Television, especially talk shows, presents an opportunity to present racist ideas to a mass public and to be in the lime-
light.[40] The racist activists also enjoy shocking audiences with their
ideas: "We go on talk shows and get out a whole bunch of statistics
before they cut us off. We had fun doing this too, made it a game."

The belief in a Jewish one-world order dominating the government
and media is based on more than anti-Semitism and xenophobia. It
draws on a number of seemingly unrelated concerns shared by many
Americans, including fears that the government is reducing personal privacy, worries that parents lack control over their children's education,
and a sense that social, economic, and cultural change is accelerating
(signified in part by the transformation of corporations into monopolies). Racist groups elaborate these mainstream ideas to teach that they

are all part of the same problem of Jewish control. Typically, the fears of a southern Klanswoman about computers, the financial system, corporations, media, and the government appeared together in her insistence that

The one-world order is fast approaching and the computers have taken over 95 percent of all transactions, 90 percent of all communications, and as far as payroll and management it's almost 100 percent. So one-world order is here and it's backed by Jewish money and Jewish organizations. Although they're the ones that openly said, "No, we're against it," they're secretly in it. They're all a part of it because they own the government, they own a percentage of the government, the media, [and] our Federal Reserve system.

Women learn to express their discontent in anti-Semitic tones; another Klanswoman told me that she was "tired of working and my hard-earned tax dollars going to the very ones who hate me . . . tired of the government interfering in my private life . . . tired of the Jew-controlled government teaching my child what they want him to believe . . . tired of seeing my white brothers go to prisons for standing up for their rights." Her words convey a desire for personal autonomy, a belief in local control of the schools, and a suspicion of police and prosecutors often found in progressive politics. But here these ideas are framed by racial hatred and bigotry.

The points of overlap between racist and mainstream ideas help racist groups recruit ordinary people. They can draw on long-standing racist ideas widely shared among mainstream whites about African Americans and other racial minorities, but there are fewer established prejudices and concerns about Jews. Racist groups therefore rely on more diffuse fears about society, government, and the economy that can be steered in an anti-Semitic direction, once again building their outlandish ideas (this time, of extraordinary anti-Semitism) on more accepted views. Consider the following three statements, the first from an antiracist woman who supports private gun ownership and the second and third from two Aryan supremacist activists:

The worst-case scenario I can think of is that laws are passed that basically ban all firearms, which leads to confiscations. So that every person who has a concealed weapon license, which is basically every law-abiding person, gets their doors stormed in and their firearms

confiscated, and their cats killed, and whatever else they want to do while they're there.

Look at Waco and the Weavers and stuff. I mean, they choose to move away from society and then all of a sudden they're getting their house burned down or getting shot.

Existing laws ensure total control of and by local, state and federal agencies over all decisions made by the parent, with regards to the welfare of the child. . . . The tragedy at Ruby Ridge in Idaho [i.e., the Randy Weaver confrontation], involving the murder of a mother and her child, was all that anyone needed to see as proof of this brutal control.[41]

Here what separates the racist from the nonracist is only the idea, expressed later in the racists' stories, that the government they fear is controlled by Jews.

Widespread social concerns about the decline of family values also are a foundation on which racist groups can build, teaching that the Aryan family will face destruction in a ZOG- dominated one-world government. An Aryan supremacist told me that the biggest problem facing society was "Jews [who promote] the loss of family structure and the values that are instilled into children in a family structure." Another insisted that "the adversary, whoever you want to call them, is destroying the family values in America, because they are the root of any good nation and if they destroy the family values, they will destroy the nation." What distinguishes the words of these racist women from those of mainstream conservative women is not their conclusion that the family is dying but their choice of the party responsible for its downfall.

Such similarities do not merely indicate that effective racist activists learn to speak in politically acceptable terms. Rather, they suggest that organized racism persists because its ideas overlap with more conventional ones. Citing ZOG influence, a Klanswoman declared: "I'd say we're one step away from vigilante activity in America, when you see people calling the Klan instead of the sheriff's department. But of course we are not ourselves ready for that."

Manipulation of Racial Strife A third element of anti-Semitism that racist groups teach their recruits is the belief that Jews are orchestrating a "race war," which is often linked to the imposition of the "one-world order."

"I feel the new world order will trigger the race war and I think the new world order will be enforced by 1998 to 2000 and the race war will follow soon after that," explained a Klanswoman. Racist groups teach that Jews manipulate and benefit from tensions between whites and African Americans, thus instructing members to tie their hatred of racial minorities to anti-Semitism. A midwestern Nazi told me, "When I first joined [my group], it was for dislike of blacks. Now I realize the Jews are controlling their puppets, the blacks, for their own means." Another woman confided that "the Jews have used blacks like a tool to take over America, [like] a battering ram."

Most women foresaw an armed struggle between Aryans and all other races manipulated in their battle by unseen Jewish controllers. One midwestern white supremacist told me, "A race war is coming. *They're* predicting one—even the government knows it's coming." These women generally view the coming race war as inescapable. It is the culmination of forces that are unseen and unstoppable. Whites, they insist, must prepare themselves for this inevitability by practicing techniques of survivalism and by paramilitary training. Many thus claim to maintain a substantial cache of foodstuffs, along with emergency medical supplies, water, guns, and ammunition, in remote rural hideouts. The cities, they imagine, will be under the control of armed bands of African Americans, Hispanics, and other people of color, all operating under the careful watch of their Jewish overlords.

Some are certain that this racial conflict will occur, though they are hazy on its timing. A Klanswoman and a racist skinhead commented, respectively:

I would say a race war is inevitable, but I couldn't say when. I have lived in the country all my life so I'm not living around other races, but if a race war does hit the country, of course I know which side I'm on.

I think [the country] is going to either explode and there's going to be either a racial war or something really soon because of all the racial tension and all the problems. . . . Because a lot of white males, regardless of whether or not they are racialist, are upset at how much is being taken from them.

Other women present race war as simply the unfolding of inevitable historical dynamics, as did a Christian Identity woman and another skinhead:

A race war is inevitable because when you mix, cohabitate races, when you have them dwelling together, it is unnatural for them . . . and when you put opposite people in a situation together it will cause unrest.

The race war is here and has been going on since biblical times [with] Euro-Americans, Asians, Africans in competition for air, land, and water.

The idea of "race war" is often tinged with a general apocalyptic sentiment among organized racists. As noted above, this notion sometimes is grafted onto other racist ideas, such as the belief that a one-world government will soon be imposed. At other times the apocalypse foreseen is literal, rooted in biblical notions of an end-time battle between good and evil and Christian Fundamentalist prophecies of the end of the world.[42] In either case, the race war predicted is powerfully dualistic, playing out an absolute contrast between Aryans and their demonic Jewish enemies.[43]

VIOLATING RACIST BELIEF

We have already heard Margaret's fumbling attempt to recount the beliefs of Holocaust denial. Although much of her adult life has been dedicated to violent neo-Nazi activism, she ultimately wavered in her commitment to a core tenet of Holocaust denial—that claims of genocide during World War II were manufactured for the financial and political gain of Jews. Such equivocation is found among many racist women activists, as their private racial beliefs sometimes veer from the official positions of their organizations. Those expressing ambivalence may be highly committed to their groups, as their own public statements aligned with the groups' agendas make clear; they include active, long-term members and even leaders.[44]

Some women make statements that disregard, even distort, the very principles that are central to the mission of racist groups.[45] A member of an explicitly Nazi group said she liked the group because "it doesn't really place the blame for a lot of things you know squarely on one particular people—like, say, the Jews or something." Others dismiss the idea that they were drawn to participate in the group because of its beliefs; a middle-aged woman claimed that she joined the Klan simply because "you can meet celebrities . . . you know, [referring to talk show

Klansmen] people you see on television." Another maintained that the leader of her openly Nazi group was different from other racial leaders, whom she characterized as "more hate-filled": "[His is] a whole different approach to all of this. I sometimes think he's not really one of them. I think maybe he's not. He might be on a secret mission from God or something."

There were also discrepancies between the public statements and the private actions of racist women. Nearly all the women I talked to, including those in leadership positions, admitted doing things that were explicitly or implicitly banned by their groups.[46] When I asked a Klanswoman about abortion, which her group strongly opposes, she replied, "Oh, Lord. I have to tell you, I had one myself. I think it's a perfectly private thing. . . . It should never be part of a political platform. Not an issue out in public." Another woman explained that "the Klan is against abortion, but I think it should be left to the individual. It wouldn't be right for myself, but better to have an abortion than to abuse it. But the Klan is dead set against it, as are my brothers and my family."

It is not uncommon for racist women to ignore the prohibition against personal contact with outsiders. Conspiracy-based movements seek to limit or ban encounters between their members and those who might puncture the conspiracy's logic. But many women racists continue to maintain ties to outsiders, including those of other races, religions, nationalities, and sexual orientations. Almost one-third of the women told me of mixed-race or homosexual family members with whom they were on friendly terms.[47] A young neo-Nazi leader on the West Coast disclosed that her best friend was married to an African American man and that their children played together. An Aryan supremacist in New England told of being involved in a lesbian-dominated goddess-worship group; she dismissed the suggestion that her participation ran counter to the antihomosexual politics of her group by saying, "Oh, we're just great friends . . . none of us really believe in the label thing." A skinhead from the West related her efforts to maintain a friendship with a non-racist friend: "I tried to talk to one of my friends, you know, [saying] 'Really, it makes a lot of sense.' And she's like, 'Listen, I'm one of the only people that still talks to you from high school. Don't do this to me. Don't put me in this situation.' And I was, like, 'Okay.' And we're still friends to this day."

Like participants in other social movements, women racial activists disregard particular creeds and conventions of their groups that are at variance with their personal goals or allegiances. Such inconsistencies can result in bizarre twists; for example, a neo-Nazi woman covered with swastika jewelry and insignia claimed that she was interested in getting to know Jewish people but explained that "they generally stay away from me. They demand a certain kind of loyalty and if you're not loyal to their interests you can't be their friend." For these women, "collective identity"—what the sociologist William Gamson refers to as the process of defining "being part of a 'we' who can do something"[48]—can be highly fragmentary, as they selectively adopt group agendas and identities.

Such ideological distancing enables women to participate in racist groups whose goals and agendas—largely forged by the beliefs of male racist leaders—are not fully consonant with their lives and relationships. A woman who distributed vicious antigay flyers later confided to me, "I don't agree that gays deserve AIDS, deserve to die, but that's what [my group] says," and hinted that she had friends who were lesbian. As these women became racist activists, they adopted the ideas that least threatened their own lives and personal commitments; the rest they simply ignored. In a particularly striking example of putting family concerns before ideology, one dedicated neo-Nazi took her son to a Jewish psychiatrist to seek help for problems caused by the family's violent clashes with the police and antiracist skinheads.

The contrast between the ideologies of racist groups and the expressed personal beliefs and daily life practices of their women members can be seen clearly in the stories of three women: Alice, Lucy, and Shirley.

Alice

In the story of Alice, a neo-Nazi, we see one way that organizational propaganda and the personal stances of racist activist women can differ. Though a recent series of prosecutions and civil cases has weakened the group, one of the most prominent neo-Nazi groups that include women members has been the Movement for White Resistance (MWR), which espouses an anticapitalist, anticommunist, anti-elitist, and racist philosophy, claiming to take the side of white working people against both race mixing and capitalist exploitation. It appeared in the early 1980s with a declaration decrying the fate of the white workers in the era of deindustrialization and calling on Aryan "soldiers" to take up arms to resist. MWR leaders are extremely critical of others on the right, such as David Duke and many Klan leaders (whom they see as not radical enough), as well as the new Christian right (whom they view as brain-washed by religion).

At the time of our interview, Alice, a twenty-seven-year-old woman from Michigan, had been associated with the MWR for eight years. She initially heard of the group through her older brothers, who were long-time members; they persuaded her to join the women's affiliate. While in the MWR, Alice met and married Rex, a skinhead who later became peripherally involved in the MWR. They had a five-year-old son. Ever since Rex was sentenced to prison for armed assault, Alice had become more heavily involved with the racist movement.

As a teenager, Alice had high ambitions for a career. After she joined the MWR, however, her racist politics clashed with those of teachers and other students, and she found it too hard to continue in school. She completed a GED and hoped to begin college, but being a racist activist once again stood in the way of her education. When her husband was arrested, Alice became the sole support of their son, and she decided to defer college until her husband's release. In the meantime, she worked odd jobs, most recently as a waitress at a local restaurant. She had no clear occupational goal; she saw her life as mainly "getting through daily routines, dealing with society the way it is in my own way."

Alice's beliefs both mirrored and contrasted with the doctrines of the Movement of White Resistance. Like others in the group, Alice favored "separating ourselves from the nonwhites." Indeed, she claimed that her interest in racial activism stemmed from her disgust at interracial couples. When asked what she saw as the biggest problems facing society today, Alice quickly listed "race mixing, [interracial] dating, marriage"; and, consistent with MWR propaganda, she attributed the world's problems to "Jews, NAACP, and the government," singling out Jews as the most powerful "because they get the votes." She concurred with the neo-Nazi view that a race war is coming, though she hedged about the timing: "I feel that [a race war] is due. I don't know if it's anytime soon. I feel it will be in the future." Like many racist leaders, Alice insisted that she did not hate other races, she "just chooses not to socialize with them"; but when asked her vision for the United States in the future, she presented a scenario that was far less benign: "I'd like separation . . . if we have to live together I'd like punishment handed down to people of different races. I think the future will turn to violence. That's why I'm looking for a mostly white state if possible, a better place."

The most striking difference between Alice's rhetoric and MWR propaganda lies in what is missing from Alice's comments. Nothing in her

three-hour interview suggested that Alice was interested in global eco-
nomics, the decline of the middle class, or corporate ravaging of the
environment—issues that are key to how the MWR construes racial
politics. Indeed, on a number of issues Alice's views were at odds with
some of the basics expressed in MWR propaganda. While the MWR
insists on armed resistance as the only way to avenge the wrongs done
to Aryan citizens, for example, Alice argued for a more cautious, electoral approach to racial politics. The best way to change the situation
of "Jews, NAACP, and the government" running the world, she told
me, was "just to get better people in office and in the political spotlight."
Though violent confrontation is a major recruiting tactic of MWR, Alice
believed that the racist movement will be built simply by "getting the
word out so people notice."

This emphasis on less violent forms of racial confrontation did not
demonstrate a disagreement with MWR propaganda stressing armed
resistance. It instead reflected Alice's pragmatic concerns as a single parent with a husband in prison. Although she admitted that she was initially attracted to the MWR because of its reputation for violent rhetoric, she now believed that its literal battles, such as street fights with
African Americans, "need to stop or all our people will be in prison."
Taking a longer perspective on the goals of racial politics, Alice cau-
tioned that violence leads to the incarceration of racial activists, thereby
preventing them from influencing their children. Yet her differences with
the MWR had not lessened her commitment to the group or to the
struggle for white supremacism.

Alice's views on issues of gender similarly reflected her life experiences, drawing on but not perfectly reproducing the gender ideology of
the MWR. Asked if she had any personal contacts with African Americans, for example, Alice related a standard racist account of an African
American co-worker, whom she described as "a typical black male [be-
cause] he likes white girls." Although MWR literature presents white
women as victimized by African American men, Alice painted a quite
different picture: "I'm pretty much a bitch to him, I put him in his place."
That assertiveness also fueled her criticism of feminists, whom she attacked not for intruding on men's prerogatives, as does MWR literature,
but for being "too wimpy. They're not strong enough to get along by
themselves." Yet she by no means embraced a feminist ideology. Like
many women in the racist movement, Alice was torn between an aggressive assertion of white female privilege against white men and all
peoples of color and an equally powerful conviction that the future of

white supremacism rests on procreation by white women. Being in the MWR, Alice maintained, made her "think about my race more than I ever did and I just want to have babies, babies, babies, to help myself and my race."

Other disagreements with the MWR may have reflected Alice's unfamiliarity with the organization's positions. Despite the virulent attacks on David Duke that pepper MWR literature, for example, Alice immediately identified Duke when asked to name her political heroes. Duke, she maintained, "feels the same way I do . . . he knows what he's talking about, about integration, schooling, the race mixing."

Lucy

Lucy, a member of the Ku Klux Klan, dissented from her group more explicitly and in greater detail. A thirty-year-old from a small town in Tennessee, Lucy was a high school graduate. At the time of our interview she had no concrete plans to attend college, but she expressed a vague desire to earn a degree that would enable her to work in child care. She was working as a cashier at a local video store, was married, and had no children.

Lucy's interest in the Ku Klux Klan began in high school when she was persuaded to attend a Klan meeting by her cousin, a recent recruit. Lucy said she was impressed at the meeting by "people [who] could stand up for themselves and not be ashamed of it and really act on what they believe in." Through her cousin she was introduced to a regional Klan leader who successfully urged her to attend those meetings. Eventually, she decided to join, and she persuaded her husband to join at the same time.

I was more for it, but he kind of wanted to join, but he just wouldn't you know, put that last foot forward, and when I made my decision he said, "What are you going to do?" And I said, "Well, I'm going to join." And he said, "Are you sure?" and I said, "Yeah, you can join with me." And he was like, "Well, if you join, I'll join." But he wanted to, so I can't really say that I made the final decision, but with me joining, it let him take his last foot and step in the doorway.

Lucy echoed the fraudulent message projected by some modern Klan leaders: that the Klan is a benign organization supporting the interests of white people. She maintained, "It's just being involved in something you really want to do. . . . Just like a big family." In line with the Klan's recent efforts to deny its racist views, Lucy insisted that her Klan membership did not mean that she was racially bigoted or even intolerant of other religions or sexual orientations: "In school my best friend was black . . . I've got a family member that's bisexual, and the Klan's supposed to be against that. So you know it's just the person, not the race, not the religion. If I'm gonna like you, I like you for *who* you are, not *what* you are."

Her departures from the Klan's ideology centered largely on issues of gender. Like many Klanswomen, Lucy was dissatisfied with the limited role she was allowed within the Klan. Furthermore, she argued that the Klan's agendas were influenced more by men's desire for aggressive combat than by racial ideology. Lucy saw racist violence as necessary but often lacking a strategic focus, propelled mainly by men's desires for physical superiority. "The biggest issue," she indicated, "is probably the minorities and the whites. They've all gotta prove something and that's the way they think they gotta prove it. 'Oh, I'm a white guy and I beat up a black man yesterday.' . . . And, you know, it's a power kick. They all want it and that's the way they think they gotta go about getting it."

Shirley

Shirley, a twenty-four-year-old member of a Christian Identity (CI) church, provides a very different story of ambivalence. At the time of our interview, she was living near a group of other Christian Identity members in a remote rural area outside a midsize city. Recently married, she had no children. Like many other young Christian Identity adherents, Shirley's commitment to Aryan supremacism started at an early age when her parents became involved with a CI group in the far West. From that point on, Shirley's life was increasingly shaped by precepts of Christian Identity. Her schooling, religious education, employment, and social life were largely in CI-affiliated schools, churches, and youth groups. Shirley had a high school degree, but her plans for future education were complicated by fears of the "indoctrination" she would receive in a secular university.

More than was true of Alice, Shirley's beliefs and actions mirrored the CI groups to which she had pledged her life. In part this agreement was an outgrowth of her early socialization into Christian Identity ideologies, but it also reflected the all-encompassing nature of many CI groups, whose members generally avoid significant contact with the non-CI world. Shirley avidly embraced both the white and Christian

supremacist beliefs of Christian Identity and its confrontational organizational tactics. She particularly liked "its aggressive stance toward
the need to have a movement for white people in America." Asked to
name her political heroes, Shirley picked the Confederate Civil War general Robert E. Lee for what she regarded as his great military accomplishments against formidable odds.

Shirley—a woman raised and continuing to live in an isolated racist
community—presents an extreme case. But even she disagreed with one
of the main principles of her group, the idea that childbearing is an act
of racial conviction for women. When talking with me about her life,
Shirley admitted that although she'd "like to have a few children," she
was not interested in raising a large family of children for the movement.
Although it does not seem momentous, such an assertion challenges the
fundamental place of women in Christian Identity politics.

Unlike Shirley, most racist women were not raised in racist activist
homes. Rather, they began to associate with organized racism as adults
or teenagers. And it was in racist groups that they refined their ideas
about enemies. They learned to fashion ideas of everyday racism into
an ideology of extraordinary racism that in turn deepened their commitment to organized racism as a way of guarding the white race from
its enemies. Racist groups draw from the political mainstream. Core
elements of racism targeting African Americans, of xenophobia, and
even parts of anti-Semitism supply platforms on which racist groups
construct extraordinary ideologies about enemies that seem plausible to
their members.

The term *enemy* means something very different in organized racism
than in other social movements. Most movement activists differentiate
themselves from an outside enemy: environmentalists see corporate pol-
luters as the enemy, good government movements target corrupt politicians, and peace activists identify advocates of war. To a certain extent,
the group defines itself and enhances its commonality against an opposing group. But in organized racism, the process takes on far greater
importance. Both the casual banter among members and the central
texts of the movement exhibit a highly developed and vicious notion of
racial enemies.

Having a well-defined enemy is crucial to a movement that lacks other
immediate payoffs for its members.[49] Being a racist entails high costs,
and the idea of fending off a worse fate can provide partial compensa-
tion. As a white supremacist women imprisoned for an assault on a

minority group person put it, "Now I'm a criminal so it's like my life means nothing. So, the only thing I hold on to is my beliefs and my son." The notion of an enemy helps solidify racist identities by creating a sense of mutual besiegement. There is an "us," because we face a common racial fate. This unity holds even if the definition of who constitutes an enemy is vague. Raphael Ezekiel notes that one southern Klan leader "is fuzzy about the nature of his enemy when we are sitting and talking. Whenever I try to point to the identity of the enemy and get straight [his] enmity and the grounds for it, he slides off into trivia or repeats barely relevant scraps of movement pseudo-history. . . . [T]he category enemy lacks substance."[50]

In addition, racist groups have little sense of political alternatives. They are unable to envision the future because of their ambivalence toward other whites, their presumed allies, and also because their members and leaders often are interested in simple slogans rather than ideas. These groups, unlike most political movements, contain few "intellectuals." Lacking a developed vision of the future beyond empty calls for a "white homeland" or a "Jew-free" country, the racist movement focuses on detailing the threats faced in the present.

Racist women zealously parrot the attacks on African Americans, Jews, and Hispanics found in racist propaganda, yet, as with believers wholeheartedly committed to religions whose rules they ignore or whose principles they privately contest, their statements and behaviors are sometimes contradictory. When women recite vile anti-Semitic ideas but retain Jewish friends or promote the Klan yet criticize its principles, they demonstrate that even participation in an extremist movement such as organized racism does not force a complete change in beliefs or personal choices.

The ideological and behavioral latitude of organized racism is partly a function of decentralization and of a desire to heighten recruitment, which makes groups reluctant to sanction members.[51] But it also results from the broad compass of extraordinary racism. Although hatred of Jews and racial minorities is always at their core, racist groups embrace, in varying degrees, other ideas and values, including militarism, gender hierarchy, patriarchy, and nationalism,[52] as well as individual achievement, aggression, courage, authoritarianism, conformity, and the need for a strong state.[53] Perhaps the ideology of extraordinary racism is best seen as fitting the description of modern racism offered by the political theorist Étienne Balibar: "a number of racisms, forming a broad, open spectrum of situations" rather than a "singular, monolithic racism."[54]

This broad scope permits some variation in belief and practice among its members even while the central focus on whiteness and its enemies is maintained.

Scholars of culture often point to the "polyvalence" of texts,[55] seen as containing multiple, even contradictory messages that can be adopted differently by various audiences rather than as conveying one consistent message. As discourse analysts find, people use "different interpretive repertories to accomplish different actions,"[56] and racist activists are no exception. Members at all levels of racist groups actively construct and interpret racist understandings in accordance with the specificities of their own lives. While these inconsistencies of practice and belief rarely seem to hinder women's practical allegiance to their group's agenda, they may, as the next chapter discusses, make the racist movement more fragile.

A neo-Nazi group's simple but powerful
graphics clearly denounce interracial
sexuality.

Above: White power activists
demonstrate in support of police
after a racial shooting in 1982.
(Photo courtesy Ted Dunn.)

Right: This cartoon suggests
that men's racist activism will result
in sexual access to white women.
(Courtesy Resistance Records.)

Above: An advertisement in a white power music magazine emphasizes tradition in appealing to women. (Courtesy Resistance Records.)

Right, top: Appeals to the need to protect white children are common in racist recruiting drives. (Courtesy The New Order.)

Right, bottom: To recruit women, this neo-Nazi flyer appeals to their concerns for the safety of their children.

Save Me!
I don't want to live in a crime-infested, black jungle.
I don't want to be raped or murdered!
Please, don't let them hurt me!
Save Me!
Save *all* the White children.
Our future is up to YOU !!!

Aryan children need more to cling to than Teddybears............

They need a future !

Above: Racist gatherings bring the whole
family together, as in this group portrait
of a white power gathering in 1992.
Note: Here and elsewhere faces have been
obscured to respect privacy rights.
(Photo courtesy Ted Dunn.)

Right, top: A Klan member makes his
allegiances clear on his wedding day in
the 1980s. (Photo courtesy Ted Dunn.)

Right, bottom: This skinhead flyer graphically conveys both the maternal and the
activist roles of racist women.

Above: This Nazi recruiting flyer places a woman front and center in the group.

Right, top: The racist salute clearly identifies the stance of these activists at a gathering in the 1990s. (Photo courtesy Ted Dunn.)

Right, bottom: Cross burning at a Klan rally. (Photo courtesy Ted Dunn.)

Above: A racist salute is almost de rigeur in any group portrait, such as this one of women at an Aryan fest in 1991. (Photo courtesy Ted Dunn.)

Right, top: Skingirls. (Reprinted with permission from *Skinhead Street Gangs* by Loren Christenson, Paladin Press, Boulder, Colorado.)

Right, bottom: Music is often used to promote racism, especially among youth, as this skinhead flyer suggests.

ARYAN
SUMMERFEST 93
SATURDAY, JULY 24, 1993 - ULYSSES, PENNSYLVANIA

TRI-STATE TERROR PRESENTS:

BOUND FOR GLORY
THE VOICE
AGGRAVATED ASSAULT
NORDIC THUNDER

Plus Special Guests (to be announced)

TICKETS ARE: $15.00 IN ADVANCE OR $20.00 DAY OF THE SHOW

ROCK & ROLL FOR THE MASTER RACE

LIVING AS A RACIST

THE PLACE OF WOMEN

Deep in rural Pennsylvania, eighteen young women gathered on an out-door stage to be photographed for the cover of their group's newsletter giving a collective Nazi salute at the 1992 Annual Aryan Festival. Some held babies. One of them spoke for the group, announcing that white Aryan women were now ready to do battle with ZOG (the Zionist-occupied government) and its white traitor supporters and that the threat of neither imprisonment nor death could deter them from this mission.[1]

That same year, the Aryan Women's League (AWL) published a eu-logy to a woman they characterized as "epitomiz[ing] Aryan woman-hood." They extolled her "legacy of absolute loyalty to her husband, her children, and her Race, which she served all her life." Particularly noted was her deepening racist involvement over her forty-five years of political activism, which began in her young adulthood. First a Girl Scout leader and Republican Party activist, she later worked on behalf of American Independent Party presidential candidate George Wallace; she then married a midwestern Klan leader. Her political career culmi-nated when she became the Klan's state secretary and, during her hus-band's imprisonment and in defiance of federal authorities, operator of a racist publishing house.[2]

These two vignettes of racist activism are quite different, but both present women in familial as well as racial roles. Women are mothers of babies; women are politically supportive wives who parade the vilest form of racism. To those victimized and disgusted by organized racism, such images are frightening and confusing. They suggest that women's family-oriented activities not only can expand to a politics of caretaking, justice, and resistance to capitalism, colonialism, and imperialism, such as that displayed by the Argentinean Mothers of the Plaza de Mayo or by mothers involved in environmental justice movements in the United States, but also can become deeply entangled with reactionary and bigoted interests. These images highlight women's familial concerns being used to support agendas of racial supremacy.[3]

Depictions of racist women often are tinged with gender ambiguity. Using the historian Joan Scott's insight that gender "provides a way to decode meaning and to understand the complex connections among various forms of human interaction,"[4] we can see several such ambiguities in the montages of organized racism. The women gathered on the Aryan Festival stage are not posed with husband or boyfriends; they are depicted with other women, not as wives of racist men. Their pledge to do battle with ZOG is presented as their view, not that of male intimates. The AWL eulogy of a woman who lived her political life largely overshadowed by a more prominent racist husband seems to adhere more closely to conventional gender roles. Yet the AWL glorifies her as a model of "Aryan womanhood" by describing—probably erroneously—her increasing racist commitment as a personal decision, not as acquiescence to the political ideas of her husband.

As racist groups reach out to recruit women, it is increasingly important to examine their gender-specific appeals. How does the racist movement reconcile its desire for women as members with its historically deep masculinist emphasis? What roles do women play in racist groups and how are these changing? Might issues of gender become a weak spot in organized racism, a point of tension between its strategic need for unity and growth and its ideological commitment to a male-dominated racial struggle?

IMAGES OF GENDER

Gender is unquestionably an important organizing principle for racist groups.[5] Aryan masculinity is venerated as the bedrock of the white race, racist politics as the litmus test of masculine prowess. Assumptions about masculinity are crucial, as the methods used by racist movements to appeal to white men make clear. Throughout modern U.S. history, racist groups have trumpeted the idea that white men are in imminent danger of losing their proper economic, political, and social place to undeserving white women and to nonwhite men and women. To protect their long-standing racial and sexual privileges, racist groups declare, white men must support movements fostering racism, xenophobia, and sexual conservatism.[6] Emblematic of such pronounced emphasis on masculinity are the names of the bands—Extreme Hatred and Aggravated Assault—featured at a white power music festival billed as a "Whiteman's Weekend."

Stereotypical traits of masculinity, especially physical strength and aggression, are presented as both the prerequisite and the consequence of white racist activism. *Manly* traits make the Aryan racial warrior. Conversely, battling the enemies of Aryan civilization heightens masculinity. Indeed, the trappings of modern organized racism—from its militarized uniforms and command structure to its aggressive rhetoric and practices—project a sense of hypermasculinity, an exaggeration of masculine ideals.[7] Thus three young men on the cover of a skinhead music magazine are championed as prototypical male racial warriors: their shaved heads and arms tattooed with Nazi insignia mark them as racist, while their linked weapons denote both masculine prowess and a racist collective activism. A woman pictured inside the cover provides a starkly contrasting image of racist womanhood as passive and ethereal.[8]

White women have little obvious role to play in such racial politics. If maleness is asserted through political activism on behalf of one's personal or racial family, then its presumed opposite, femininity, must be passive—that which is defended by masculine activity. Indeed, from the decline of the women's Ku Klux Klan of the 1920s until the 1980s, organized racism was mostly a masculine enterprise. Solidarity among racist activist men was based on the exclusion of women, as well as of all members of groups designated as racial enemies.[9] Women rarely were recruited to any but the subordinate positions of helpmates or intimates of male racists, and racist propaganda uniformly denigrated or dismissed women, seeing their only functions as supporting racist men and educating racist children. Strikingly, much of what Martin Durham in his study of the British fascist National Front terms the "overwhelming masculinity" of the extreme right has persisted in the face of increasing numbers of female members.[10]

Although racist propaganda until recently targeted a male audience almost exclusively, racist groups have not been silent on issues of women and race. On the contrary, they consistently traffic in ideas about gender to promote themselves as the best way to ensure the superior position of Aryan men. Such ideas appear most graphically in demeaning and brutalizing propagandistic images of women from racial or religious minority groups. The women are portrayed as animalistic, sexually aggressive (or, conversely, asexual), and predatory (or, conversely, passive: as victims of domination and cruelty by nonwhite, non-Aryan male intimates or family members). Women of color, Jewish women, and other "non-Aryan" women are depicted as irresponsible "baby breeders" or sexual seductresses, and they are presented as threats to the racial standing and self-respect of Aryan men.

That several of these images are contradictory (for example, women as passive yet predatory) goes unnoticed in racist propaganda, though as I discuss later, these contradictions do concern racist activist women. There is little acknowledgment of the conflict between strongly condemning abortion and promoting births by white women, who are expected to breed the new racial generation, and advocating the opposite for women of color and non-Aryan women. Neo-Nazi groups, in particular, tend to support access to abortion for Jewish women, women of color, and women in third world countries. At the same time they view access to abortion for American Aryan women as a plot inspired by Jews seeking to "deplete the white race"; it succeeds insofar as "women give their bodies to be abused and mutilated by Talmudic butchers."[11]

While racist groups' portrayals of nonwhite and non-Aryan women are uniformly negative and degrading, their ideas about white Aryan women are more mixed. Most racist groups simultaneously advocate gender and racial subjugation, but often the two impulses combine in complex ways. Both because they seek to broaden their appeal and because they have little interest in ideological consistency, leaders of racist movements tend to have what the historian George Mosse calls a "scavenger ideology"—a system of beliefs that annexes pieces of other ideologies.[12] Around the racist and anti-Semitic core of modern U.S. racist groups can be found views as disparate as a belief in alien invasions, faith in homeopathic healing, and concern for animal rights. In such an ideological stew, a variety of ideas about Aryan women can coexist with dedication to hard-core racism.[13]

In creating an image of white women, racist groups draw on the widespread tendency of the middle classes in Western societies to equate women with virtue, along with frivolity and shallowness.[14] They portray

Aryan women in four general and somewhat contradictory ways: as ethereal Nordic goddesses and racial victims, as potential "race traitors," as wifely supporters of male racial warriors and bearers of the next generation of Aryans, or as racist activists in their own right.

Goddess/Victim

The idea that white women are racial victims is captured aptly in the description by Vron Ware of the "enduring image of a seemingly passive, but wronged white femininity."[15] The notion has been central to every racist movement in U.S. history, used to justify assaults on men of minority races in retaliation for the threat they are presumed to pose to innocent white women.[16] For example, a cartoon widely distributed in the contemporary racist movement shows a powerfully built African American man kicking sand at a white couple on a beach and threatening to rape the woman. "Mac," a scrawny white man, decides to fight back by subscribing to a racist newspaper and tattooing himself with swastikas. These strategies prove successful, as he gains both an impressive physique and the attention of attractive white women. He becomes known as "Nazi of the Beach."[17]

The cartoon's theme is painfully familiar; its refrain closely echoes, among other tragedies, the Reconstruction-era Klan lynchings of African American men that often were "justified" by false charges of sexual interest in white women. Like these, the cartoon links a feminine racial victim to masculine racial violence. If white women represent innocence and potential racial victimization, then white men represent actual, engaged racial agency. As Mac adopts Nazism, both his body and the white (male) racial community are strengthened. White women, however, remain unchanged. They are still potential victims, though now their male protectors are more powerful. Thus a message of white female victimization is really a statement to and about men, declaring that racial violence is necessary to maintain white male superiority.

This message is conveyed often. Neo-Nazi and Klan groups issue mountains of cartoons, flyers, lyrics, and articles that portray African American men as rapists and victimizers of young white women, Nordic-looking goddesses as the archetypes of white womanhood. To suggest that whites are simultaneously victims and victors, both perilously endangered and about to vanquish, racist groups peddle images of white victimization as well as those of white strength. Underscoring their warning that white children are in danger of becoming an "endangered species," they distribute photos of white children captioned, "We will never forget, never forgive! We will forever be vigilant in our endeavor for our children's future. A White future!"[18]

Portraying white women as racial victims gives them a role in racial politics that does not challenge traditional notions of women's place.[19] A good white woman must guard against racially inspired threats to her children and family. Pamphlets circulated by white supremacist women's groups portray Aryan women as the crusaders "fighting for white survival," responding to "a non-White crime wave which makes our cities unsafe for our families" and "the brain-washing, by the schools and the media, of White youth with racial self-hatred and genocidal race-mixing propaganda."[20]

Race Traitor

Another view of white women is much less benign: male racist members imbued with deeply sexist ideas easily cast these women as their antagonists. In the mildest form of this antagonism, women are seen as weakening men. Richard Butler, titular head of the white supremacist compound Aryan Nations, commented that "drugs, alcohol, and women have destroyed the manhood of two thirds of the white race, really. Two thirds of the white race is mentally castrated."[21] He is hardly alone in expressing this sentiment; racist propaganda often warns that sexual and romantic entanglements with women deplete the energies that white men require for racial warfare. Women are personal obstacles in the way of collective racial agendas.

More significantly, white women become racial traitors by being sexually intimate with nonwhites, thereby eroding Aryan racial purity. Twisting the motif of woman-as-victim into that of woman-as-*willing*-victim, a major racist publication provocatively asks, "Is Nordic Womanhood Worth Saving?" The answer, the unnamed author concludes, is clear: "to accept that she is free to destroy our race by mating with alien males is to accept—in advance—the face of our own extinction. Survival alone demands her rehabilitation."[22] In a similar vein is a lengthy poem titled "The Saddest Story Ever Told," distributed by several racist groups. It reads in part:

> When a White girl marries a negro, her sun of life goes down,
> And glaring spots of sun appear on her white wedding gown.
> And White and black men stand aghast, while viewing this strange role;
> And mutter, "they will wreck themselves and damn each other's soul."

All other crimes may be forgiven when prayer its power fulfills;
The scheming crook may find new hope, and even the man that kills;
But all my prayers can never clear my baby's mongrel skin,
Nor make him White as driven snow, nor cleanse my soul of sin.[23]

This depiction of white women as both sexually and racially promiscuous is consistent with the racist movement's general preoccupation with white women's sexuality.[24] While white women are revered as chaste racial goddesses, the possibility that they might respond to the sexual attention paid by minority men also makes them feared. Drawing on a mainstream cultural sense that women are innately "disorderly," some racist groups portray white women in interracial affairs as not fully accountable for their racial errors, as the unwitting dupes of predatory men.[25] The women thus lack either the racial commitment or the personal strength to resist the advances of sexually voracious men, despite the potential harm to the white race.[26] A recorded message on a telephone "hate line" for Aryan women declares that whites "have been programmed to feel guilty for everything—slavery, the so-called Holocaust and such" but warns that race mixing "is one guilt that the white race has not been charged with and they should be [since] the more race-mixing that continues, the better [chance] the Jews have of controlling the United States."[27] Relationships between white men and nonwhite women are less often discussed in organized racism; perhaps such discussion is taboo because of frequent speculation that some male racist leaders have secret nonwhite girlfriends.[28]

Using both sexual prudery and sexual titillation—a mixture common in racist movements[29]—racist women embed their admonitions to white women against interracial sex in sexually graphic images, decrying "young women who fondle these black greasy ballplayers" and claiming that "the Klan could do a lot of good, especially with young white girls who keep falling for black guys." Frequently, racist groups point to white girlfriends of prominent African American men as a harbinger of "the death of the white race." The final warning of one flyer is particularly ominous: "Whiteman, look at the beautiful woman you love. Whitewoman, think about the future for your children. WHITEMAN, THINK. The decision is for this generation. Your children will be outnumbered fifty to one, by colored people who have been inflamed to hatred of our people by the JEWSMEDIA. . . . YOUR FIRST LOYALTY MUST BE TO YOUR RACE, WHICH IS YOUR NATION!"[30]

The demand that white women avoid interracial relationships can be couched in profoundly hostile language. A flyer distributed by one Nazi

group, addressed to "'SLUT' OR LADY," explicitly attacks the racial loyalty and moral standards of white women who associate with nonwhites
or listen to music produced by nonwhites. Even more vindictive is a
"dial-a-Nazi" phone message that wishes death on white women who
tarnish the racial crusade of Aryan men by engaging in interracial sex:
"What has happened to you, Aryan woman? Have the hypnotic spells
of some Kazar Jewess lured you to her bed, or perhaps the blubbering
lips of some stinking, black, idiot ape have convinced you to partake in
miscegenation? Whatever the case or cause may be, may you die a slow
and painful death. You have abandoned the last of the Aryan heathen
warriors in their darkest hour of need."[31]

Wife and Mother

Because they are deeply concerned with destiny, reproduction, and identity, racist and right-wing extremist movements typically place great emphasis on women's roles as wives and mothers. In a study of right-wing
extremism in France, Claudie Lesselier finds that "at the heart of every
racist and/or nationalist system the same function is assigned to women:
they are called upon to transmit the blood, tradition, language, and be
prepared to fight if necessary."[32] Similarly, Italian fascism depended on
the "spiritual collaboration of wives and mothers" to make families
responsive to its political agendas.[33] Modern U.S. organized racism, too,
promotes the idea that Aryan women will produce a new white generation. As a neo-Nazi group put it bluntly, "the Aryan women hold the
key to the future existence of the white race."[34] Their role is linked to
the fear, often expressed by racist activists, that high minority birthrates
and white women's interracial affairs have brought the white race to the
brink of demographic destruction. Only the birth of white children in
great numbers can secure a numerical advantage over nonwhites. Thus
almost all racist groups churn out images of Aryan women as mothers
of infants and young children.

Though the racial procreation entrusted to white women is portrayed
as essential, it remains decidedly secondary to the activism of racist men.
As mothers, white women do not have to take conscious racist action.
Rather, they safeguard the racial future through their passivity and adherence to conventional gender norms. Simply by acting on their instincts, Aryan women are "doing their part for the white race." As they
become pregnant or nurse babies, they fulfill their racial destinies. Consider the striking adulation directed toward Vicki Weaver, a Christian

Identity supporter who was killed in 1992 when federal agents besieged her family's Ruby Ridge, Idaho, home in an effort to arrest her husband, Randy. Hit by a bullet as she stood in her doorway, infant in arms, Vicki exemplifies for many in the racist movement how innocent, noncombative white mothers are imperiled by government forces—a portrait that ironically ignores Vicki's actual outspokenness in defense of her beliefs.[35]

Racist propaganda also portrays white motherhood as a deliberate strategy of racial warfare. In the newsletter *White Sisters*—published by the Aryan Women's League, a neo-Nazi women's group—mobilizing white mothers is seen as key to an Aryan supremacist future. Pointedly attacking traditional modes of racist activism, these white supremacist women assert that "one Aryan baby born in a small town is worth much more than a dozen Klan rallies."[36] Mothers also are seen as safeguarding white childhood; thus a recruitment flyer for the racist Church of the Creator mimics ads for abducted children with its stark message about a "missing" future for white children. Moreover, an Aryan's mother's strength and protectiveness toward her children can extend to the entire white race. A graphic of an Aryan woman on a racist flyer depicts her heavily muscled arms encircling a sleeping baby, framed by symbols of Nordic Aryan history.[37] A poem by a Christian Identity mother of three tells of "the lifegiving delights of the Aryan woman's bosom"; she claims that it was pregnancy that led her to accept the importance of racist organizing for herself and her children.[38]

In addition, racist groups glorify women who perform the wifely supportive roles that enable white Aryan men to maintain their racial vigilance. Racist wives are accorded a special, although decidedly subordinate, role in the racist movement. They are wives to the movement as well as to movement men, acting both as personal sexual accessory and as collective supporter and admirer of racist men. As a Nazi man writes, "I love the white woman not as a goddess but better yet as a feisty full loving individual and inseparable part of the line of mothers and teachers of our race."[39] The impersonality of that role is demonstrated in a sexually explicit "Poem for a Norse Man," distributed by a neo-Nazi group:

The Norse Man
Stands beside me,
Within the
Circle of life.
Serpents upon his arms,

We face the sea.
He is entering the spiral maze
Upon his thundering steed,
Into the garden within,
To plant the final seed.[40]

Even widows of slain racist men are assigned a role in the racist movement. A frequently mentioned racist icon is Mary Snell, whose husband,
Richard, a member of the white supremacist Covenant, Sword, and Arm
of the Lord (CSA), was convicted of murder and executed in Arkansas
on April 19, 1995, exactly one year before the federal building in
Oklahoma City was bombed. She is esteemed for her "lady-like toughness" in lobbying for Richard's release, for maintaining his racist newsletter in his absence, and for preserving the memory of Richard's racist
cause after his death.[41] Other racist widows, too, are presented to the
world as survivors of racial atrocity; their grief is displayed as evidence
of the victimization of racist activists, and their determination to carry
forward the agendas of their dead husbands is praised.[42]

Female Activists

To recruit women into organized racism, a number of racist groups now
include images of women as racist activists in their own right, along
with stock images of women as victims, traitors, mothers, and wives.
Earlier racist propaganda aimed more exclusively at recruiting men,
sometimes promising to provide women from racial and religious minorities as movement prostitutes for "the few whites that can't get any
'stuff' for some reason."[43] Today, however, the picture painted offers a
broader welcome that includes women.[44] One male neo-Nazi, writing
an article (as its title declares) "from a man's point of view," describes
the idealized comrade-wife as one who "has strode beside myself and
other warriors into full impact combat [and] was strong, healthy, and
spirited."[45] Some racist groups even decry nonracist religions for their
purported subjugation of women, criticizing the negative "attitudes toward women [that] are handed down by the major religions of Moslem,
Judaism, and Judeo-Christianity [whose] belief structures tend to be
Middle Eastern and anti-Aryan"; in contrast, "qualified women operate
at all levels of [white] separatist activities."[46]

Groups that want to recruit women as individual members rather
than as the wives or girlfriends of male members are particularly likely
to portray women as racial combatants. Thus one flyer announces,

"White racially-conscious women, if you have any wits left about you, flee the Judaic and Judeo-Christian insanity and join the throngs of Aryan women warriors."[47] A "hate line" message appeals to women as a potential collective force as it urges, "[F]ind the purpose and need of the Aryan woman today, and meet the mighty host of women that take the Zionist pig by the ears."[48] Arguing that "white sisters" are necessary in organized racism, a women's neo-Nazi group claims that women are needed as movement activists, not only as racist mothers or wives. They hasten to clarify, however, that they are "not a feminist group" but rather one that works "side by side with our men"[49] More strikingly, they express concern about women's subordinate status in organized racism, although they insist that women's activism need not create conflict with racist men:

Do you feel the path to victory is through gossiping, backstabbing and petty jealousies? Of course not! So why does it continue to happen? Are these some of your reasons? 1) you get no respect from the men? 2) you feel you have no place in the movement? 3) you have nothing more constructive to do with your time? The AWL is here to offer you an alternative. The AWL women have a definite place in the struggle for White victory, but it does it by working together with the men not as separate extremes. Jewish media love to see White Aryan men and women battling each other and therefore destroying our cause.[50]

Portrayals of female racist heroines are used to attract women to the cause. These heroines are a diverse lot. Among those praised are women involved in earlier progressive as well as right-wing movements, such as the Russian wives of the attempted assassins of Czar Nicholas I in 1825, who supposedly saved their men with heroic feats; Margaret Sanger, who in 1921 founded the organization that became Planned Parenthood and is heralded as a "eugenics visionary" for allegedly focusing her birth control efforts on neighborhoods where poor black women were concentrated; and Mary Bacon, one of the first highly successful female jockeys, whose recruitment address to a Ku Klux Klan rally in Louisiana in 1975 earned her public notoriety as "the Klansman's Jane Fonda."[51]

Vignettes of female racist activism featuring Jean Craig and her daughter Zillah appear in a great many different racist venues and present a more ambiguous picture. Typically, Jean is portrayed as a heroine, her daughter as an example of women's political duplicity. Jean, a Wyoming grandmother at the time she became involved in the racist movement, had a difficult early life; she suffered through abusive marriages, years of economic struggle as a single mother, and a serious car accident. Then, with the help of funding from a vocational rehabilitation program, she began attending the University of Wyoming and thereby gained more stability in her life. At about the same time, Jean was introduced to Christian Identity by her aunt and began to attend CI groups. Her involvement in racist politics deepened as she met greater numbers of racist activists through her visits to a Christian Identity church in Colorado. Eventually, Jean became associated with a racist underground gang known as the Brüders Schweigen or "The Order," organized in 1983 to eliminate Jews and the ZOG from the United States. Her role in The Order's June 1984 murder of Alan Berg, a Jewish radio talk show host in Denver, led to her conviction on federal racketeering charges. Members of The Order were also implicated in a string of other crimes, including plotting the assassination of a federal witness, counterfeiting, bank robbery, and armed assault.

Like her mother, Zillah is presented as having experienced many problems in her early life, including an involuntary commitment to a mental health institution at sixteen and an unwanted pregnancy at seventeen, after which she and her mother became estranged. Independently of her mother, Zillah became involved with Christian Identity through a family member. Through CI she became acquainted with Robert Mathews, the founder of the Brüders Schweigen, with whom she had a child and who was later killed in a shootout with federal authorities. Despite her personal feelings for Mathews, Zillah ultimately served as an informant for the FBI against her mother and others and testified against them at their trial for sedition.[52]

The images of white women found in racist propaganda—victim, race traitor, wife and mother, and activist—are intended to prod women to join racist groups through both promises (offering them a range of ways to contribute to the racial cause) and threats (maligning those women who stay on the racial sidelines). Yet those women who become active in the racist movement find themselves playing roles less important than they are promised.

WOMEN IN RACIST GROUPS

Women's activities in organized racism differ considerably across groups. In general, Christian Identity and Klan groups tend to emphasize women's familial and social roles, while women in some white power skinhead and other neo-Nazi groups are involved in more direct action, playing what I term "operative" roles. But these distinctions are often blurred. Groups overlap in their memberships and women move between groups. Even groups that share a similar racist philosophy vary in their treatment of women members, reflecting their different histories, their leaders' ideas, and their balance of male and female members. In general, the roles of racist women fall into three categories: familial, social, and operative.

Familial Roles

The most common activities for women in organized racism are racial elaborations of the domestic roles to which women are traditionally assigned.[53] Racist activist women are expected to assume tasks associated with creating and nurturing a racist family. Because some segments of organized racism, especially Ku Klux Klan groups, emphasize that organized racism is "like a family," the scope of those tasks is not clear. Sometimes, the racist family is invoked to refer to women's responsibilities to their husbands and children. At other times, it denotes women's obligation to sustain a collective "family" of organized racists. Many racist leaders try to create a familial atmosphere by stitching together political and recreational activities that promote loyalty and commitment among their followers. As Robert Miles of Aryan Nations told one reporter, "No one who joins these circles is ever without family. Each of us is the father and the mother, the brother and the sister of every white child who's within our ranks."[54]

Nearly every Klanswoman I interviewed partly framed her discussion of organized racism in terms of family, claiming that organized racism promoted "family-like" qualities of caring and mutual responsibility among its members. Although, as I show later, many Klanswomen have specific criticisms of their groups, on an abstract level they insist that the Klan's ideal follows a family model. "Everyone's real supportive and, naturally you're going to have your little arguments here and there, but . . . basically, they're all real supportive, just like a big family," concluded a Klanswoman. An Aryan supremacist claimed that her racist colleagues were "part of my life, like family." A Nazi said that the thing she liked best in the group was "the camaraderie and the sense we get of having an extended family. The kinship we feel is probably the most important thing to all involved." Another claimed that "the unity between people who live so far apart is amazing. It is its own family." A southern woman made a Klan rally sound like a family reunion: "We'd all be together. The guys would play football. And it was like a big family, togetherness. It was the perfect utopia." Just as threats and conspiracies are understood by racist women largely in terms of their impact on immediate family and on daily life, so too the "virtue" of being in a racist group is often expressed in terms of its impact on self and family. A member of a violent Aryan group summarized how she felt about the group by saying, "It's given me more purpose and commitment in my life and I think it's helped me get closer to . . . my family, my friends. It's strengthened bonds of commitment."

The family sought by the racist community is more than just a metaphor. European fascism was built on existing cultural practices and norms, including those that governed family life.[55] Similarly, modern organized racism is based in part on familial expectations and ideologies, however distorted.[56] This invocation of family life also enables those within the racist movement to draw on codes of behavior and understandings by which personal relationships are fashioned and judged. As they learn to understand organized racism in terms of familial qualities, recruits to racist groups apply their expectations of familial relationships to those within racist groups. For some members, this analogy is positive, bolstering their commitment to organized racism. But for others, including many women, the equation of family life and racist group life exposes painful conflicts. Women whose experience in racist groups does not measure up to idealized portraits of family life—those who find racist groups oppressively male-dominated or male leaders patronizing or dismissive of women—feel cheated and resentful. Others find that the emphasis on family life contradicts the demand that they sever relationships with family members outside the racist movement.

Families are expected to serve as platforms for racist recruitment efforts. Modern neo-Nazi and some Klan groups enlist women and adolescent girls, hoping to absorb entire families. In a Nazi publication a reporter described a rally to which "many brought their families. Loving fathers and mothers watched their children play all across the compound with the pure Aryan children from other families. I saw with my own eyes what we all are working so hard to achieve in microcosm. A pure White nation made up of happy, successful White families working and playing together under the protection of the Swastika."[57] A Klan leader commented that "you couldn't join the Klan unless your whole family came in at the same time. It was truly a family of families."[58]

In most racist groups, women are expected to mother their immediate families as well as the larger racist "family." Except in a few racist skinhead and neo-Nazi groups, women racists are told to fulfill their obligations to male intimates and to the racist movement by bearing Aryan babies. Cautioning racist men that "selecting a proper mate is the only way to give us the possibility in life to improve the heritary [*sic*] makeup of the coming generation," racist groups make it clear that racial obligation includes racial procreation. Such pronouncements are particularly frequent in Christian Identity and neo-Nazi groups that emphasize long-term planning for a racist future. This maternal responsibility is made explicit in the recruiting efforts of some groups that seek to win the "birth-rate war" by enlisting race-conscious white Aryan women who will give birth to a large number of children.[59]

In reality, the childbearing patterns and expectations of racist activist women are more mixed than the glorification of fertility in racist propaganda might suggest. On the one hand, several women I interviewed spoke with enthusiasm about their potential or actual contributions to increasing the white population, including one neo-Nazi who described being in a racist recruitment video "pregnant and strolling down the street with my baby and [being] so proud." Similarly, a skingirl interviewed by sociologist Mark Hamm commented that "what people don't know is that the [skinhead group] are strong into family values and strong antidrug. There are 11 women in our group and 8 are pregnant. This is the most important way we can carry on with the white power tradition."[60] An eighteen-year-old woman interviewed by a reporter at an Aryan Fest prided herself on supporting the white movement even before she had her own babies by contributing toward movement drives for "cribs, baby clothes, [and] diapers" for "white families starting out."[61]

On the other hand, many women in my study who were childless at the time of their interview expressed a desire to have no more than three or four children. Although a few predicted vaguely that they would have "a big white family" or that they wanted "as many [children] as possible," most were like a neo-Nazi who alluded to pressure in the movement to have many babies, commenting that she would have "of course more than the typical one or two that the women of today want" but insisting that she was "not really aiming for ten either." A skinhead said that she supported the idea of having a lot of children—"at least four"—but that she was not willing to begin having babies until she and her boyfriend were financially and geographically stable and "prepared to raise our children in a decent environment." Another, an aspiring racist, told a reporter that the emphasis on babies—the insistence of male skinhead leaders that "the purpose of intercourse is to have as many white Christian babies as possible"—made her and her girlfriends reluctant to pursue their involvement in the racist movement.[62] Women with children and those older than thirty tended to be the most conservative in their childbearing goals. Most claimed that they did not want any additional children beyond the one or two they already had. One Klanswoman lowered her voice as she confided, "My husband wanted seven kids. I had two. I don't want any more." A skinhead, pregnant with her first child, concluded that she would have "only as many [children] as we can afford. I wouldn't want to deprive children of what they need just to have more." Some women even elaborated medical steps they had taken to ensure that they would not again become pregnant.

Racist women are also held responsible for socializing their children into racial and religious bigotry. They often provide verbal instruction in the norms of racist living, such as direct admonitions "to stay away from nigger children"; sometimes their cautions are more indirect. For example, a skinhead mother recounted a conversation she had had with her elementary school–aged daughter, a story oddly preceded by the mother's assurance that "I don't push her to believe any beliefs." "My daughter understands," the mother insisted. "She knows she's a special person. . . . It's the little things, [like] when she didn't know what a black kid was, I explained that she's different because of color, to let her know that she shouldn't be involved with nonwhite."

The children are ushered into a world of racial and religious hatred at a very early age. Homes are strewn with drawings, photos, flyers, videos, and pamphlets filled with vicious lies and threats against racial and religious enemies. In one house, a child's high chair featured a handscrawled swastika on the back. In another, children's crayons lay on flyers denouncing Jews as inhuman. Still others displayed pictures of lynchings on living room walls or newspaper clippings about the bombing of the Oklahoma City federal building on refrigerator doors. Male leaders of racist groups, too, are involved in efforts to socialize youths as racist activists. A particularly pernicious means of targeting the very young is the racist comic book, like the *New World Order Comix* published by the National Alliance and distributed by skinhead groups.

Children have easy entry into the spectacle of organized racism. Toddlers learn that Jews are the offspring of Satan. Their older siblings learn to call nonwhites "mud people" as readily as other children learn the names of video games. From birth, some Klan children are installed in a "Klan Kid Korp," preparing them for a life of racist activism.[63] Garbed in miniature Klan robes and flaunting imitation torches and guns, they are introduced to racist activism as fun and frolic. One woman told me, "At night, the lighting of the crosses, that is a big to-do. The men, of course, were in the front lines, the women were there, and there were lots of children, too, lots of children running around and they were just so happy." Racist women extend this socializing further, creating networks of like-minded families in which their children can find assurance that their views are correct, even typical. Some children of racist families attend Aryan-only schools, where they can find white supremacist friends. Others are homeschooled, a method that almost all racist groups promote if not require to prevent children from becoming "double-minded" as they learn different racial values at home and in school (even in Christian schools).[64]

Some children are assigned minor tasks in racist groups; thus, in one Klan chapter "the kids fold the pamphlets and put them in plastic bags and then take them at night and throw them onto lawns." They also are prompted to secure children in other white supremacist groups as pen pals, an effort intended to deepen their racist identity and create a network of future activists. One such letter, credited to "Jessica," age six and in the first grade, starts out with the neutral statement that she likes "to skate and play with my best friend," but it ends with a message that seems to have been fed to her by an adult: "I love the white race and I want to keep my race alive." Similarly, "Kimberly," a thirteen-year-old, describes her "red hair" and her interests in "TV, roller blades, talking on the phone" and then adds, "I am proud to be white." Writings purportedly by racial activist children, though perhaps actually penned by adults, are found both in newsletters aimed at the young (e.g., *Little Aryan Warrior's*) and in propaganda issued from adult women's racist groups. An eight-year-old girl asks other children, "Are you tired of . . . [s]itting on your butt, watching the Cosby Show? Letting other kids make fun of you? Then do something about it NOW!"[65] A twelve-year-old girl is presented as the author of a poem titled "Being White Is Not a Crime," which reads in part:

White and proud
That's what I am
Storming the streets

Getting rid of the trash.
What's wrong with knowing
your race is strong?[66]

The extent to which parents succeed in transmitting racial hatred and racial activism across generations is unclear.[67] Some women—especially women who grew up in Christian Identity households, married CI men, and are homeschooling their children in CI philosophies—claimed that they learned racism in their families. A female founder of a skinhead gang credited her Klan mother for her political "consciousness." Another woman recalled that her father had warned he would kill her himself if she was ever involved with an African American boy. Another woman said that her schoolteacher mother "raised us to be aware that even though all people are in fact people, there are differences between the races." A Christian Identity adherent said that she suspects that during her childhood her uncle was a member of the Klan:

I remember going to a situation that they call a rally. Now I know what it is. When I was little, going to where I remember all these men talking and I remember my dad saying, "Be well behaved" and so forth. And I remember other kids. I got to play with other kids. It took many years before I realized that my uncle took me to a Ku Klux Klan meeting. I didn't even know what it was. It was a giant picnic, is what I thought. But when the men talked, I remember that you had to be hush-hush and you can go out and play with the other kids but don't disturb the meeting.

But socialization from adult relatives is not the only or even the most likely route into adult racist activism. More than half of the women I interviewed had no immediate or extended family members who were racist activists or held strongly racist views. Some women insisted, in the words of one, that their parents "secretly agreed" with their racist views or might be "closet racists," but many admitted that their parents' racial views were much opposed to their own; their mothers, fathers, or both "believed that everyone's equal" and even had played some small part in civil rights or other progressive movements. One said her father was victimized by the Klan when he was sexually involved with a non-white woman, another that "my parents would have a massive stroke if they found out that I was a racist." Only logical contortions enabled one skinhead to reconcile her views with her upbringing: "The whole time I was young I was taught that racism was awful, that you just weren't racist, you just didn't judge someone on the basis of skin color. And I still believe that way. . . . I don't care about skin color. It's just that I don't agree with multiculturalism and I know that race mixing hurts society."

Moreover, the claims of those women who told me that they came from a family of racists need to be treated skeptically. Some seemed to identify a continuous strain of racism in their families only in retrospect, after they themselves had become racist activists. Women would present themselves in their life stories as descended from a proud line of white racist warriors—but when I asked for more details, they could not name any specific racist forebear. One white supremacist did admit, with chagrin, that both her parents were racially tolerant; still, she insisted, "I haven't met any of them, but somewhere down the line in my family there are some grand dragons or grand wizards [of the Klan] or something." Similarly, other women mentioned cousins, uncles, or distant relatives who were reputed to be in racist groups.[68]

A less obvious but also important role played by women racists within the family pertains to their control of family consumption. Just as some progressive movements have struggled to politicize consumers' choices,[69] so too racist groups try to channel the money they spend into sympathetic hands. Some urge their members to boycott products certified as kosher.[70] Several women I interviewed claimed to avoid these foods, though most could not identify the symbols that marked rabbinical endorsement (a recent inventory of such symbols posted on a white supremacist women's group Internet webpage may increase their awareness). Other groups encourage the bartering or trading of goods and services among racist activists and support vendors who sell racial paraphernalia.

At least a few women use their positions in racist groups, or those of their husbands, to benefit from racist purchasing. Some try to support themselves through their racist activities. A widow of a prominent racist activist sells "Aryan crafts"; Aryans, her advertisements claim, should buy from her rather than purchasing goods from major corporations ("who knows where the money is spent!") or frequenting "the mud [i.e., minority] infested, Jewish inspired shopping malls."[71] Another woman runs an enterprise called "Cathie's Celtic Corner," and yet another hawks racist gear in ads in racist magazines.[72] One woman sells "hand crafted N.S. [National Socialism] banners" along with Viking statues, etched glass, and other wares.[73]

Social Roles

Women also must act as the social facilitators of racist groups, an expectation nearly as deep-seated as that making them responsible for
bearing white children and raising them as racists. The importance of
this role has grown in recent years as racists have sought to increase the
longevity of their groups.[74] When social ties are strengthened, members
who have individual identities as racist activists come to view themselves
as part of a larger social movement, developing a "collective identity"
of racist activism. In describing an "incubation period during which new
collective identities are formed . . . in submerged social networks out of
view of the public eye,"[75] the sociologist Carol Mueller captures how
social networks among its members support organized racism. Social
ties, as discussed in chapter 1, strongly influence people to join racist
movements; in addition, as members of racist groups come to know each
other in social as well as activist settings, they reinforce one another's
commitment to the goals of organized racism. They create the "oppositional subculture" by which organized racism is sustained over time.[76]

Racist groups have proven remarkably successful in structuring the
social lives of their adherents around movement activities. When I asked
racist women how much of their socializing takes place with others in
the racist movement, their estimates ranged from 50 to 100 percent,
with most guessing 85 to 90 percent. As a Klanswoman told me, "Once
you get into the Klan, it becomes your whole family, all your socializing,
all your parties." Racist women give a variety of explanations for their
predilection to spend free time among fellow racists. These include mutual protection ("a lot of people like us are afraid we will be hunted";
"we look out for one another when one is in trouble") and loyalty ("I'm
totally secure in my trust in everyone in [her group]"). They also cite
reinforcement of their beliefs ("I like being with people who share my
beliefs"; "you do not need to defend your beliefs to anyone because they
already share your views"), lack of access to other sets of friends ("when
I decided I was going to be a skinhead, I lost a lot of friends, but I gained
friendships I can count on"), and a perceived need for rapid and accurate
sources of information ("everyone just updates on events that I should
know about that are excluded from normal papers"). It is women who
are responsible for making racist group life work, for creating rallies
and meetings that leave people with a positive feeling. They often succeed; a skinhead remembered that her first Klan rally "was just like a
big reception; it was a lot of fun." A neo-Nazi similarly recalled being

surprised to find that a racist event was "kind of like a big powwow or something. There was no cross burnings or screaming."

A flyer advertising a neo-Nazi event promises a day of fellowship and racist learning, along with a social time of music and meals at a local banquet hall—meals served, of course, by "the ladies." Such gendered division of labor is common among racist groups; thus, for the social hour following a strategy meeting at the Aryan Nations' racist compound in Idaho, a sixty-year-old woman played the organ and baked cookies.[77] Although women remain in charge of providing meals for racist events in many groups, some leaders deny that such gender-specific assignments demonstrate women's marginality to racist operations. In the *Aryan Research Fellowship Newsletter*'s report on the Aryan Nations Youth Conference, a spokesman for the group claimed that women prepared meals on-site only to protect the gathered male racists, who otherwise would have had to buy meals in town (where they might fall into the hands of local police or antiracist activists).[78]

The emphasis on survivalism and self-sufficiency in the racist movement may heighten this gendered division of labor in the future.[79] One racist women's group sees its responsibility as "first aid, child safety, [and organizing an] emergency information guide, maternity clothes exchange, Aryan Alphabet Coloring book, Aryan Parent's Newsletter, [racist] P.O.W. art collection and fund."[80] Christian Identity women are organized as "White Nurses," preparing to heal the broken bodies of Aryan (male) combatants in the coming race war.[81] Another group defines women's roles in the racist movement as midwifery, child care, and survival cooking.[82] Barb, an Aryan supremacist, instructs new women recruits that "woman's big responsibility is to be ready to fight to raise children (no drop off day camps), and be ready to offer other women a shoulder to cry on. Many young women today didn't have a parent to teach them to cook from scratch (even the generation past had that problem and turned to TV dinners); to hand sew, and now women must learn it themselves and teach their children." The wife of a prominent Aryan supremacist—whom one racist skinhead woman described to me, without intended irony, as "like Donna Reed . . . a very nice, wonderful, matronly woman"—Barb is a model racist social facilitator. Her role is doggedly maternal, coaching younger skingirls "how to make our men happy and the importance of being good parents, and make sure we're eating nutritionally, and does anyone need vitamins?" At the racist compound where she lived, this model homemaker would "have us stay and make muffins and coffee and bring them out to our men [but] she'd go through the roof if a man stepped in our flowers 'cause she had these gardens all around the place."[83]

Acting as social facilitators, women are central to efforts to create links between organized racist groups and outsiders. Indeed, women's greater participation and visibility in the racist movement are probably responsible for making it more accessible to mainstream populations. Because women seem incongruous in organized racism, they lend an air of placidity to racist gatherings and seem to lessen the threat that such groups pose. Women holding babies, schooling children, or serving chicken at buffet tables can to some degree "normalize" racial politics. A journalist recounts: "I see a Nazi sitting with a latte at an outdoor bistro table. This Nazi has no swastikas, no tattoos, no combat fatigues. Instead, she has a chic red bob, blue tinted sunglasses and a small son. If I hadn't seen her heil the Nazis at noon, I would only see a pretty mother in her early 20s enjoying the late evening sun."[84] Racist women acknowledge their role in this effort, noting that their involvement helps racist groups convey a sense of the ordinariness of racist activism; in the words of one woman, they "portray a positive image [of] honor and integrity."[85] After several members of his group appeared on a TV talk show, one male racist leader commented: "the women did quite well, dressing modestly, using proper makeup and proper arguments. The men should have stayed at home."[86]

Racist women also take more deliberate steps to gain entree to mainstream populations, seeking connections with sympathetic outsiders and attempting to recruit new members into the movement; they act as the racist equivalents of what, in her study of the African American civil rights movement, Belinda Robnett calls "bridge leaders."[87] A Nazi group declares its members "advocates [of] a community form of activism" and urges them to get out and meet people, so that they might show by example "the society that we would like to see." In so doing, "we will do much to break the image that the Zionist controlled newsmedia portrays about white nationalists." Among the varieties of community involvement suggested are "running for public office, engaging in business, and generally acting as responsible citizens, all while being openly known as National Socialists."[88]

Many neo-Nazi and Klan groups practice some form of community "outreach." One woman described the work of women in her group on behalf of animal protection, which they support as an affirmation of "mother nature" against the masculine "cowardly excuse for power called 'sport killing,' . . . the need in their pitiful lives to establish a sense of dominance." Some go further, claiming environmentalism and animal rights as issues for white racist activists since "it is not necessary to carry on a race if there is not a world to live in."[89] Such efforts, along with programs in self-education, first aid, and survival cooking, are described by a member as "projects that bring respect in the community so *they*'ll listen."[90]

Racist women understand that groups of women who seem innocuous can attract people into racist politics. They are fully aware that most people enter the racist movement through personal contacts with existing members, and they work to create the opportunities that make such recruitment possible. Bible study groups bring ordinary women into contact with hard-core racists. Animal rights turn into Aryan rights. One recruit told of attending a women's meeting billed as a Christian apocalyptic "preparation for end times"; she thought that "it would be boring—but it turned out to be excellent and exciting, with all the women who participated (and most did) taking part and exchanging ideas, really great." Although she expressed disappointment that "many things listed were not covered in depth due to time running down," the list of topics shows a strategic mixture of fundamentalist Christianity, self-sufficiency, and racism, with lessons on women in Scriptures, home birthing, healing with herbs, and homeschooling tucked between workshops on "how to use the system" and revelations about domestic spy satellites and secret inoculations with microscopic "transformers" meant to "track our people."[91] Perhaps the greatest threat posed by modern organized racism is seen not in the highly visible parades of middle-aged Klan members, who inevitably are far outnumbered by anti-Klan demonstrators, but in the mundane advertisements for toddler car seats and Aryan cookbooks that appear in white power newsletters and on Aryan electronic bulletin boards.

Operative Roles

The operative roles taken by women in organized racism range from routine clerical tasks to informal (and, very occasionally, formal) leadership and paramilitary activities.[92] Most racist groups allow women to take part in public activities, though such participation is less common in Christian Identity and some Klan groups.

Women are found as formal leaders in only a handful of groups, but they often exercise informal leadership. Recognizing women's importance as informal leaders challenges the common assumption that all racist leaders are men.[93] That erroneous impression is created by the extreme difficulty of gathering information about the racist movement: most scholars and journalists rely on the public statements of self-appointed racist spokesmen like David Duke. Moreover, the ostentatious organizational titles that racist men customarily bestow on each other—Grand Dragon, Imperial Wizard, Commander—misleadingly imply a hierarchical structure of authority. Though their titles suggest that they command the obedience of hundreds of followers, these men may in fact enjoy little more than token allegiance from a handful of marginally committed group members. Conversely, those who actually lead racist groups may have no titles.

If we focus on the practices of leadership rather than on self-enhancing claims or titles, the picture we see is different and more complex. "Leadership," in the sense of providing group cohesion, mediating conflict, developing political strategies, and nurturing collective identity, often is concentrated in the middle and less visible layers of racist organizations. These leaders, though not always women, are the right-wing equivalent of what the anthropologist Karen Brodkin Sacks terms "centerwomen": those who maintain and strengthen social groups.[94] Racist centerwomen command racist groups very differently than do male racist leaders. Men's leadership in racist groups typically is described as manipulative, distant from followers, and simultaneously contemptuous of racist group members and dependent on their adoration and respect for self-aggrandizement.[95] In contrast, women's informal racist leadership is more elusive, indirect, and personal. It may also be more effective and more dangerous. One woman noted that the male leaders "think of me as being all for people on their side. That's how they look at it, too. 'On our side.' (Laughs) No, no complexities involved, right. They think of me as one of them, but yet not one of them. I know they have a hard time accepting me the way I am." Another distinguished herself from male leaders by noting, "I don't go for titles or offices or anything. I don't care about them." And a third downplayed her influence in the organization, saying that she was interested only in "routing the sociopaths out of the movement."

One way of exploring such differences in racist leadership style is suggested by Dick Anthony and Thomas Robbins's distinction between "norm-rejecting" and "norm-affirming" religious groups.[96] Norm-rejecting groups, like male racist leaders, favor heroic uniqueness and individual enlightenment over conventional behavior. Norm-affirming groups, in contrast, are formed around strong beliefs and strict rules.

Women racist leaders who operate in the fashion of norm-affirming groups may be able to nurture more sustained commitment to their groups, to have more success in recruiting new members, and to be less likely to alienate potential recruits. As one woman recounts of members of her group: "The girls look up to me. They're still going to dress their way, the way they do and I only suggest. I suggest you don't have your hair this way [she used her hand to demonstrate the very short hair of 'skinheads']. I suggest you grow your hair out. . . . If there's a little bit of hair you get along in the world much better." Another notes the problems faced by young recruits, which need to be addressed by older members such as herself: "[Her group]'s gonna have to work on these young people. And show exactly what's gonna happen, that you're all right."

Priscilla, a Klanswoman who declined to describe herself as a leader because she had no official title, but who nonetheless admitted that her work was vital to her group, similarly nurtured activism. She recounted her efforts to gently persuade recruits to attend public marches, an escalation of their engagement that entails greater personal danger and risk of exposure than do private rallies or meetings. While male leaders make harsh demands, insisting that recruits risk everything for the movement, Priscilla uses a subtler and more personal appeal. "I've been on rallies. I've been on marches," she informs me. "All they have to do is send a flyer and I will have everybody show up. That makes me feel good because they respect me that much. I don't tell them, 'Hey, you have to take your last dime and spend it on gas and starve to death to get there.' . . . I'm not like that. I'd say, 'Hey, it'd be great to have you.' "

Several women, in describing recruitment efforts, make it clear that they are practicing leadership indirectly and through social ties. One tells me, "I have a way of speaking in grocery stores, department stores. I approach people out of the blue, not as a [racist group] person. But if they look at something, I make a comment and that leads into something else. 'Cause they get into a conversation with me and then I try to explain some things. I don't bring up [her group] or nothing. No, I don't do that. But I try to educate them, I try to throw out little things that might make them think." Other women dismiss their male comrades' attempts to thrust racist literature and flyers into the hands of potential recruits as "ineffective."[97] One woman insists that her low-key approach is more productive, especially for recruiting women: "I'd say, 'Come over. We'll get together, we'll talk, we'll have some fun.' I mean, we have picnics where all the kids play together, all the women get together. We cook our meals, you know. We sit around, we talk about how the kids are progressing, what they want in their lifetime, in their lifestyle."

Women's informal leadership does not stop with recruitment. Racist women also play an important part in creating the social community of racism and in easing new recruits into that social world. A white supremacist tells of her efforts to guide young women in the practices of racist activism: "I've got girls that tell me, 'Lookit, I got a new tattoo,' and I'm, like, 'That's nothing to be proud of, that's stupid. It'll poison your blood and when the race war comes you can't give blood. . . . Don't go out and get tattoos and shave your head 'cause nobody's gonna listen to that.' To me I think they're a lot better if they get themselves an education, a steady job, a nice place to live, than think about having tattoos." Such instruction in daily life as a racial activist suggests a form of leadership quite different from that provided by the battle-worn male warrior glorified in racist literature. Women like this white supremacist mediate between the proclaimed goals of racist groups (for example, to foment a race war) and the actions that bolster such goals. When she instructs "her" girls to avoid tattoos and shaved heads and to pursue education and jobs, she is creating an organizational space in which complex personal identities can be configured as personal and collective identities of racist activism. Perhaps even more frightening, she is attempting to make possible something heretofore unknown: a long-term and intergenerational racist movement. In nudging her young charges to become more effective and dedicated racist activists, this middle-aged woman illustrates how women's practices of informal leadership can secure racist goals.

Women's operative roles in organized racism are not limited to private acts of leadership. At least some women participate fully in direct action. A Norwegian racist women's group, Valkyria, uses a paramilitary approach to organize against prostitution and pornography. Its members take part in strategy meetings with men and train with weapons.[98] Terrorist actions by women racists, though still uncommon in the United States, are on the rise.[99] Among the women I interviewed, about one-third reported that they had been arrested for violent acts in connection with racist activism, usually for assault; more than three-quarters claimed to have been in a physical fight with members of minority groups.[100] One woman, notorious for her public role at the helm of a major Nazi group, proudly described her physical prowess on behalf of white supremacy in a 1994 interview with *Mademoiselle.* As the "three-year reigning champion" of the hammer toss, she and her husband-to-

be, the male champion, won the honor of "getting to light the ceremonial swastika"—a startling outcome for the daughter of wealthy parents
who had earlier studied photography at the Art Institute in Chicago.[101]

Women's public activism can serve strategic goals for racist groups.
When racists confront antiracist protestors, the participation of women
can discourage retaliation. A journalist watching a Nazi "flag parade"
in Idaho observed: "Three young women with babies in strollers salute
the Nazis. Immediately, they are surrounded by screaming protesters.
One young Nazi mother cradles a baby in one hand and uses the other
to punch a young man repeatedly in the face until he is bloody. A young
Nazi man who is with her stands back and lets her be the warrior. The
strategy works: The man who has been beaten will not hit a woman."[102]

Women usually take operative roles that are less public. Some work
to support racist prisoners. A number of racist publications carry letters
purporting to be from the wives and families of men imprisoned for
racist activities, decrying the conditions in which their menfolk are
forced to live or lamenting their difficulties in visiting the prison. In a
typical example, the wife of a man apparently imprisoned for racist
terrorism writes:

*Our life changed dramatically . . . when my husband was arrested,
stood trial, and was convicted . . . we were expecting the birth of our
son. . . . After our son's birth, I relocated to where we now live, and
became a welfare recipient. What a colossal nightmare! [My husband]
got moved . . . farther and farther away from us and deeper and
deeper into the more violent penitentiaries. Our visits stopped as the
costs of visiting were way out of sight. . . . [Then] people found out
and some support began coming in. From that time on, two groups
have sent regular support and best wishes, one group was you [Bounties
Bestowing . . . Blessings Bequeathed] folks!*[103]

Racist prisoner support groups maintain lists of prisoners seeking
correspondents. They claim to screen them all to ensure that those on
their pen pal list are white and Christian, but they note that not all are
"political" (i.e., racist activist) prisoners hoping to communicate with
racist comrades; some are potential recruits. Although such groups claim
to do nothing more than give a prisoner "the security that someone
cared enough to assist with his/her family needs," their real purpose
clearly is to distribute the racist writings of imprisoned racist leaders,
to free racist prisoners, and to supply racist propaganda to prisoners.
Under innocuous names like "Bounties Bestowing . . . Blessings Be-

queathed," they link racist activists outside and inside prison walls and may help strengthen racist networks in prisons, such as the notorious Aryan Brotherhood.[104]

Most of women's—and men's—actions in racist groups are more mundane, although not inconsequential. The women I interviewed described hours spent photocopying literature, making flyers, distributing propaganda, spraying racist graffiti on buildings and highways, writing to current and potential racist activists, promoting and managing white power bands, stamping public library books with racist messages and phone line numbers, and tucking racist literature under windshield wipers and house welcome mats, in grocery bags, and in racks of restaurant menus. Others work the Internet, seeing it as a way for racist women of all ages and levels of experience to recruit others "without ever leaving home or taking away from their families."[105] These actions are largely ineffectual as means of recruiting new members to the racist movement, but they help spread a message of intimidation to the potential targets of racist groups.

In her study of women in the late-twentieth-century Italian underground, Luisa Passerini observes that "the discovery of a specific female identity—beyond the illusory mimicking of male models, in the organization and in the armed struggle—comes later than the fundamental decision to get involved."[106] Those in modern organized racism have no specific female identity as yet. Women's roles are in flux, neither submissive (as tradition demands of women) nor clearly activist (as racist propaganda suggests). But we should not see women in today's organized racism as simply mimicking male models. Their experiences in organized racism, no less than those of men, are highly gender-specific. Women enter racist groups because of contacts and issues that reflect their places as women in the larger society. And once inside organized racism, women find themselves pushed to follow several and sometimes conflicting paths: to shape the racial family, to bolster its social networks, and to assert themselves as leaders and activists.

Specific Women's Groups

Women's activities in organized racism vary according to the gender composition, ideological orientation, geographic location, and idiosyncrasies of particular racist groups and leaders.[107] Such variation becomes clearer when specific groups are examined. In some, women are quite marginal; in others, they are central players, though often engaged in different kinds of activities than those of racist men.

Aryan Women's League A particularly prominent women's racist group is the Aryan Women's League (AWL), an affiliate of a men's neo-Nazi group, White Aryan Resistance (WAR). AWL claims a unique mission in the white supremacist movement, distinct from that of men, and recruits among young female skinheads and neo-Nazi sympathizers.[108] Its newspaper proclaims the centrality of "courageous young women warriors" to the struggle for white victory, searching for historical examples of female role models among Nazi leaders or mythical Viking warriors.

Some AWL flyers recruit women without using particularly gender-tailored appeals. One asks potential recruits to join "[s]hould you want to break the habit of being part of the sheep and are willing to fight and fight hard now."[109] Another plays on fears of racial threat, invoking affirmative action, immigration, declining school quality, crime, political corruption, and foreign economic control to persuade women to "join with the thousands of your White kinsmen and kinswomen."[110] Others aim specifically at women; for example, one appeal bundled with a copy of the AWL newsletter called on "today's racially conscious woman" to join the "White Nationalist movement."[111]

The Aryan Women's League sees creating an Aryan culture and a self-sufficient economic and social support and educational system as key to the future of the Aryan race. It sponsors a baby fund to subsidize Aryan child rearing, noting that "procreating our Race is the only way in which we survive" and insisting that every Aryan couple should strive to have three or four children.[112] To that end, it publishes an Aryan parents' newsletter and collects maternity clothes and store coupons for an Aryan bartering exchange. Cautioning that "the Jews have long controlled the market; selling up clothes, crafts and everything else under the sun! We think it's high time that we support our own!" the AWL runs a baby clothes exchange for "the numerous Aryan families that need your support." It sells items billed as "useful to your Aryan family," ranging from an Aryan coloring book (advertised with the slogan "Don't let your child be forced to color what all the jews have prepared for him! Let your child learn about their history while coloring!") and an Aryan cookbook ("dozens and dozens of delicious recipes compiled from Aryans around the nation!"), to AWL T-shirts ("with a picture of a beautiful Aryan child with slogan, 'for the children' "), instructions on canning food, and an "Aryan P.O.W./Martyr Collage" that includes a free laminated photo of "one of our most valued heroes, Mr. Bob Mathews."

Consistent with its anticorporate stance and its concern for the future of the Aryan race, the AWL is also militantly pro-environment, opposing the logging of old-growth forests and the use of disposable diapers. For members of the AWL, like many in the neo-Nazi movement, the Aryan future lies in the Pacific Northwest, where they see environmental spoilage as low and racial purity as high. They endorse the "Great Northwestern Territorial Imperative," encouraging a paramilitary white supremacist network to colonize the Pacific Northwest as an all-white, all-Aryan homeland and then secede from the United States.[113]

Ku Klux Klan Women Several Klan groups have been very outspoken on the issue of women in the Klan. According to one Klan leader from the southern mountains, "Without the women, we wouldn't have the Klan,"[114] a sentiment that appears to be gaining ascendancy. Some Klan groups have publicized their commitment to the advancement of women in the organization. As early as 1987 a major Klan chapter insisted, despite all evidence to the contrary, that "women hold a very high and exalted position in the eyes of the Ku Klux Klan." Though the Klan propaganda continues to tout the belief "that our women find their greatest fulfillment as mothers of our children," it blames "international finance" (i.e., Jews) for retarding the advance of white women in this country.[115]

One woman who has achieved some prominence in a Klan is Rachel, the daughter of a Klan leader. She comes from a lengthy line of racists. Her paternal grandmother was an adherent to an early Christian Identity preacher, Kenneth Goff, who in turn was a disciple of the fascist Gerald L. K. Smith. Her father attended Goff's Soldiers of the Cross Bible Institute, where he met his future wife and subsequently launched his career as a Klan leader and CI preacher. One journalist characterizes Rachel as her father's "pride and joy . . . [his] proof that the patriot movement is not composed of losers and misfits." In high school she was a cheerleader, beauty contest competitor, newspaper editor, and participant in the Future Homemakers of America—summed up by her father as "average American people."[116] She is featured at the Internet site of her Klan group on the "Aryan Women's Page," which lauds women's roles as mothers and racial activists.

AMISH Aryan Mothers Inspiring Something Hopeful (AMISH) surfaced in the late 1990s in Pennsylvania, perhaps connected to Aryan Nations. The organization and its "Christian women's newsletter" claim to be run and produced by women; they closely follow the Christian Identity view of women's submission, insisting that "a woman's responsibilities [are] what the Bible says." "Men are to rule over women," the group declares; "it is obvious in both nature and most importantly the Bible." One woman claims that she and a girlfriend "were often very excited" while attending the Aryan Nation Congress and began to "high jive but realized that it was not very Aryan like"; they therefore substituted their own creation, a "Nazi curtsy."

Like other adherents to Christian Identity, those in AMISH mix biblical commands with the vilest white and Aryan supremacism. Two of the founders personally testified that "while striving to follow the laws of Yahweh, we noticed that a great sense of joy and happiness has come into our lives [so] we both feel strongly about sharing our experience with as many Aryans as possible." They also produced a racist and anti-Semitic variant on the children's song "The Teddybears Picnic" for readers to "enjoy . . . as much as we do":

> If you go out in the Idaho woods, you'd better be white as snow.
> If you go out in the Idaho woods, be careful where you go.
> There's crosses burning bright and hot.
> There's Hitler heiling, guns are cocked.
> Today's the day the Aryan's [sic] hold their Haaate Fest![117]

Valkyrie Voice A self-defined National Socialist women's group, Valkyrie Voice (VV) asserts an active women's presence in the racist movement, against "those [racist] men who long for 'seen but not heard women' [a] desire that evolves from an alien culture." VV draws on ancient Nordic and Viking motifs, asserting that these are politically enabling for racist women, because "the tribes which we derive from (Celtic, Nordic, etc.) did not produce a feeble breed of Aryan women. So why should we modify our instinctive behavior into being meek?" Their message is unambiguously violent and Nazi, promoting such tracts as the infamous *Turner Diaries,* which allegedly inspired the bombing of the federal building in Oklahoma City; the "Writings and Teachings of David Lane, P.O.W.," by an imprisoned member of the terrorist group The Order; and Hitler's *Mein Kampf.*

The stance that members of VV take toward the issue of women as reproducers of the Aryan race challenges some traditional racist philosophies. Though they emphasize this contribution of Aryan women, noting that "[f]or some [women] childbearing is the extent of their involvement (which is an obvious necessity and the greatest gift a woman can give to her race)," they also acknowledge that "for others this does not satisfy their desire to advance our people." To those men and women who see the need to have women "restricted from thoughts or actions that are beneficial to our people's future," VV has an unambiguous response: "those who disagree have no place in our resistance, period."

In other ways, VV's supporters promote conventional notions of women's place in the movement, particularly about women as mothers. Messages directed at women chide them to "get all their drinking and fighting out of their system before they become parents." Aryan mothers, they insist, should learn first aid for "bullet, knife, and other serious wounds" and become emergency medical technicians. They should work toward food self-sufficiency by gardening and by canning their food, "not only for preparation for a race war, but [because] relying on the system makes you another host for the parasitic Jew." Mothers should also breast-feed babies, homeschool older children, and learn martial arts and how to use firearms to "take care of yourself and/or your children in a necessary event."

In VV, racist women express anger against what they perceive as abusive treatment by racist activist men. One woman, who claims that she was "led into the racial 'scene' under false pretenses," attacks racist men who get drunk, fight over "petty differences [to] make others regard you as tough," spend their time watching TV or nursing drunken hangovers, ignore or neglect their children, or justify promiscuity or adultery on the grounds that "it creates more babies for our race." They have, she concludes, replaced the original fourteen words of the racist movement ("we must secure the existence of our race and a future for white children") with the notion that "racial pride should only be taken seriously until it affects your personal life."[118]

United White Sisters An organization very different from VV is United White Sisters (UWS), which urges women to work with men for the good of the racist movement. In flyers and propaganda riddled with spelling and grammatical errors, members of UWS address disaffected racist women. "We as individuals," they insist, "must put personal differences aside (since can Aryan armies truly expect to be victorious when there is squabling in the ranks?)." Acknowledging tensions between women and men in racist groups, UWS nonetheless concludes that "it is imparative to our survival that we work together!" Fully subscribing to the racial and anti-Semitic agenda of the larger racist movement, UWS paints a scenario of imminent doom for Aryans, because "ZOG [is] throwing descent White folks into jail for knowing the truth."[119]

Warrior Breed Like members of other skinhead groups, those in Warrior Breed insist that they are not really an organization, but "merely a group of friends united by the love and concern of our Race." Despite this, women in the group promote racist rock and roll, attack ZOG, and encourage "natural family planning, ecological breastfeeding and home schooling."[120] Their propaganda is very similar to that produced by other segments of the racist movement, but Warrior Breed also distributes material targeted more specifically to young girls and boys. These include a "skinzine" that claims to feature "news, reviews, art, tattoos, and commentary" but is in fact largely a vehicle for selling white power music tapes and clothing emblazoned with Nazi insignia.[121]

Warrior Breed also counsels skinheads on how to survive without being employed and how to secure money from the government. Their suggestions include claiming to be an alcoholic in order to receive government disability and getting services and resources from free clinics, food banks, and churches. "I always wear my grungy duds," claims Warrior Breed activist Robyn, adding ironically, "it makes me feel more like a communist begging for food."[122]

Christian Identity Women Christian Identity women tend to express the most traditional view of women's roles, drawing on biblical justifications for the subordination of women to their husbands. CI's philosophy is summed up by Cheri Peters as encouraging "all women to fulfill their ancient roles as wives and mothers, that there may be proper male leadership in the nation." In her column and her radio broadcasts, she urged wives to practice submission to their husbands and men to exercise command over their wives. CI insists that "a Christ-like woman wants a man who takes the lead and shows male dominance" and that women "cannot and will not be happy in a man's world because our Creator did not make us to find our fulfillment there."[123] Notwithstanding this deferential stance, Christian Identity women also are commanded to show determination in living CI principles. Asks another CI woman, "are your convictions strong and sure enough that you have planned who will care for your children if you are called to prison for your faith? Are you prepared to die for the convictions that you have?"[124]

Sigrdrifa A recent addition to the racist Internet world is Sigrdrifa, which proclaims itself "The PREMIER Voice of the Proud White Woman on the World Wide Web." Declaring that it "is not the oldest, nor largest, women's group in our struggle," Sigrdrifa nonetheless claims to provide a comprehensive range of help for "white women taking a stand for their great race and rich heritage." Among their offerings are a help network for white parents who wish to teach their children racial pride, a support system for new and expecting Aryan mothers, a home-schooling curriculum, a guide to home canning, an address list of prisoners of war combined with a "white prisoner book drive" to collect reading material that imprisoned Aryan racists "might find interesting," and links to a wide variety of white supremacist Internet sites.[125]

CONFLICTS OVER WOMEN'S ROLE

The introduction of women into the racist movement has not been without controversy. Many men are hostile toward women members and unsure what role women should play in a movement that historically has characterized itself in idioms of fraternalism—as a clan, a brotherhood, a community of like-minded men.[126] Moreover, the effort to create a "racist family" has been hampered by a disinclination to interfere in the private lives of members, particularly the power of men over their wives and children. And although a few women and groups describe themselves as "white supremacist feminist" or insist that it is possible to combine "white power with women power,"[127] organized racism has found it difficult to incorporate issues of women's rights. As a result of these problems, many women members become dissatisfied, sometimes openly unhappy, about life in white supremacist groups even as they continue to support racist and anti-Semitic goals.

Conflicts within Racist Groups

In public, racist leaders often insist that women are treated as men's equals in the racist movement. Indeed, it is increasingly common for women to be a focus of racist speeches and propaganda. One neo-Nazi group proclaims, "We believe that without our women the movement will never achieve victory. [Our group] supports the equality of the sexes. We encourage the men of all political organizations to start showing more respect for the ladies. Our women should stand and fight with us."[128] However, this verbal support for women's rights does not imply any sympathy for feminism, which most male racist leaders routinely blame for deforming Aryan women. Racist propaganda decries the feminist movement as Jewish-controlled, as a conspiracy led by such women as Gloria Steinem and Betty Friedan to alienate white Aryan women from their male counterparts,[129] and as an assault on the masculine strength necessary for white victory. One racist newsletter put it bluntly: "feminism is the means to weaken Aryan masculinity, promoted by the international Jew. . . . [T]he Jews started this emasculation with the young intending that they never become real men who, someday, could challenge their worldwide supremacy."[130]

Many racists leaders encourage their female recruits to hold good jobs. But some groups, especially those associated with Christian Identity, see the employment of women outside the home as part of a Jewish plot. They argue that Jews use their economic dominance to force Aryan women to work and then gain control over the Aryan children left unsupervised by at-work mothers. For them, Aryan women who work for wages, or even those in college, are racial enemies: they further Jewish goals.[131]

Most of the women I interviewed were highly critical of the feminist movement. They saw it as controlled by Jewish women and lesbians and as pro-abortion and antifamily. They characterized feminism as "disgusting," or "a bunch of ugly women trying to get the spotlight," and made such statements as "Gloria Steinem should be shot." However, some women did not share this blanket condemnation. One dedicated Nazi credited feminism with indirectly strengthening the racist movement, "because, before women's lib came about, our movement was ten years lacking [behind]. We [women] wasn't able to do anything and now we can hold office . . . , we can have authority where before we had none." Other women racist activists drew on the rhetoric of feminism to demand rights for Aryan women and to decry the misogyny of contemporary society. When a skinhead publisher spoke of the "male-dominated society" in which she "had the [work] experience [while] the men had the power and the salaries," she echoed the frustrations of many progressive women. It is the perceived *cause* of the problem—in this case, Jewish control of the economy—that sharply distinguishes her racist ideas about male domination from nonracist ones.

A few male leaders even admit openly that men have found it difficult to regard women's issues as important to racist agendas. One, commenting on television coverage of gang rapes, claims to be frustrated by the cavalier response of fellow racist activists: "When I discussed this matter with several racialist friends (all male) over the next few days, I encountered a disheartening reaction. They all agreed that rape was a bad thing [but that] it was essentially a 'woman's problem' and that as such it fell outside the overall scope of racialist interests." Such attitudes, he continues, reflect a narrow view of women that could cause additional problems for the racist movement:

Any discussion of women's rights and feminism within the Movement usually ends abortively with the unchallenged assertion that the whole topic is an artificial one concocted by Jewish communist lesbians to further divide and weaken the White race. Such an attitude is fundamentally un-National Socialist. . . . Too many male racialists live in a dream world of their own fantasies when it comes to women. Home is the only place they should be, it is felt, and cooking dinner and having babies are the only things that they should be doing.[132]

Another male leader, discussing the formation of a neo-Nazi women's group, traces its problems to the reluctance of racist men to accept women as their comrades:

The biggest problem the [group] has with recruiting is the men *not accepting their women as counterparts in this race struggle, therefore pushing their women into the closet when racial matters and confrontations arise [because] . . . most men have chosen dainty little dormice as mates who will kiss their ass and give them no feedback at all. . . . [M]ost men in this situation are afraid that if their mate gets involved with other women, she will become even more harsh. . . . White racially conscious women are most beautiful when they are in battle. . . . Any man who feels threatened by his woman if she wages a few battles of her own might as well hang it up because he is no man at all, let along a White Warrior! Men who enslave and oppress their women are egotistical losers and "boyish" inside.*

His earlier fears about women activists, he concludes, were misplaced: "I was predicting gossip and ceaseless nonsense. . . . It was not happen-

ing like that at all. The gossiping, glamour girls weeded themselves out
. . . were excommunicated and could not reap the harvest of victory and/
or glory."[133]

Ku Klux Klan groups, in particular, have hotly contested the place of
women in the racist movement. On the one hand, some male Klan leaders have been among the most outspoken in their desire to recruit women
into the racist movement. For the most part, however, those Klanswomen have been seen as a means of bringing into the movement more
men—their husbands and boyfriends. This approach is the reverse of
earlier efforts, whereby women were recruited through boyfriends and
husbands already active in the Klan. But the underlying premise remains
the same: the Klan is an organization of men. As one Klan leader told
me:

A lot of [racist] men today, and this is true . . . a lot of men are a
bunch of woosies. OK, I'll put it that way. Their women, girlfriends,
and wives wear the pants in the family and in the relationship now.
. . . So, in order to bring in men, the men will follow the women.
It's sort of a reversal. If a wife is against the husband's being involved,
you can just about forget the husband's hanging around for long
once the wife starts complaining about the lack of attention she's
getting. . . . The other way, if the wife is into it, she'll drag the husband
along. I've seen that too many times to ignore it, so we don't hold
women back from promotions or climbing the ladder. We can't afford
to not let them have whatever positions they want to work for.

Despite his protestations that the Klan is an "equal opportunity" pro-
moter of its female and male members, very few women have been given
positions of power in any Klan groups. In fact, the Klans may have more
gender inequality within their organizations than any other groups in
the racist movement, with the exception of Christian Identity sects (with
which many Klan leaders are affiliated).

Klanswomen are acutely aware of gender inequities in the organization. One woman said that she was not interested in recruiting her grown
daughter, because if her daughter joined the Klan, there "wouldn't be
anything for her to do. She could go to a few rallies or picnics, but
wouldn't be allowed to go to the real meetings. There would be basically
nothing." Another made a similar point, telling me that "the Klan is
male-oriented, totally sexist. The men still run it, as far as the offices
go." Yet another woman, who had been in the Ku Klux Klan a little
more than three years, expressed her disillusionment with the gender

politics of the group, saying that "they acted as if women were equal [to men] but once you are inside the Klan, women are not equal at all."

White supremacist skinhead groups present more varied and more extreme gender practices.[134] Many skin groups are intensely male-dominated and violently misogynist: skinhead boys and men refer to their female comrades as "oi toys" and feel it is their privilege to dominate and exploit their girlfriends, wives, and female comrades.[135] A Klan leader cast himself as an advocate of women's rights by pointing out to me how he differed from skinheads:

I've noticed [the skins] have a different attitude. Their men regard the women as sort of a biking attitude; you know, they're there to serve the man and they keep 'em off the front. Sort of on a pedestal, but yet they can look down on them at the same time. . . . In fact, one woman told me that the skinheads from Pennsylvania, this is what she said, at least one group look upon women as cattle. . . . So I think it's a false sense of protecting the women. They won't have them out on the front lines. They're going to keep them behind the scenes, so they can have the refreshments ready when they get back from the demonstration.

Almost all racist skinhead propaganda projects images of extreme masculinity as central to racial activism. The pamphlet *The Code of the Skinhead*, for example, begins with a quotation from the philosopher Friedrich Nietzsche predicting that "a more manly, war-like age is coming, which will bring valor again into honor!"; and movement 'zines commonly define skinheads as young men "that love to have fun, beer, and girls (not necessarily in that order)."[136] A statement titled "I Am the Wife of a Warrior" makes it clear that women belong distinctly in the background when racial warfare is being waged by skinhead men: "My vows to my warrior-husband are as strong as fine tempered steel. . . . I am subject to long, lonely nights of worry and tears, while my warrior-husband fights our battles. I suffer his defeats, as I celebrate his victories. . . . Should he be wounded, I nurse him back to health, so that he can return to the forefront of the battle. I support my warrior-husband in all ways and through all circumstances [because] my warrior-husband fights for me."[137]

Oddly, however, skinhead women are often the racist movements' most physically aggressive women, and at least some prominent skinhead women publicly confront the sexism of male skinhead culture.[138]

As the message on one hate line asked, "Why do so many male skinheads and other males in the white resistance simply degrade women, get drunk, yell 'white power' and little else? Well, the answer is these are not Aryan warriors. . . . These are punks who use race as an excuse to be antisocial."[139]

Even skinhead women who are not physically combative may not conform to the image purveyed in skinhead propaganda. A twenty-two-year-old skinhead, living with and supported by her skinhead boyfriend, was nevertheless willing to challenge him when her relationships outside the skinhead world conflicted with the beliefs of her group. Her mother's sister was openly lesbian, and she commented that she "didn't really mind . . . [to me] it wasn't really a big issue, [although] to some skins it was a huge issue." Specifically, she recalled that her boyfriend was "appalled" when he found out that she had been frequenting a local gay and lesbian dance club. "I had gone in there a few times and when he found out he went nuts. But it wasn't that big of an issue at all for me. . . . Hey, to each their own. It's not something I'd be into."

Conflicts within Personal Relationships

In a treatise on recruitment, a women's neo-Nazi group argues that it is difficult to recruit women into "our movement" because of the *personal* behavior of male racist activists toward their female partners and wives. Warning that "the poor treatment that Whites of the opposite sexes give each other these days [and the resulting] deep emotional scars inside our kin" have political consequences, it urges movement men to recognize the political "dangers of promiscuity" and stop "discard[ing] partners like garbage."[140]

Such sentiments are not unusual among racist activist women. In his study of racist skinheads, the sociologist Mark Hamm found a good deal of conflict over issues of sexual promiscuity. For example, a Texas skinhead and high school honor student reported that "this guy [who was married] got caught sleeping with another girl [and] she got her ass kicked."[141] On national television, Moli, a self-described Nazi, boasted: "I don't have a man in my life right now because I don't want one right now. The one who I choose is going to have the same beliefs as myself or I won't want him at all. I'm very proud of myself and I'm not giving up my beliefs for no one."[142]

In an appeal that is titled "A Woman's Opinion: (Scary Thought,

Guys?!?!)," members of a neo-Nazi women's group ponder how to recruit more "solid women" (those who "think for themselves") into the
racist moment. They assemble the following quiz for men:

> *Q. You are at a gig. You see a beautiful Aryan Woman. What do you do?*
> *A) Go over and talk to her and try to score before your girlfriend returns*
> *from getting you yet another beer.*
> *B) Stare and make crude comments to your buddies about how you would*
> *like to get her into bed.*
> *C) Get your girl & then go meet this other woman and her boyfriend. It is*
> *always great to meet Racial Kin—especially another Sister!*

After a complaint that ironically draws on racist propaganda about Aryan women as goddesses ("We are just sick and tired of seeing our Sisters
and potential sisters degraded and insulted when we know we deserve
so much more since we are the 'ultimate symbol of love and beauty' "),
women are presented with the following scenario:

> *You are arguing with your boyfriend because you believe that he*
> *doesn't show you the respect that you, as an Aryan Woman, deserve.*
> *He claims that he has utmost respect & would die for any Aryan*
> *Woman yet, the night before he was with the waitress at the bar doing*
> *. . . well, you know! Does this sound familiar? I think it is time to*
> *re-evaluate your "meaningful" relationship with this so-called Man![143]*

The struggle over gender roles in racist activists' personal relationships is evidenced in many women's gripes about being dominated by
their male partners. They complained that male intimates wanted to
control their every action, often in the name of racist solidarity:

> *He didn't want me working. I wanted to work. I wanted to go to*
> *school. So I took part-time classes at [the local] community college*
> *and I worked part-time. He chose my friends. Almost all my friends*
> *from high school I was not allowed to see. In fact, there are three*
> *friends that I still remain close with that he will just go bonkers if he*
> *knew.*

> *I remember one time [a friend] came over to the house and Jerry did*
> *not care for her, didn't want me hanging out with her. It must have*
> *been my birthday or something, that would have been the only reason*
> *why she would have been allowed to be there. And she and Jerry*
> *got into a heated argument about something and she ended up swearing*
> *at him and telling him exactly what she thought about the whole*

white power movement and this and that. And he just looked at me.
And he said, "Get her out of here." Not in those words. And she
got out of there. And I only called her from work from that point on.

In their conversion stories, the women tied their fears mostly to male members of minority groups. Some described the danger they felt from hostile men at public racist events; one recalled, "[Anti-racist activists] got ahold of me and almost killed me. . . . I literally had to fight for my life. . . . All I remember is all of a sudden, whoom, all these people were running from here and here, not far from me. [I thought], 'Oh shit, they're gonna kill me if they get ahold of me.' They're yelling, 'Kill the Nazi, kill the bitch.' . . . I was scared for my life." When pressed to describe their private lives, however, some talked about feeling threatened by their male racist comrades. Several told of being beaten by racist boyfriends or husbands. Indeed, racist women are often stereotyped as victims of domestic violence, though it is unclear whether they are more likely to suffer violence from their male intimates than are women in the general population. But the problem is serious enough that male racist leaders were forced to act publicly against one prominent leader after he was arrested for battering his girlfriend. Moreover, battered racist women have few avenues for help. As members of racist groups, they distrust and fear the police; and few believe that their networks of racist comrades are likely to prevent further occurrences or punish the perpetrators.

Almost all women racists spoke of difficulties in their personal lives caused by their activism, difficulties that are compounded by a lack of support from their male partners. Despite the racist imperative to produce many white babies, some said they had trouble juggling commitments to children and to racism. One woman noted, "I used to sit for hours and hours and fold literature. I'm into being mom now. I don't care. Let the literature pile up." A Klanswoman complained bitterly about her husband: "He's been at more rallies than I have. But you know I have to work and I can't really be there and work at the same time. And the bills have got to be paid." A male Klan leader confirmed these rigid gender expectations in his uncritical explanation of his inability to maintain a stable relationship with a woman: "Girls that will put up with this [Klan life] are hard to come by. You know, I thought I had one, this girl here I dated for about two and a half years. She was a good girl, but, you know, when she'd want to do something on the weekend, I'd say, 'Well, we got a rally.' "[144]

In recent years, the racist movement's emphasis on becoming a surrogate family for its members has further complicated women's lives. In an interview with a reporter, a twenty-two-year-old woman who wanted to be a nurse to aid white people points to the personal costs of the pressure on women to have many white babies: "Reproducing a white child is a great thing. . . . But it's the thing to do, especially with a lot of skinhead girls, to have white children when they are very young. A lot of the girls quit high school."[145] Another woman decries what she regards as the limited scope allowed women in the Klan: "Klan men see women as breeders and most women in the Klan feel they should produce babies for the white race."

Gender differences are seen clearly in pen pal columns designed for Aryan singles. Thus the White Aryan Resistance offers the "Aryan Connection," a personals column for those seeking racially suitable dates and marriage partners that encourages "sports, camping, dancing or whatever Aryans would aspire to"; and on the Internet, racist women and men can use "White Singles" to advertise for politically like-minded partners and spouses.[146] Ads from racist women request men who are stable and family-oriented; almost none refer directly to racial beliefs or practices. They seek "a hardworking skinhead who wants a family," or "a responsible, respectable, and active male," or "a serious relationship/ husband to settle down with and have a big family." These criteria are consistent with the personal dreams that racist women narrated in their life stories, which almost exclusively envisioned interpersonal harmony, a happy family life, and a stable marriage. In contrast, racist men advertise for women with explicitly political requirements, searching for "an 'anti-women's libber' who is free of any all non-White influences," or someone "who loves and fights for her racial survival."[147]

Studies of successful social and religious groups find that members often have a deep emotional attachment to, even love for, their groups.[148] Such attachments are rarely seen among women in the racist movement. One Klanswoman could recall no names of those in a group to which she had previously belonged and had described as "like family." Another said that the Klan "seemed like the perfect utopia at the time, but now looking back, I remember other things." Still others found themselves depressed at the nature of their groups, which they viewed as self-defeating and fractionalized by "squabbles about petty ideological differences." "The picture I had in my mind was a lot different than it finally turned out," commented an eighteen-year-old who had moved

to Idaho to enter into a polygamous relationship with a white supremacist.[149] Indeed, it is hard not to notice the air of forced conviviality at
racist gatherings—there is likeness and common purpose, but little sign
of the intimacy, excitement, and spontaneity from which deeper social
ties are fashioned. While its agenda of racial terrorism and vicious Aryan
supremacism puts the racist movement chillingly far from the mainstream of American political life, the hollowness at its core mirrors obstacles to social connection that are widespread in modern America.

In chapter 1 I discussed the deep sense of resignation that colors many
racist women's life stories, a sense of obligation rather than passion for
racist activism. They talk of finding themselves in a racist movement
that they support but that does not always support them, and they hesitate to involve their children, particularly their daughters, in the life of
organized racism. Some women do describe feeling empowered by being
a racist activist. But others paint a more negative picture. They rarely
see themselves as racist heroes or warriors, talking instead of having
made great sacrifices to be in a movement that has given them little in
return. The image of women's activism projected in racist propaganda
and in the speeches of racist leaders does not match the daily experiences
of the average woman in a racist movement that remains very ambivalent about its female members.

Racist women react to this gap between their expectations and reality
by tempering their involvement with racist life in various ways. Despite
intense pressure, racist women resist severing connections with friends
and family from the outside. Publicly they concur with racist ideas, but
privately they refuse to enact those that intrude too deeply on their personal relationships. They proclaim their undying zeal for racism, but
they search for boyfriends and husbands who are responsible and stable
rather than politically inspiring. They work to recruit others, but their
support of even the main tenets of organized racism is less than whole-
hearted.

The experiences of racist women in many ways resemble those of
women in other social movements. In progressive groups, women often
find themselves expected to perform maternal and wifely roles: they are
usually responsible for nurturing a family feeling among activists, sustaining family life, socializing children, and ensuring that purchasing
decisions reflect the movement's goals, and they bear the burden of creating and maintaining social ties among members. There, too, women
are often found in middle-level and informal leadership positions. Racist
groups are also like other groups in failing to provide their women mem-

bers with a sense of satisfaction to compensate for their internal short-
comings. It is not difficult to find progressive women echoing the de-
spondency expressed by racist women who think their movement will
never become more accommodating to them or to other women.

But in other ways, women in racist groups are in a very different
situation. Organized racism, perhaps more than any other social movement, is intensely concerned with biological reproduction. Racist groups
are obsessed with ensuring the purity of racial bloodlines, determining
race from racial markings, and increasing white birthrates. To racists,
reproduction can never be left to chance. It is the racial destiny and
obligation of Aryan women to produce large numbers of children. The
centrality of biological reproduction overshadows other roles for
women in racist groups, and it is a particular source of discontent among
women.

Moreover, unlike those in more mainstream social movements, racial
activists differ greatly from the larger white society from which they
seek recruits. Their commonly held ideas about race, religion, and government seem bizarre and frightening to outsiders. To recruit members,
racist movements must make themselves appear more normal, less
threatening. Presenting women in the movement as fulfilling traditional
gender roles is key to achieving that end. When racist women take part
in everyday activities such as food preparation or child care, they can
seem reassuringly similar to women in the rest of society. The very ordinariness of their tasks can disguise the racist and anti-Semitic goals at
which they aim. Thus racist groups favor positioning women members
where they will come into contact with outsiders while engaging in the
most normal-seeming and gender-traditional functions possible, even
when women want—and are promised—a broader set of roles within
the movement.

Finally, like other extremist and marginal groups, racist groups embrace conspiratorial ideas, which are wedded to strict internal hierarchies of authority meant to shield members from outside influences and
dangers. Racist groups teach their members that they are the targets of
attacks from the government and racial minorities. They teach them to
depend on the group for protection. This mind-set favors tightly controlled groups with minimal input from rank-and-file members, perpet-
uating male leadership.

These features suggest that the road to gender inclusion in racist
groups will be a rocky one. Plans to fuel a sustained revival of white
supremacism in the United States by recruiting many women are not

likely to be successful.[150] The number of women members may increase, but there is no certainty that women will be central figures within racist groups, or even remain in them for long. A more likely outcome is that the interpersonal conflicts and political disillusionment experienced by racist women may contribute to the demise of organized racism.

A CULTURE OF VIOLENCE

Two huge logs lashed together in the shape of a cross lie on the ground in a remote clearing in the southern mountains. As a long day of speeches draws to an end, most people head to the food station to claim the remaining sodas and chips. A few walk in the opposite direction—men into pickup trucks, women into station wagons. They drive away, returning soon after with containers of kerosene and gasoline stacked next to bags of chicken and tubs of potato salad. Women carry the food back to the group. The men drag the accelerants across the field toward the cross where other men, younger and more raucous, arrive and join them. Women and children begin to drift over. As they start to splash fuel on the cross—first carefully, then haphazardly, the men become more agitated. The crowd segregates. Men move closer to the cross. Women and children retreat to the perimeter of the clearing.

Once the cans of gas and kerosene are empty, most people head for the headquarters building to change into their uniforms. Soon a line of women and men forms, all dressed in black trousers with white shirts neatly pressed despite the stifling August weather. Most have Klan or Confederate badges on their sleeves or pockets. Their heads are bare. Their feet sport black Doc Martens, work boots, or sneakers. Children walk beside them, dressed in smaller versions of the adults' clothes. The children are laughing, talking about how this cross compares to others, whether it will take "too long" to burn and take time away from their snacks and play before bedtime. In vain, parents plead with their children to be quiet. As they walk toward the cross, another group appears on the steps of the headquarters: men and women in full Klan regalia. With hoods to mask their faces and white robes to hide their clothes, they too march toward the cross. Except for the children, the crowd is hushed, expectant.

When everyone has assembled, two men hoist the cross aloft. Outside the ring of Klan figures, two other men begin dousing rag-tipped poles into a bucket of kerosene and lighting them. As these are distributed through the crowd, even the smallest child falls silent. One man orchestrates the ceremony, directing the crowd to set the cross ablaze with their torches. A line of uniformed figures is instructed to stand, then kneel, before the fiery cross. Hooded figures surround them as they solemnly recite a pledge to defend the white race against all enemies. By the time the cross crashes to earth, sending sparks spilling across the dry, dusty ground, the initiates are celebrating their "naturalization." They have become knights of the Ku Klux Klan.

This is organized racism as cultural spectacle. For their victims as well as their members, racist groups are defined by cultural displays—by symbols, rituals, coded language, striking clothing. And it is by such displays that they are marked over time and across generations. Organized racism rests in collective memory as crosses set ablaze, waves of black-booted storm troopers, and swastikas—images that are shorthand for the vicious ideas, the murderous acts. To some, these have an emotional lure, stimulating interest in racial agendas. In others, they evoke visceral revulsion. The accoutrements of today's racist groups—like those of their predecessors—signal the terror of racist agendas as surely as do speeches and flyers. Nazi shock troops of yesterday have been replaced by gangs of brutal white power skinheads, but burning crosses and fascist insignia still telegraph the presence of racist ambitions. Yet despite such conspicuous trappings, we know relatively little about the culture of modern organized racism. Paradoxically, their ubiquity may account for the lack of rigorous attention to racist cultural spectacles.

Some observers, surprised at the overlap of racist and mainstream culture, regard racist displays as simply *banal*.[1] A reporter at a large gathering of neo-Nazis commented, "Everyone was so common, so average, so mannerly and nice." She was struck by the similarity of these neo-Nazi parents to parents everywhere, as they held children and boasted of their accomplishments. Even a young woman's offer of a gingerbread recipe on a swastika-festooned flyer that demanded "white power" and "death to race-mixing" did not disturb the observer's assessment of the event as seeming benign.[2] Such interpretations of racist culture are grossly misleading, however. As important as it is to understand the culture of white supremacism, it is critical that we not lose sight of the racial agendas bolstered by such displays. As the cultural theorist Edward W. Said notes, a full analysis must recognize the tension between understanding historical-cultural phenomenon as "willed human work" and retaining a sense of "the alliance between cultural work, political tendencies, the state and the specific realities of domination."[3]

Other observers stress the fearsome nature of the racist movement but regard its culture as meaningless: they attempt to *see past* racist cultural displays in order to focus on the political agendas that lie beneath. Studies that focus on the correspondence between a movement's ideas and the group interests of its adherents are particularly likely to follow this pattern.[4] Such work has been important in challenging the notion that racist activists are irrational agents who ignore their own interests, but it has downplayed the extent to which culture shapes people's sense of what is in their individual or group interest. Moreover, those who view racist culture as meaningless, like those who find it benign, fail to notice that racist groups are knit together by commonalities at least as much of cultural practices as of beliefs. Indeed, for the newest recruiting targets of racist groups—teens and women—cultural spectacles and ritualized practices may be particularly important. For teens, whose racial and political attitudes are just developing, and for women, whose stance toward organized racism can be deeply contradictory, the power of cultural spectacle (along with the social ties of racist communities discussed in chapter 4) secures their allegiance to racist groups. Thus, any explanation of organized racism that attends only to the attitudes of its members or to the political ideologies of its groups will be flawed. Many of its recruits find racist culture and sociability, as much as politics, to be at the heart of organized racism today.

From imposing displays mounted by groups, such as Klan crosses set in courthouse squares, to the seemingly trivial adoption by individuals of white supremacist styles of hair and clothing, organized racists use racist cultural practices to assert their hostility to what they see as the dominance of liberal, racially egalitarian ideas. They thereby flaunt a racist variant of the "arts of resistance," practiced in daily life, that the political scientist James Scott found among dominated groups. Like the resistance acts of peasants who wear forbidden colors or of slaves who laugh behind the backs of their masters, the cultural practices of racist groups can seem politically insignificant unless understood in the context of the powerful forces (here, those of racial equity) against which they feel they are arrayed.[5] Adherents of the racist movement view themselves as the victims, their cultural practices simply as defensive acts of resistance.

Recent theories that view culture not as dogma that constrains behavior (as did older notions) but as social practices displayed in public systems of meanings are particularly useful for understanding the cultural core of modern organized racism. This scholarship has been especially attuned to the relationship between culture and social action, exemplified by the sociologist Ann Swidler's idea of culture as a "tool kit" with which people fashion strategies of action. Culture, in this sense, consists of "symbolic vehicles of meaning, including beliefs, ritual practices, art forms, and ceremonies," as well as "informal cultural practices such as language, gossip, stories, and rituals of daily life."[6] Significantly, such an understanding of culture does not presume that people draw on cultural symbols, rituals, and behavioral guides in uniform ways for a particular set of ends. Conversely, Swidler's observation that people create similar cultural scripts when they confront the same social institutions explains why racist groups whose beliefs may differ markedly from one another on many issues continue to use identical symbols and rituals (such as swastikas or cross burnings) to mark their opposition to racially integrated societies.[7] Moreover, it suggests that racist cultural practices, rather than statically expressing group dogma, can themselves shape meaning. Because of the flexibility with which individuals can use cultural tools, racist cultural practices mediate between the rigid ideologies of racist groups and the variety of beliefs held by their members.[8] In other words, racist cultural practices help forge a shared racist agenda among a somewhat heterogeneous membership.

The study of organized racism not only draws on new cultural theories; it also contributes to them in three ways. First, it enables us to examine how cultural practices can be mobilized toward racist ends. Racist culture is more than a backdrop against which racist actions take place. It also is the means by which racist activists devise common strategies. Culture sets the boundaries of the racist movement by defining who is included in the "us" and who is the "them." It gives significance to actions (such as street assaults) that otherwise would seem meaningless. And it is what gives racist practices longevity, infusing swastikas or Klan hoods with meanings that endure over time and that translate into new situations.

Second, an examination of organized racism provides insight into a particular intersection of culture and social movements: it reveals how social movements can be organized *through* culture. Most other research focuses on how cultural practices sustain the commitment of political activists, especially under conditions of extreme oppression or political marginality.[9] By analyzing racist groups, by exploring how cultural practices can generate collective racist action, we can fulfill Scott's injunction to study "the immense political terrain that lies between quiescence and revolt."[10] Here, the differences between today's racist movements and those of European fascist states are instructive. In Mussolini's Italy, for example, fascist leaders sought to weaken association among citizens in favor of a mass culture through which the state could exercise control over individuals.[11] But racist movements that are far removed from state power, like that in the United States today, work to strengthen cultural and social ties among those they view as potential racist activists. They use culture as a way of organizing politics.

Third, looking at racist groups helps us explore how movement culture can nurture violent and repressive political actions. Most research on culture and social movements focuses on progressive social movements and thus examines how liberatory and egalitarian cultural practices shape politics.[12] In contrast, the study of organized racism reveals how group hatreds can be absorbed into the culture of a social movement and how politics can be forged through the symbols, imagery, practices, and even aesthetics of violence. By concentrating on women's involvement in racist cultures, including cultures of violence, we can go further, to explore how cultural tool kits are used in specific, gendered ways.[13]

CULTURE AND RACIST ORGANIZING

The relationship between racist culture and racist organizing is complex. Culture often is assumed to be a *product* of social groups, but culture also can *shape* social groups—as does racist culture. In part 1, I identified and discussed the three components necessary for becoming a racist: making contact with racist groups, learning to identify oneself as a racist, and developing a commitment to racist activism. Each of these processes is nurtured by racist cultural practices. Racist culture helps entice people into racist groups, forge an individual and collective racist identity, and consolidate commitment to racist action. In these three ways, racist culture shapes the organization of racist activists.

Culture as a Movement Lure

That racist culture can lure recruits into organized racism is most obvious among young white supremacists—not surprisingly, given the importance of cultural practices to teenagers, especially young teens.[14] A young West Coast skinhead describes how her racial identity, as well as her subsequent racial activism, was organized through cultural practices: "I had always been kind of a bit different than your average teenager. I dyed my hair and wore combat boots, so you kind of attract a different type of person. So I got invited to [a skinhead] holiday evening and I met people that I knew were white supremacists." An older neo-Nazi activist from the Northeast notes that music has particular power to mobilize and recruit young people into organized racism: "I believe music has the potential to get through to the kids like nothing else. The great thing about the music is, if a kid likes it, he will dub copies for his friends, and they will dub copies for their friends and so on. This has the potential to become a grassroots, underground type movement, which we see happening already."

More established racist groups, such as Ku Klux Klans, regard all white Christians as potential members. For such groups, cultural practices like wearing robes, group singing, and participating in racist picnics are important not to differentiate friend from enemy, but to create a sense of commonality that can attract recruits. For newer and more fluid racist groups, in contrast, the boundary between friend and enemy is ambiguous. Not all white Christians—or even all white racists—are potential allies, and determining what is a properly white or racist or Aryan or skinhead way of being is a matter of great concern. Assaulting members of minority groups does not clearly signal who is part of the white power skinhead movement, because sporadic physical confrontations are commonplace between youths of different races, sexual orientations, and nationalities. Nor is espousing white supremacist principles a reliable indicator of movement adherence, because knowledge of racist ideology is thin, even among committed activists. Groups like white power skinheads therefore rely on cultural practices—skinhead haircuts and enjoyment of white supremacist music—to separate true racists from those who simply hold racist attitudes. For them, being in the racist movement means participating in racist culture: group affiliation is defined by cultural appropriation. Music, dance, use of graffiti,[15] and personal adornment mark adherence to a common racist agenda, differentiating allies from adversaries and potential recruits from potential victims. Establishing oneself as a bona fide racist means adopting a set of cultural tastes, and these tastes, in themselves, confer racist authenticity.

The young women I interviewed mentioned music and fashion repeatedly in describing their arrival into organized racism. These retrospective accounts do not necessarily accurately describe how these women were transformed into racist activists, but they do indicate the importance of cultural markers to new recruits. The story of a young California skingirl pivoted on her discovery of a racist musical underground: "How I really started believing, thinking, in that white separatist sense and then got all white supremacist, it was really through the music. There's a whole other genre of music out there that no one ever hears about, and it's real powerful, especially at that awkward stage where no one exactly knows who they are. It gives you an identity, it says you're special, you know, because you are white." For her, the racist movement was defined by its music and by the racial identity that such music could confer.

Culture and Racist Identity

Cultural practices also secure racist identity. To be a racist skinhead means to be part of a musical subculture of loud, hard-core music with viciously racist lyrics. Many young racists see such music as key to reviving a movement they regard as floundering under the lifeless leadership of older Klan and Nazi leaders.[16] To them, music is a way to energize organized racism through emotion rather than through ideology.[17] As the head of a white supremacist record company noted, new racist music "operates on an entirely different level than the cold, dry, rational approach of our predecessors. Music can chill you to the bone, raise up your spirit, and make you want to explode with energy and vibrancy. It has the power to reach you on the deepest emotional level."[18]

Skinhead racist culture includes violent dancing, all-night parties featuring alcohol and drugs, and a presentation of self through specific hairstyles and clothing. Until coached by older white supremacists on the dangers of being so visible to law enforcement,[19] white power skinhead men typically shaved their heads completely or adopted extreme punklike styles. White power skingirls favored a variant of this style, shaving the sides of their heads and retaining a long, blond-dyed swatch of hair down the middle, or cutting their hair with stark feathering that echoes other punk and hard-core styles. Both male and female white power skinheads typically wear Doc Martens boots, jeans, and black jackets and festoon themselves with many racist and violent tattoos, body piercings, and metal and cloth insignias. The iconography of racist art, especially among white power skinheads, also is highly stylized, featuring bold, aggressive graphics.

Women racist skinheads claim to be personally empowered by the cultural practices of organized racism. Although other women generally talk of organized racism as little more than a refuge from the vulnerability they feel in other areas of their lives, some skingirls boast that their physical appearance—their visible tattoos, body piercings, striking hair colors and styles, and military-type clothing—commands respect from other racist activists as well as from enemy groups:

I'd seen a [Klan] rally going on and I was, you know, checking it out and shit. And I walked right up on it and they were tripping out [in awe] looking at me.

The people I hung out with, I was the only person that would walk through niggertown with my Mohawk [haircut] and not worry about it. And so they were like, "Damn, you know, that bitch has balls." I'm like, "Damn straight." . . . I don't care how big they are or whatever. I'll fight anybody and that's how I feel when I'm on the street.

Such boasts suggest why some may find racist cultures appealing. Not only do racist groups promise a sense of personal identity and a collective culture, but they also afford their members a sense of control over the circumstances of life, a feeling of self-empowerment, and an expectation that they have authority over others. This response to the culture may also help explain why some young people drift back and forth between racist and antiracist skinhead groups: both offer similar trappings of music, alcohol, friends, causes to which one can be committed, clear identities, and a sense of power over a defined group of enemies. Though racism trivializes, circumscribes, and nullifies the lives of those it deems to be enemies, it can bestow on its exponents a sense of individual and collective power, however illusory.[20]

While white power skinheads are enmeshed in the cultural trappings of violent racism, other neo-Nazi groups use culture in a different way to secure racist identity. Aryan supremacists, especially those who adhere to Christian Identity or Odinist ideas, employ quasi-religious rituals or kinship gatherings. The feeling of unity that the historian Mabel Berezin argues was an aim of Italian fascism—where "public spectacle was an arena of political emotion, a community of feeling, in which Italians of all ages were meant to feel themselves as fascists"[21]—is the goal of racist rituals. A white supremacist newsletter describes the "new sight [that] has appeared in the forests. . . . An Aryan wedding at dawn; as the sun just breaks above the horizon"; the article's author encourages readers to write for a copy of their Aryan wedding ceremony.[22] In its report on a Nazi "Youth Conference," a publication of the Idaho-based Aryan Nations similarly includes a lengthy description of two weddings:

[The groom] wore the S.S. officers formal evening wear and [the bride] wore a beautiful white lace dress, and a veil with a long train, accented with flowers around her head piece. Dress, veil and the Mother's Cross she wore, produced an earlier era setting for the traditional wedding. [The second groom] and [the second bride] wore traditional skinhead attire. . . . Both ceremonies were impressive, each in its own way with the commitment they made to themselves and their race. . . . [F]ollowing each ceremony—as they descended the aisle together, they were saluted by 40 skinheads and brownshirts. Receptions followed with beautiful tiered wedding cakes.[23]

These weddings may have borrowed from traditional rituals, but they ended on a decidedly racist note, with one of the new brides lecturing the crowd on racist and gang conflicts in her hometown and proclaiming that "our people need re-organizing and unifying."

The ordinariness of such racism—the banality of evil, in Hannah Arendt's sense—is found also in other cultural forms. Racist groups sponsor white power skinhead dances where young teens learn racial hate along with new dance steps. Neo-Nazi compounds hold Aryan baptisms along with family camp outs, picnics, and ball games. Much neo-Nazi culture is home-based, taking the form of homeschooling, survivalist rituals, and efforts to create a modern version of Hitler's Aryan supremacist folk community. When asked to describe her group, a southwestern Nazi adherent told me: "It's living comfortably with a nice-sized family in a community with like-minded families. My family lives off of the land and I homeschool my children. We live free from government intervention and I am able to keep and bear arms to protect my children when necessary. Basically put, it's a Jeffersonian ideal."

The Klan, too, has developed a set of cultural practices meant to heighten racist identity. These range from the ubiquitous cross-burning ceremonies to elaborate rituals that denote ranks in the Klan to a vocabulary of coded Klan words. Such practices can be highly effective; a southern Klanswoman commented about her initiation, "I liked the cross-burning ceremony. It's just really, it's beautiful. There's nothing else. . . . They got up there and [a leader] did this ceremonial speech and you got your knight[hood], 'cause you got to get through your stages [of Klan ranks] before you reach this far and it was beautiful when the crosses went up. Probably other than my son being born it was the most beautiful thing I ever saw."

Developing a racist identity is made easier when cultural practices instill a sense of common purpose. Klan life is organized to maximize the opportunities for members to feel themselves part of a Klan world, to be in situations in which they can identify themselves as racists. A woman from a mountain state Klan recalled one such episode as she described a cross burning that served as a memorial service for the wife of a Klansman. "They had a special little meeting for him, that they got up and give speeches for him and everything," she remembered. "And it was real touching, I mean, they were real supportive. I mean, everyone was definitely sympathetic because, you know, she was a great lady."

But not all racist groups agree on what forms of racist culture are appropriate. The question of music can provoke especially hot disputes within organized racism. A number of older racist women passionately derided the musical tastes of their younger counterparts, arguing that the music's lack of aesthetic value undercuts its claim to be authentically Aryan. Young racists, declared one of the older women, "put out this music which they have the nerve to call Aryan, see 'cause Aryan in my opinion is Strauss, Beethoven, you know. They put out this stuff that's, like, terrible, sounds awful, and they slam themselves into each other when they play it. It's [a] total degenerate form." And unlike the younger racists, who view music as crucial to their racial evolution, older white supremacists rarely cite current musical tastes as evidence of racialist commitment, though some said they would listen only to music by those they considered, often erroneously, to be German Aryan composers (such as Tchaikovsky). Others noted that music had played an important role in their racial development in the past, but no longer did so, underscoring their belief that changing musical tastes is part of political maturation. Only younger and less politically aware racists, they implied, need music to shape a racist aesthetic. White power music is an initial stage in becoming a racist, one that experienced racists have progressed beyond; those who continue to listen to white power music reveal their personal and political immaturity. As one neo-Nazi told me when I asked her whether she still listened to the white power bands that earlier had been important to her, "No way, they're terrible." Others expressed similar sentiments:

[As I grew up] I still wanted to go to my concerts. I saw some of the most beautiful concerts. You name it, I've seen it and it was great. That was my main goal, to make sure I had extra money for my concert tickets.

[White power] is not my type of music, but the kids need it. They listen to it.

Culture and Racist Commitment

Cultural practices also help translate racist identity into active commitment to racist politics. This transformation occurs in three ways: when organized racism is certified as an interpretive community for its members, when group history and tradition are evoked, and when racist cultural institutions are established.

Racism as an Interpretive Community Among some groups, the culture defines acceptable racist practices. For them, being part of organized racism means deferring to its cultural as well as ideological dictates. Many people are racist, but one's authenticity as a white supremacist is conferred by a collective judgment of the "interpretive community" of organized racism.[24]

Studies that focus on men are likely to overlook the importance of cultural interpretation in racist groups. The gendered nature of leadership in white supremacist groups means that men usually claim authority over what they view as public, important decisions, leaving to women the less visible decisions that they regard as trivial. Thus, it is often women who serve as arbiters of cultural acceptability in racist groups. Since many of these informal "cultural leaders" are older than the young recruits who form the bulk of new members, older women also find themselves mediating generational conflicts over racist culture. For example, an elderly Aryan supremacist woman described how she counseled young recruits to avoid insignia that would reveal them to the authorities or keep them from blending into mainstream society: "Don't mark your body with your belief system. You can flaunt your beliefs with a badge, a pin, an armband, a patch, a shirt, but then you can take it off when you don't want to. With a tattoo it's very hard. And they don't find out until it's too late that they can't get certain jobs when they mark themselves." Realizing that such practicalities are not likely to persuade young skinheads who are fiercely attached to such cultural practices, she sometimes used another tactic with especially recalcitrant teenagers. She would tell them that some markers of skinhead identity (clothing) are acceptable, even if others (tattoos and bald heads) are problematic: "If you have your jacket and your boots and braces, fine. But that's all you need. You don't need to go out and get tattoos and shave your head bald to prove a point. 'Cause nobody's gonna listen to that anyway. The only thing that's gonna do is cause you aggravation up the road."

This emphasis on clothing (or musical taste) as a barometer of racial maturation relies on cultural practices to mark the passage from racial self-consciousness to unself-conscious acceptance of racialized common sense. Those who use overtly racist symbols in public or who adopt an exaggerated racist style, according to this logic, are movement novices. Over time, the group member's use of racist culture is expected to become more subtle, showing that racism has become an integral part of how he or she thinks and lives. Culture, in this sense, is most powerful when it is least obvious.

The notion of appropriate cultural markers presupposes a general acceptance of the racist movement's authority to interpret and dictate cultural practices and tastes. This assumption is evident in discussions of racist style. One young woman told me: "Once you start listening to [white power] music, becoming familiar with the lyrics, you repeat them, you start to believe them. The more you associate with a certain crowd of people, the more you start to adapt their sense of style." Thus one way in which culture organizes behavior is by defining which style is authentic. Codes of style can be more precise than codes of behavior or belief. An Aryan supremacist group that is loath to prescribe how their members should act, even at public rallies, nonetheless establishes itself as the arbiter of acceptable dress: "Several members have asked us at the main office, 'what kind of SS uniform is acceptable?' Since the old wool tunics from Germany are hard to find, and dying them is a mess, we have switched to black BDU or SWAT uniforms. We recommend that collar tabs be sewn directly on the jackets."[25]

Nevertheless, style can be elusive, even within the highly elaborated rules of skinhead culture. It is not possible to learn racist style once and have done with it; rather, the style must constantly be relearned, and to stay current one must be actively immersed in the racist community. One skingirl noted, "It seems like every person that used to have the shaved heads and the [Doc Martens] boots and the [swastika] T-shirts is now doing that whole greaser, rockabilly image thing."

Although young white power skinheads and some young neo-Nazis and Klan members favor particularly dramatic cultural displays through clothing, body piercing, tattoos, and haircuts, the cultural markers of racism are not solely a province of the young or of new recruits. Older and more established racist activists, too, place a premium on shared practices of self-presentation. For them, racist style generally requires some form of uniform in public displays and in formal rituals, from the hoods and robes of the Klan to the militaristic attire favored by neo-Nazis. Even in private gatherings and daily life, there is an expectation that activists will wear some racist item of clothing or insignia.

At the same time, cultural markers can be points of tension, especially between younger and older white supremacists. To many young racists, visible racist symbols are important signals of racist pride and racist identity. They are a means of attracting attention, demanding recognition, declaring the wearer's fringe status, and marking his or her stance against authority. To some older white supremacists, however, obvious racist markers retard the progress of the movement by making it less appealing to potential recruits from mainstream society. This disagreement reflects differing views of the politics of racist culture. Young racists see cultural practices such as tattooing and head shaving not simply as markers of personal and collective taste but as effective *means* of politics. Nazi and Klan insignia and symbols need to be displayed openly because such displays flaunt the threat of racial terrorism. In contrast, some older racist activists find these to be only *expressions* of racist politics, manifesting a racial agenda that is best kept from public view. Misplaced racist signification, in their view, can disable collective racist politics.

Other older racial activists do, however, support a muted form of the in-your-face cultural terrorism of skinheads; they mix racist insignia and conventional attire in a mild form of racist action, which at the same time affirms their allegiance to organized racism. These activists will wear a badge, pin, belt, patch, bit of embroidery, earrings, body piercing, hair design, or tattoo that refers (usually obliquely) to organized racism and then delight at the puzzlement and concern that the symbols evoke. A West Coast woman recounted the effect that her Klan badge had on others: "You walk into a restaurant [wearing this], and they'll clear everyone around from the tables from you. And you got to sit in the middle table 'cause they're afraid you're gonna start something." Others brag about provoking a reaction through titillating shows of racist insignia: letting a coat drop open in a store to reveal a quick glance at a Klan badge, rolling a sleeve in a restaurant to show part of a tattoo, or devising clothing symbols that suggest without precisely replicating a racist message or symbol. Such displays are not intended, as are the skinheads', as forms of terroristic harassment. Rather, they are meant to provoke reactions that mix fear with confusion, creating incidents that create unease with little likelihood of drawing physical retaliation and that furnish a humorous story to share with fellow racists.

For established racists as well as for their younger counterparts, racist style is based on confounding established cultural codes. One elderly woman, a seamstress who sewed badges on shirts for a number of Klan chapters, told of the trouble she had securing appropriate material for her work after clerks at the local police uniform store she frequented became suspicious of her large purchases of standard-issue white shirts. She dismissed my observation that these seemed to be generic shirts that could be purchased in any department store, reiterating that Klan shirts had to be from a store that supplied police uniforms. Although she was unable to supply a reason for that stipulation, it was clear that "Klan style" rested on the perversion of clothing used by authorities.

Culture shapes action in ways that transcend precise explanation or even acceptance, as the seamstress who knew that Klan shirts should be made from police shirts, but did not know why, illustrates. Similarly, skinheads who are unable to explain the historical importance of black boots in right-wing extremist politics would sacrifice their lives to safeguard their boots. Klan members who cannot give even the most rudimentary explanation for the insignia that they wear so proudly or the peculiar formations in which they march also reflect this pattern.

Racist Tradition Cultural allusions to racist history also shape racist commitment. Studies of social movements make it clear that ideas about tradition can be used to mobilize people politically.[26] But evocation of tradition can be problematic for racist groups.

Consider first the Ku Klux Klan. All Klan groups glorify racist tradition. Indeed, the Klan's ability to recruit members and inspire fear in enemies depends on its association with the large memberships, political victories, and violent history of earlier periods. Modern Klans use

traditions from the first Klan in the ritualized choreography of "naturalization" in which attendant knights form a circle (*kuklos*, from which
"Ku Klux" is derived, is a transliteration of the classical Greek word
meaning "circle"). Klan robes and hoods mimic clothes worn by nineteenth-century night riders to shield their identities as they terrorized
blacks and those whites deemed their enemies. Klan history also is
evoked in the burning cross, a stark symbol of earlier periods of lynchings; in Klan "homecoming marches" in Pulaski, Tennessee, the site of
the 1865 founding of the first Klan;[27] and in the militarized hierarchy
of command, harking back to the nineteenth-century idea of the Klan
as an army of liberation for the white South. Until recently, when local
authorities made it inaccessible to the Klan, efforts to identify with past
Klan glory also included pilgrimages to Stone Mountain, Georgia, a
monument to the Confederacy fashioned on the site where in 1915 the
Klan staged its twentieth-century rebirth.

However, Klan leaders who are interested in mobilizing larger numbers of members by refashioning the public image of the Klan find that
negotiating their tradition can be very tricky. In his study of members
of the British National Front, Michael Billig noted that traditions of the
past are consequential only when they have an impact on the present.[28]
Members who wish to use the Klan's history to inform its present must
maneuver precariously between what the sociologist Erving Goffman
calls "front stage" public pronouncements and "back stage" private
talk,[29] since traditions from earlier Klans do little to support the efforts
by some Klan leaders to reframe the organization in a more mainstream
direction. Relying on the Klan's reputation for racial violence to attract
avidly racist members and at the same time recruiting mainstream whites
for a "new Klan" is a delicate balancing act, and the contrast between
the Klan's front and back stages has created dissatisfaction and faction-
alism in some Klans.

Despite these problems, Klan history continues to be evoked, even in
the most mainstream-oriented Klan groups, both because Klan leaders
need an image of terrorism to placate their most violent members and
frighten their enemies and because these traditions hark back to a past
when white power was closer to absolute. An elderly Klanswoman saw
it as her duty to acquaint younger recruits with white supremacist history: "Stories of how the [local] university was racially exclusive [in the
past] startle them. They didn't realize that you had to be white, that they
didn't even have any Jewish teachers." But the Klan's reliance on tradition can alienate some of its members as well as frighten off potential

mainstream recruits. When Klan leaders attempt to ward off challenges from competing racist leaders by asserting that they are the true heirs to the Klan's legacy, some rank-and-file members find such embrace of tradition foolish and even counterproductive. Women members, in particular, claim they feel demeaned and excluded from rituals that glorify the Klan as an all-male fraternity, complaining of the gendered subcultures inside the Klan:

It's the same old thing over and over again. They [male leaders] hone [the rituals] down till they make themselves into total paranoid basket cases.

You see when there's a big gathering, it's the men [who are] parading and it's the women you see doing the cooking.

The use of tradition creates other problems for the Klan as well. Evoking tradition requires, even as it instills, a sense of commonality, a notion of the "us" whose memory is being evoked as a guide to actions in the present. Much as nationalism presupposes an "imagined political community,"[30] so too racist politics rests on an imagined community (here, of racial similarity). But the boundaries of an imagined racial community have shifted considerably over time in the Klan: it began as one constituted of white, Protestant, southern males after the Civil War; then shifted in the 1920s to one of white, Protestant, northern and southern native-born men and women; and later became one encompassing white Protestants, Catholics, and atheists of both sexes. Today, the definition of who can be in a white supremacist movement is being stretched even further, as past sentiments of "America first" collide with new interest in an internationalist "Pan-Aryan" community. Such efforts are resisted by members who cling to more strictly nationalist definitions of a "klannish" community. Thus, many Klans continue to attack immigration, and only a few have inched toward a postnational imagined community that would encompass right-wing extremists from Europe and elsewhere.[31]

Among neo-Nazis, the use of tradition requires even greater contortions. Neo-Nazis are both handicapped by the xenophobia of many members who find it difficult to identify with German symbols and Nordic/Viking legends and wary of celebrating a past in which European Nazism was defeated.[32] Yet neo-Nazis still find the symbols and rituals of past political glory useful; for example, a seminar held for youth recruits interspersed calisthenics and martial arts instruction with a memorial service for Hitler and other "fallen comrades" and a swastika lighting.[33] Neo-Nazis and other white supremacists sign their names in movement correspondence above the number "88," a reference to the eighth letter of the alphabet that begins "Heil Hitler." Hitler's birthday is often celebrated by racist groups, and turgid texts of World War II history from a Nazi viewpoint are owned, if not read, by many neo-Nazis. The occasional discovery of former German Nazis or concentration camp guards in hiding in the United States and elsewhere also occasions great interest among neo-Nazis, who staunchly denounce the deportations and trials of these war criminals.

Today's neo-Nazis romanticize the past as a time of racial purity, no class conflict, and gender harmony.[34] They see the defeat of German Nazism as simply one stage—a temporary setback—in a process that will end in Aryan victory. To them, the imagined community of Nazism includes far more than Germany. It rests on a Pan-Aryanism that stretches from ancient Viking communities to white Europe and North America. Aryans, they insist, have a common history of victimization, from the hardships of Viking explorers and colonial settlers in the Americas to postwar Zionist assaults on German Aryans. A middle-aged Nazi woman demonstrates this reasoning: "And I'm sorry if that happened to those people, but at the same time if you go back in history, there's an awful lot of white ancestors that went through the same kind of hell one way or the other. . . . White people, from Nordics from many moons and history ago . . . went through a lot of hell in order to exist to this day." Neo-Nazis use Nordic religions to fashion a more noble Aryan past and a modern Pan-Aryan community. Symbols from and references to ancient spirituality pepper neo-Nazi literature and music and, less often, the talk of neo-Nazi activists.[35]

Women members often express ambivalence about such use of tradition. A middle-aged neo-Nazi woman complained about her group's celebration of Hitler's birthday: "I didn't like that kind of hero worship of Adolf Hitler. Because even though I do understand his ideology and I agree with a lot of the points of it, I would rather not put his mark on it, you know, because of [people's belief in] the Holocaust and all that stuff." Another neo-Nazi attributed the defeat of Hitler to "moral" failings, which she located in his use of ancient Aryan beliefs:

I'm not much for Hitler. I guess I understand the things that he taught, but I don't really necessarily forgive him for going about it the way he did. I think that most of his beliefs were ones that had been there already from the Aryan forefathers [who] worshiped Odin and Thor. But he put it into a political ideology format and then it failed. It failed because of different things, but I think that there was a real moral reason that caused it to fail.

A third noted that continuing to celebrate Nazi traditions made it difficult to recruit members: "I don't think that most people would still think that the Nazis were number one or anything even if they proved it [the Holocaust] wasn't true, so sometimes I see that as almost a futile thing."

But even when women object to some aspects of neo-Nazi culture, the rituals of culture still bind them to the group. Those who say they do not like the Hitler cult still scrawl "88" on books and letters, attend celebrations of Hitler's birthday, learn war trivia, and wear uniforms modeled after those worn by German storm troopers.[36]

Racist Cultural Institutions Racist culture also requires institutions to sustain it over time. An important one of these is the white power music industry, which consists of small recording companies, distributors, music magazines, and promoters. The white power music industry peddles its brand of racial hate through tours of white power bands and sales of white power music in racist stores, in mainstream sales outlets, and on the Internet. Launched in 1993 and taken over in 2000 by National Alliance founder William Pierce, the white power music company Resistance Records and its associated magazine, *Resistance,* are seen by many as critical to the future of the white supremacist movement. Resistance Records has promoted music by such bands as No Remorse, Nordic Thunder, and RaHoWa (Racial Holy War), who feature violent racist and anti-Semitic lyrics. Like the more mainstream music business, racist music is run almost entirely by men, despite its appeal to both female and male audiences.[37]

White power music helps create racial commitment with lyrics that romanticize white racist politics, driving home the message that racial pride requires racial action. It also hammers out the theme that music is a means of racist politics, not an end. *Resistance* features advertisements for various white supremacist groups and inspirational profiles of white supremacist leaders, luring white power music fans who lack other focus in their life into racist groups.

CULTURE AND RACIST VIOLENCE

The core of white supremacist culture is violence. As actions, beliefs, and talk, violence suffuses the world of organized racism.[38] Indeed, violence may be the only theme that is as common in the life stories of individual racist activists as in group propaganda. This observation holds true across organized racism, from Ku Klux Klan chapters that claim to have renounced violence in favor of electoral and legislative efforts to skinheads who boast of their violent practices and neo-Nazis who embrace terrorism as an explicit strategy.[39]

The voluminous scholarship on collective violence suggests that societal, internal group, gender, and ideological factors all contribute to the violence of organized racism.[40] The societal conditions on which many studies focus include competition between members of racial groups, provocation or limited response by authorities, and inadequate social control of individual behavior. Less directly, socially induced feelings of isolation, powerlessness, and uncertainty in the face of social change are associated with individual propensities to violent behavior that may fuel collective violence. In addition, studies find that violence is more likely in groups in which advocates of violence gain status while proponents of conciliatory responses are marginalized and in groups that adopt violence as a means of building solidarity or expressing collective bravery. Violence also results from hostile confrontations with authorities or from the encouragement of those whom Donatella della Porta describes as "entrepreneurs of violence," members who push toward more radical and sustained forms of violence.[41]

Although less frequently addressed in the scholarship on violence, gender-specific circumstances are important in shaping violent behavior. Social expectations of aggressiveness or efforts to limit men's power may propel men to violence. Women's violence can stem from their attachment to violent men, from efforts to prove their toughness to comrades, or from conditions that make it impossible for them fulfill their traditional maternal or feminine roles.[42]

Much research also makes it clear that ideologies generally can promote violence. Certainly, the ideologies of belligerence on which racist groups are founded target members of minority groups and their allies for harm. As David Theo Goldberg argues, "Violence is inherent in racist discourse. Subjects are defined in general by the discourses of difference. So subjects recognize themselves for the most part only in contrast to others."[43]

Yet considered individually and together, these antecedents of violence provide only useful clues to, rather than sufficient explanations for, the nature and extent of violence evident in racist groups. Though they clearly contribute to racist violence, they cannot explain its ubiquity in some segments of the racist movement, its practice as a celebratory aspect of daily life. And they provide only a limited understanding of why some white power skinheads inflict horrific violence on fellow white power skinheads, friends, randomly chosen members of majority groups, and even themselves, as well as on those they perceive to be members of racial, ethnic, religious, or sexual minorities.[44]

This latter aspect of racist culture—the way that violence and terror can be casual, seemingly without direction or purpose—often puzzles outsiders. Usually we assume that racist violence is reserved for vulnerable minority communities, an assumption that holds true for most extremist right-wing groups in Europe and for many white supremacist groups in the United States.[45] But a significant amount of violence in the racist movement is also directed at allies. Violent confrontations between racist skinheads and self-defined "antiracist skinheads," in particular, can have an eerily fragile connection to ideology, as people move from racist to antiracist skinhead groups, and back again, for reasons having less to do with politics than with shifting friendships or the availability of parties, drugs, and alcohol. Such violence appears to be engaged in largely for its own sake. To be sure, the level and randomness of violence among skinheads might be due to the psychological and political immaturity of these young racists, and violence among older racists might reflect their own sadistic or masochistic tendencies. Yet such explanations do not tell us why the practice of racist violence is so inconsistent and chaotic.

We can better understand racist violence by seeing it not only as driven by societal, group, gender, and ideological factors but also as a cultural expression that includes, but is not limited to, acts of hostility toward racial enemies. This approach to thinking about violence has several advantages. First, it highlights the relationship between violence and racist identity. Violence affirms people's understanding of their collective interests as racist activists, defining those with whom they share interests and those against whom they must struggle. Second, thinking of violence as a culture makes it easier to understand why racist groups can attract members from many social classes. If we view violence as the product of deprivation and pathology, how do we explain why some children of liberal, economically secure parents become racist activists?

But if we envision violence as a culture, the appeal to both privileged and deprived classes is more conceivable. Third, seeing violence in cultural terms enables us to explore how violence can *create* organization among racists rather than simply being the *product* of racist organizing—how it can unify racists and attract recruits.[46]

The culture of racist violence has two facets, which I label *strategic violence* and *narrative violence*. Both are found or advocated in most racist groups, but narrative violence is more pronounced among newer or loosely formed racist groups such as the white power skinheads, while strategic violence is more common in older Ku Klux Klans and some neo-Nazi groups.

Strategic violence is aimed at those whom white power advocates deem to be their enemies;[47] it is exemplified by paramilitary survivalist preparations for race war and by attacks on members of minority groups, antiracist activists, and government installations and personnel. An outgrowth of a racist group's explicit political mission, it provides a way to conquer perceived enemies and respond to predictions of an apocalyptic future for the white race. This kind of violence is embedded in what social movement theorists refer to as "collective action frames," which are "purposively constructed guides to action created by existing or prospective movement organizers."[48]

The ideas about violence in organized racism are clear and self-conscious. Although usually careful to avoid prosecution for advocating violence toward specific persons or property, racists pose violence abstractly as an overarching guide to action, as a common resolution to disparate problems:[49] Jews should be exterminated; gays and lesbians killed; African Americans, Latinos, and Latinas enslaved, forcibly removed from American soil, imprisoned, or shot; institutions of the state attacked, dismantled, or otherwise rendered ineffective; and race traitors terminated. From the names of white power bands—Aggravated Assault, Berserkr, Extreme Hatred, and White Terror—to the celebrity profiles of Charles Manson and German SS leaders sprinkled throughout white supremacist literature, strategic violence is the backbone of racial identity and purpose. Even those groups (such as some Ku Klux Klans) who purport to renounce violence in favor of more democratic processes of persuasion traffic freely in the rituals and symbols of violence.

An article titled "To Kill or Not to Kill," published in a white supremacist newsletter, provides a particularly striking expression of strategic violence. "Many years ago, I killed an important enemy of my race," the author begins, and he proceeds to elaborate his six reasons "to kill and be proud of it":

1) The sheer pleasure of revenge ... *a certain physical feeling of full satis-faction, if not sharp sensation, to see a base enemy laid down and out.*

2) Learning self-assertion, gaining self-respect. ... *You have to have the in-tegrity and self-respect to "do the right thing."*

3) Building group consciousness, mutual admiration and cooperative sup-port ... *you can become part of a group of true friends with mutual interests.*

4) Maintaining race/national integrity. ... *Your children's children will thank you.*

5) Increasing spiritual strength for future activities. ... *Feel the strength surging through you from the sheer joy of taking control and taking action.*

6) Admittance to the Hall of Heroes/a place in racial memory. ... You will become a legend of time itself.[50]

Narrative violence, in contrast, is the seemingly meaningless practice of violence that exists as a routine aspect of daily life. It is violence as tradition and commonsense understanding, something taken for granted, seen as natural.[51] The sociologist Francesca Polletta argues that collective definitions of problems and remedies (setting the terms of "us" and "them") depend on prior, often-repeated stories.[52] Such narratives shape activist identities and form commitments to action. They are the precursors to the collective action frames, ideologies, and strategies that develop later. Borrowing Polletta's terminology, we can see narrative violence as a group story (what she calls "the story of our becoming")[53] rather than as an explicit political strategy. Narrative violence is a means of solidifying group identity and giving purpose to group life.[54]

Anthropologists ascribe a "habitus of violence" to those societies in which violence becomes simply another "dimension of living," neither meaningful nor meaningless but "emotionally senseless."[55] Subcultures like that of white power skinheads similarly infuse all social interaction with violence and coercion. Violence can bind together a disparate group of people whose political and ideological agendas may be unformed, ambiguous, or even conflicting. It is the story they tell about themselves as a group. It gives a sense of the "us" from which it is then possible to develop a politics and ideology. Belief in Aryan supremacy provides the logic for narrative violence (as it does for strategic violence), but nar-rative violence does not simply mirror ideology. Instead, symbols and practices of racist group life continually push action toward violent ex-pression.[56]

Racist women talk about both strategic and narrative violence. I was surprised at how openly they discussed violence, which is highly stigmatized in mainstream society. But, as della Porta suggests, "in biographical recollections, the selection of the information follows—consciously or unconsciously—psychological needs . . . as well as aesthetic considerations."[57] The many descriptions of violent acts and sentiments in the stories of racist women testify to the importance of violence in their lives. Indeed, some organize their entire life story as a chain of violent episodes, though the role of violence in their lives as racists may have significantly influenced those recollections. They usually depict themselves initially as the victims of violence, and later, under the tutelage of the racist movement, as perpetrators. But unlike the European left-wing terrorists whom della Porta studied, they rarely try to cast violence as honorable,[58] presenting it rather as necessary, as provoked.

Dolores, a neo-Nazi, recounted a string of violent incidents and their consequences. For her, school was memorable only for the physical assaults received and inflicted there. Her memories of neighborhoods were of street confrontations. Her marriage was presented not in terms of love but as a temporary oasis from a sea of violence. A similar story was told by Darla, a Klanswoman whose earliest memory was of violence: "The first fistfight I was ever in, I was in kindergarten. He took my spot on the merry-go-round and that just wasn't going to go with me. And he grabbed my hair and pulled a big chunk of my hair out. And I turned around and nailed him right where you're not supposed to nail a guy and got suspended for a week from kindergarten."

These women's senses of self are constructed, at least retrospectively, in relation to violence. For them, violence defines life, so the violence of organized racism does not stand out as remarkable: it is only one thread in an unvaried fabric. The random violence of skinhead life simply reflects the violence that is now and has always been everywhere. Thus, tales of violence that are implausible to an outsider seem true beyond question to these women. For example, although most racists believe that a "race war" is on the horizon, some of my interviewees claim that it has already begun, flaring just outside their personal experience. One told me, in a story already related in chapter 1, of a friend of a friend shot and killed by an African American, "simply for being a skinhead."

Joining an all-girl white power skinhead gang is one way for young racist women to navigate violence. Although rare, skingirl groups afford their members a sense of strength and power. They project an image of raw aggression, a female version of macho violence and invulnerability.

A West Coast skingirl commented: "There's a certain macho image that people do like. You always hear people speaking with a sense of awe and respect for the Mafia, you know. You even hear people bragging that they have relatives in the Mafia. I don't believe they do, but they do brag about it. So I think there's a certain segment that applauds these violent acts."

To skingirls, like their male counterparts, violence feels inevitable, in just the same way that racist views come to seem obvious. An East Coast white power skingirl recalled, critically but with admiration, such a group in her town: "The Grey Heel Girls, they wept and raged, they drank. There was Grey Heel Boys and Grey Heel Girls. And they all kind of dated each other. It's like these two little mini gangs. About ten to twelve members each. . . . If there was a fight or something needed to be done, they were the people that did it. These Grey Heel Girls, they'd rough it up. They'd be bruised and bloody and they wouldn't care. A tooth knocked out and they didn't care."

Another skingirl described watching a girl "get jumped in" to her group:

I guess there are different ways, but the time that I saw it, it was like a line and you had to walk the line. There were all these girls lined up and the first one just took a punch and you couldn't hit them back, and you couldn't scream and you couldn't cry and you couldn't wince or anything. You just had to take it and go to the next one and take it and go to the next one, and down the line. And if you could do it then you were in. But there were other ones where they just circled you and you get inside and you had 30 seconds or x amount of seconds where everyone just kicked you and beat the crap out of you and if you could get up on your feet afterwards, stand up on your feet, then you were in.

When violence is a part of daily life, it ceases to arouse comment. It becomes a commonsense strategy of action, used as the situation demands. As a lesbian skinhead noted: "Sometimes, like you walk in a bar and somebody'd look at my girlfriend. And I'd be like, 'What the fuck you looking at?' And they'd say something. And I'd take the man outside to the parking lot and fight. And I would have my knife. The blade was six and a half inches long, this wide, strapped to my leg."

But even some white power skingirls find violence in skinhead culture overwhelming. One woman hinted that it might cause her to leave the movement, remarking, "After you had not totally seen but [had] known four or five people that had been killed within two years' time, it starts to really sink in. . . . It was just crazy, crazy." Each death that she related occurred under different circumstances, but the enormity of the death toll is striking:

They said one was a suicide. Which probably it was, you know, [although] we all thought it was a conspiracy, that the SHARPS *[antiracist skinheads] got him. He was probably just torn and afraid. There was another that ratted out [became an informant] for protection and someone that was associated with him was killed. And there was another that was shot. And there was a girl, she was raped by a group of black men because she was a white supremacist and . . . then she killed herself because she said she was just a disgrace, she was used, she was dirty, she wasn't good to anyone anymore.*

This skingirl's narrative of violence evokes Hannah Arendt's insight that evil "is never 'radical,' that it is only extreme" and lacks depth.[59] We forget that truth when we impute strategy to all racist violence. Though violence is often strategic, sometimes the mere practice of violence can be nearly as important as its direction. A middle-aged western Klanswoman described, without condemnation, how the girls and boys in a visiting group of racist skinheads encouraged her cat to latch onto their arms with its teeth and claws until "blood would be flowing down their arms and they would all just laugh and laugh."

The participation of women in such bloody rituals is puzzling at first glance, for it defies our sense that right-wing violence is done only by men. But this belief is a misconception, largely based on studies done in Europe. Those European extremist right-wing groups that are vying for electoral office tend to restrict women to traditional roles. Others that, like European skinheads, more frequently engage in physical violence may be less concerned about the electorate's general attitudes toward gender, but they have few women members.[60]

In the United States, women are involved in violence, at least to a limited extent, in white power skinhead and some neo-Nazi groups. They rarely are credited when violence is committed by Ku Klux Klans and Christian Identity groups with more traditional ideas of gender, though my interviews suggest that women may participate in this violence more often than media accounts or arrest data indicate.[61] In any case, Klan and Christian Identity women are far from renouncing violence, often heartily cheering on its exercise. Women speak about the need for violence repeatedly in their life histories. Whether or not they claimed to participate in violence in the past or present, almost all imagined a future in which they would take part actively, even enthusiastically, as did a southern Klanswoman who told me: "In the future, I think that I will be fighting to make [the white supremacist] dream a reality. It won't be through [distributing] flyers either. I wish we could get what we want through negotiation, but I don't see that happening. The government will not negotiate anything. I see it all coming down to civil war." An adherent of Christian Identity made her commitment to a violent resolution of racial conflict even more explicit:

I have something I need to do. I hope that it will be helping to usher in God's Kingdom on this earth, which may sound strange to you, but what I mean is there's going to be something that goes down in America in the next, I don't know, let's say ten years. (laugh) Just to be optimistic. . . . We're on the brink of something and I want to participate in it! Maybe it's Armageddon. (laugh) Maybe it's going to be total wipeout of the world. But if it's something that I can participate in, then I will be very happy.

Racist women can also be drawn into violence in other ways than as perpetrators. One story, involving a confrontation between Sally, a very young, low-level southern skingirl, and Jane, an older and very prominent neo-Nazi, exemplifies how strategic and narrative violence can intersect in the lives of racist women. As Sally told it to me, she vacillated between anger at its unfairness and gratitude for the "valuable lesson" she learned about the "need to be tough."

I was walking downtown and I had just bought a new pair of Doc Martens [boots] and this car just screeched to a stop and this woman jumped out. I'd never seen her before in my life and I'd been a part of the movement around here for almost two years. . . . She looked at me and said, "Are you white power?" And I just looked at her and I said, "Why?" I just didn't answer her. . . . Then she slapped me and took a knife out of her pocket and she sliced down the length of what I was wearing on my boots . . . and she punched me. . . . She ended up leaving with the boots from on my feet and my new boots in the bag.

In a subsequent meeting, Jane insisted that Sally reconsider her reaction. The attack, according to Jane, was necessary to teach Sally how to act in the difficult situations she would face as a racist activist. Using a twisted logic similar to that used by racists in portraying minorities as responsible for their own victimization, Jane claimed that the assault was provoked by Sally's failure to "stand up for white pride" when asked whether she was "white power": "She sat down next to me and said [that] at all costs no matter who I was or who I could have been, 'You should have said that yes, you were white power. And you should be proud of that.' And so she wouldn't give me back . . . the boots that I was wearing because she liked them. And she had taken them from me fair and square." Thus Jane quickly and effectively conveyed a verbal message about how racist activists are expected to act on the street and a physical message about the currency of violence in racist groups. Violence confers status and leadership in organized racism, reinforcing relations of domination and acquiescence. So Sally's boots become payment for her unsolicited lesson about negotiating street encounters.

Racist women often face violence, both by men and women, at dances. It is especially common at racist concerts that feature brutal body-slamming by performers and audience members clustered in pits in front of the stage. Several white power skingirls told me of slam dances at which there was "no mercy for the weak." When someone was knocked down in the mosh pit in front of the stage, one remembered, "rather than helping them up," fellow skins—men, mostly, but occasionally also women—would "stomp them and kick them in the head with their big boots." Through white power slam dancing, skingirls and male skinheads can affirm both gender and racial identities. Like men who engage in violent initiation rites in street gangs, military units, and some college fraternities, racist men demonstrate their masculinity and their allegiance to racism through brutal encounters with other men. Deciphering the meanings of women's slam dancing is considerably more complicated. Some girls said their violent dancing, including voluntary visits to the mosh pit, showed that they were tough, that they could project an image of a powerful racist woman. Some claimed they had done violence to others, men as well as women, in the mosh pit. But others felt it was just another instance of being victimized by the very men who claimed to be their racist comrades.

Skingirls find themselves victims of horrifying violence, at the hands of fellow skins and others, in a variety of situations. In chapter 4 we looked at domestic violence among racist couples. But racist women are also threatened by men who are not their sexual partners: "A good friend of mine, Cindy, had a hammer put through her head by [a male skinhead]. She was in the hospital. Another girl lost her baby because she got the crap beaten out of her [by antiracist skins] when she was pregnant." A racist publication deplored a similar incident: "Some are very concerned with reports not so long ago of people who left a comrade to the tender mercies of a mob who beat hell out of her. We are very disturbed that people in the White Nationalist Movement would do this, first of all. Then to report on it and sort of slide over it with a casual attitude is unforgivable."[62]

Women can also be the occasion of violence between men. This is not lost on the women themselves, who talk of "their men" fighting on their behalf: "You felt like it was special being a woman, you know. Well, the men are going to take care of me. Anywhere you went there would be someone, you know, to cover your back if anything happened." And in the gendered world of racism, as in the rest of society, it is women who are responsible for redressing the effects of violence. A Klanswoman from the Midwest recalled watching as a Klansman was stabbed in a street fight: "This guy, he couldn't go to the hospital because they report things, but he needed someone to stitch him up. He had a huge gouge over his eye. So I used dental floss and a needle. And I stitched him up. And we got betadyne and it didn't get infected or anything." Another interviewee, a skingirl, spoke of the violence that surrounded her boyfriend: "I'd hate it if he was ten minutes late getting home. I wouldn't know whether he just had to work late or whether he was in jail or whether he was dead or whether you know. You just, you didn't know. I hated that. That was just the worst feeling."

Despite their praise of strategic racist violence, most racist women were ambivalent about the level of violence in their lives. A West Coast Klanswoman told me that although she wanted her daughter to follow her political lead, she would never allow her to become a skinhead, because "skinheads are just violent, just into violence." Another recalled an earlier group she had been in: "I started being a part of that [racist] lifestyle . . . You'd do everything from, you know, guns coming out . . . And yeah, it was just no fun. I was arrested a couple of times but never convicted. Charges were always dropped, thank God. Just, you know, for saying things I shouldn't have said, being at the wrong place at the wrong time." Moreover, many women believed, whether with good reason or not, that they were particular targets of antiracist demonstrators. One Klanswoman admitted—with some embarrassment—that she was afraid nearly all the time when participating in Klan events. Although acknowledging what she saw as a racist imperative to be fearless, she told stories of rallies at which she and other women were pelted by "machine gun bolts, plastic holders full of pennies, and taped rocks."

Some women worried about the political implications of violence, fearing that its advocacy would make recruitment more difficult. Their worries may well be justified: scholars generally agree that social movements are most successful in attracting recruits when their appeals overlap with ideas accepted in the wider public discourse, such as the promotion of freedom or individual rights.[63] Since mainstream discourse does not overtly support violence (though perhaps some subcultures of disaffected youth do), its role in racist propaganda may drive away older and more mainstream whites. Indeed, those in the racist movement debate whether the violence of white power skinheads will attract or repel others. In public, many racist leaders disavow skinhead violence. One complains: "I say there is something fundamentally wrong with the 'skinhead' movement if six months is the average time they remain White Activists and while in it they have managed to do a great deal of damage to the White cause by their senseless acts of murder, mayhem and vandalism."[64] They also worry about the effect that skinhead violence has on the continuity of the racist movement. As one woman told me, "We have a problem with aging activists with few replacements [because] so many white youth get caught up into the ZOG [Zionist-occupied government] prison system and discriminated against there." Striking a similar note, a young neo-Nazi woman from the East Coast said that she had begun to disagree with the amount of violence because, if it did not diminish, "all our men will be in prison."

At times, however, some admit that there are advantages to impetuous violence. Typical is one leader's simultaneous dismissal and embrace of the skinheads: "Although some Movement activists would not want to socialize on a personal level with the skins, we must also understand that these youth are willing to stick their necks out, get their hands dirty and attract media attention to problems that all White people face."[65] Another likewise describes his young allies as "skinheads all dressed up with nowhere to go [so] the frustration boils over," noting the advantage to older leaders like himself of tapping into "the youth outrage that is starting in the schools and streets."[66] Nonskinhead women, though less likely to approve of skinhead violence, sometimes praised it. A few told me that skinheads were the best racists. One woman in the far West publishes a newsletter that extols skinheads as "the most effective branch" of white supremacism. Other women said that skinheads were right to attack racial minorities, but worried that these actions were risky and not always productive. A neo-Nazi woman confided, "I wouldn't say that the typical skinhead violence helps the movement. I think it hurts it because they usually pick what I would call a meaningless target. They just swat a fly. They don't go after the problem, they go after some symptom which changes nothing. I mean, you've changed nothing if you snuff out one black on a street corner. How many blacks are there in America? Eleven million, something like that. Fifteen million?"

Debate about violence also can explicitly focus on gender. Some women worried that movement violence would increase their vulnerability to boyfriends or husbands. Others complained, as did one skinhead talking about a former boyfriend, that women suffered from the violence of their men in less direct ways:

I ended up losing a job 'cause [my boyfriend] came in to pick me up from work. I was, like, clocking out, just getting ready to leave. And it was a Hispanic manager came in and he was doing something and he made a comment. He said like "Muy Bonitta" or something like that. And [my boyfriend] just went nuts. Turned into this huge fisticuffs, brawl. So my boss said, "You know, he's bad news. I don't know why you're with him. You're a good worker, but we don't want him coming here to pick you up anymore. He's not allowed on the property." And I said, "I quit then."

Occasionally, women reflected on the violence in somewhat ethical terms. One East Coast skingirl told me the story of a particularly horrifying incident involving her friends and a fellow skinhead whom she described as "a big, tough, macho-type guy": "Someone put like mercury in his beer and . . . it was real painful. He was like screaming and crying. And he like got into his bed. . . . He was like screaming and they couldn't stand to hear the screams and so they just like beat him with baseball bats until he just quit screaming and by that time he was like dead." Although she was "disturbed" by the murder, she was most troubled by the reactions of the other white power skinheads: "Someone said, 'Well, like Dave always used to say, "Mercy is for the weak," and he obviously was weak at that point and so he got what he deserved.' . . . There were a couple of women that I remember were really upset about it, [but] others were like, 'Well, he deserved it.' Other people just didn't have no opinion either way. . . . And some guys were like real adamant, [saying,] 'You know, he deserved that.' "

It is tempting to dismiss such gruesome violence as directionless. But even this seemingly random violence, so characteristic of skinhead culture, carries a political message. It announces to the world that racist skinheads should not be messed with, that there are no limits to what they will do, that they will give their lives if necessary to maintain their group. The very heinousness of racist violence, apart from its target or purpose, strikes fear into its intended enemies. Racist activists are well aware of this response and make concerted efforts to maintain their fearsome image. In fact, they worry that failing to project an image of incipient violence will create an impression of weakness that will deter possible allies. According to one racist publication, "Meetings that are only possible with the protective assistance of a strong police convert nobody; because in order to win over the lower strata of the people there must be a visible show of strength on one's own side."[67]

In this light, narrative violence must be seen as a precursor to strategic violence, rather than simply as pointless acts of savagery. Like the raw celebration of death and violence that characterizes fascist movements and organized crime, the violent culture of organized racism has a political effect, however remote from any particular action: racist violence is a spectacle, functioning in much the same way as do racist uniforms or Nazi symbols.

The culture of organized racism is a ghastly version of a fun house mirror. In it, we see images that are familiar, yet distorted. Like any culture, it helps people locate themselves in society and history. It sets up ways of doing and ways of being that create a sense of an "us," forging collective identities and goals. It carries the sense of common purpose that brings people into social groups and makes those groups work.

Yet racist culture is frighteningly different from most subcultures. It is rooted in shared hatred of racial others rather than in a mutuality of common experiences, tastes, or values. It is fundamentally a culture of violence, which is sometimes enacted and always promised. Organized racism terrorizes not only in deeds but through its ability to project a certain image, by projecting a cultural spectacle that inspires awe in its followers and dread in its enemies.

Women who come into the racist movement discover there a sea of violence that they abhor but also find attractive. They see the brutalizing effects of organized racism's culture of violence in their own lives and in the lives of their friends and male partners. But many of them also find the violent images of racist culture to be personally empowering, at least in their interactions with outsiders. It gives them a feeling of mastery and of female potency, however illusory, that they rarely find in other social settings.

LESSONS

Racist groups threaten democratic, pluralist societies. Women who associate with Ku Klux Klan, white power skinhead, Christian Identity, or neo-Nazi groups have a conscious commitment to the destruction of racial and religious tolerance. They hold views that are deeply conspiratorial, that cast history as the product of sinister Jewish forces. Many advocate violence to achieve Aryan supremacism; almost all foresee an imminent race war that will pit white Aryans against all others, and some want to hasten this racial apocalypse.

We must do more than recognize the danger of this movement. Indeed, reports that merely heighten public fear of racist groups as a bizarre and dangerous subculture can be unproductive. When we see organized racists as an "other," as profoundly different from the rest of society, we can feel secure about our own commitment to tolerance and diversity while viewing group members as unreachable and their recruitment as somehow inexorable. This assumption is politically paralyzing. Instead, we need to know the truth about racist activists. They are not uniformly ignorant, incomprehensible, or irrational. Such caricatures hamper our efforts to understand what they are like and to lure them *out* of racist groups. Many of the women I interviewed had quite unremarkable backgrounds. Some of them combined oddly conspiratorial worldviews and viciously racist agendas with otherwise fairly mainstream lives.

While never forgetting their horrifying actions and potential, we must also see how racist groups operate like other social groups. It is a mistake to assume that the process of recruitment into racist groups differs markedly from that through which individuals enter churches, neighborhood associations, or bowling leagues—they join because of contacts with current members and, in some cases, a particular receptivity to the group's ideas. Similarly, we cannot assume that members of racist groups have a greater familiarity with or more uniform acceptance of their group's ideologies than we expect from members of mainstream religions, political parties, and the like. In most social groups, even deeply committed members may have only a shallow understanding of their group's principles, and they may show considerable variation in their beliefs. Just as the racist movement is complex and multifaceted, so too our responses to racist group recruitment and activism must be varied and informed. Challenges to racist activism can—and should— be political, legal, educational, and ideological, based on an accurate analysis of these groups and the members that populate them. Whether challenges to the racist movement involve school programs, rebuttals in mainstream media, direct confrontations, or community efforts to design alternatives to racist groups and ideas, effective opposition must acknowledge the ways in which racist ideas and actions overlap with those of the rest of society, as well as differ.

From my interviews, I have learned five main lessons about racist groups in the United States. Each points to a strategy that can help stop organized racism.

1. *Racist groups change people.* Most of the women I interviewed were changed profoundly by being in a racist group. They were taught new ways to think about themselves and other whites, whom to consider enemies, and how to change the world. They went from holding racist attitudes to being racist activists, from racial apathy to racist zeal.

It is important to remember that holding racist attitudes and being an activist are different. Racist attitudes are amenable to change through education, personal connections with minorities, and representations in the media. There is considerable evidence that diverse neighborhoods, schools, and workplaces and depictions of the heterogeneity of American life in the media and school curricula promote racial and religious tolerance. Racist activism, in contrast, includes a sense of persecution, a conspiratorial worldview, and a commitment to action that such methods are unlikely to alter. We thus need to develop a new set of strategies to reach racist activists.

2. Today's racist groups are different from those of the past. Organized racism is a product of the present, not a legacy of the past. The common assumption that racism is anchored in history makes it seem that racism will necessarily be a victim of social and economic progress. Unfortunately, time has proven a poor curative for group hatreds. For proof, we need to look no further than the anti-Semitism of the crumbling former communist world or the ethnic violence flaring in the Balkans, central Africa, Southeast Asia, and the Indian subcontinent. As the political theorist Paul Gilroy states, racism can "move tidily and unchanging through time and history [but] assumes new forms and articulates new antagonisms in different situations."[1]

Today's racist groups differ from those of the past in a number of ways. First, many racist groups now draw on apocalyptic ideas to justify violence and terrorism.[2] In addition to a global "race war," these include predictions of a millennial "last days" battle with Satan and his forces, as described in the biblical book of Revelation; secular beliefs in a coming global catastrophe following monetary collapse or military disaster; and fears of cataclysmic confrontation with federal authorities, like the FBI's 1993 attack on the Waco, Texas, compound held by the followers of David Koresh. These apocalyptic visions create a sense of urgency, and the groups often view spectacular violence as a way to hasten millennial prophecies. We therefore need to monitor more closely the racist groups that use apocalyptic imagery. At the same time, we need to recognize that the institutions on which we rely to combat organized racism—local police departments, federal authorities, churches, and neighborhood organizations—may themselves have a racist legacy, so they themselves must be monitored and guided by broad and democratic coalitions rooted in the communities that organized racism targets.

Many of today's racist groups are deeply anti-Semitic and conspiratorial. While racist groups have always hated Jews, the virulence of current anti-Semitism is striking. The belief that Jews are the literal embodiment of Satan may lead to more violence against Jews and their property. Such incidents as the 1999 shootings in Los Angeles and Chicago and the 2000 murder of a Jewish woman and attacks on synagogues in suburban Pittsburgh may increase. Jewish institutions need protection.

Although Jews and African Americans are particular targets of organized racism, they are not the only ones. Others include antiracist activists, members of progressive groups, homosexuals, Asians and Asian Americans, Chicanos and Chicanas, Latinos and Latinas, Pakistanis, Indians, doctors and nurses in abortion clinics that serve Aryan women, federal government employees, politicians, lawyers and police officers, and members and clergy of non-Christian religions. Broad alliances are necessary to defeat organized racism. Organizing around the shared vulnerability of very diverse racial, religious, sexual, and political groups—even when there is no immediate threat—can be a means of building sustained community coalitions. Remarkable efforts have been mounted in Chicago, Pittsburgh, and elsewhere to bring together diverse communities to address racist organizing. Some have been disappointingly short-lived responses to specific episodes of racist violence, but others appear likely to continue over time. Especially promising are broad-based campaigns that take on issues often ignored, such as violence against gay men and lesbians, and that focus on grassroots organizing against hate. The antiracist groups listed in appendix 3 are vital in these organizing projects.

Finally, today's racist groups rely on mass communication, especially the Internet. Many try to recruit through webpages, and private bulletin boards or chat rooms enable members to communicate unnoticed by outsiders and police. The ultimate effect of the Internet on racist organizing is unclear: it undoubtedly aids coordination, and it may make racist ideas appear more legitimate, but racist groups may find the Internet far less effective for recruiting than personal contacts. In any case, we must pay attention to online racism. Software that blocks access to Internet hate sites can help prevent children's exposure to racist propaganda, but educating children and the community at large about the vile agendas of racist groups is the best means of ensuring that their messages are received skeptically and critically.

3.   *We can prevent racist recruiting.* Most of the women I interviewed found their way into organized racism, and into its dangerous and nonsensical beliefs, by meeting existing members. We must prevent such contacts by exposing racist activists in high schools, music concerts, and social gatherings. When racists' agenda is made clear, it is harder for them to recruit.

The appeal of racist groups is social and cultural—providing a network of friends, a collective identity, and a sense of purpose—as much as political. Young people in particular find the in-your-face, alternative culture of racist groups powerfully attractive. To combat racist recruiting among the young, we need to respect alternative youth cultures that are not racist. We need to assess youth cultures accurately, challenging those that are racist but not those that are rebellious, defiant, or simply irritating to adults. Moreover, oppositional youth cultures can be valuable allies in antiracist work. Teens, especially those identified with alternative nonracist teen cultures, are best situated to discourage their peers from being lured into racist groups.

Similar steps must be taken to protect vulnerable women, whom the racist movement recruits by manipulating their feelings of victimization, anger, and fear. Women who gravitate to racist groups with worries about crime, their children's schools, their jobs, or their families might as easily find answers in community organizations, feminist groups, or labor unions. Progressive groups that seriously address the systemic and local problems that make women afraid for themselves and their families can counter racist recruitment.

4. *We can bring activists out of racist groups.* Too little attention has been paid to how people can be recruited out of racist groups.[3] If we assume that all racist activists hold rigid beliefs and are deeply committed to their cause, then encouraging defection seems an impossible task. But my research shows that racist women's beliefs are more fragile and their allegiances more complicated than those of racist men. We need to look closely at the circumstances of each woman individually. Because many maintain ties to relatives and friends on the outside, social networks may be able to entice them to leave—much as personal contacts brought them in. Disagreements and disillusionment with their racist groups also can be played on to pull them out.

To be sure, defecting from a racist group can be terrifying. As one woman told me: "I was afraid that if I just said, 'I don't want to live this life anymore, I can't be a [group name],' that I wouldn't be allowed. I'd seen what happened to people. I mean people that I knew and was friends with had died. And no one talked about it, but people knew." But despite such very real concerns, networks of friends and family help bring women safely out of racist groups.[4]

5. *Racism is mainstream as well as marginal.* We cannot understand contemporary racism by looking only at its extremes. The case of David Duke, a former Klan leader and neo-Nazi member, is instructive. Massive media attention to Duke's electoral efforts in local and statewide offices in the state of Louisiana in the 1980s and 1990s netted hundreds of interviews with Duke supporters. Yet taken in isolation, these interviews were dangerously misleading. Those who consented to them were almost uniformly lower middle class, poorly educated, and inarticulate. But the racism into which Duke tapped, and many of the votes that nearly gave him the keys to Louisiana's gubernatorial mansion, lay deep within educated, middle-class, mainstream white Louisiana. Interviews with those unsavvy or unrestrained enough to utter racist sentiments on camera or before a tape recorder are of limited value—and indeed can create a distorted image of racial hatred—unless they are placed in the broader context of racial privileges that are institutionalized and rarely acknowledged.

To understand what is fueling organized racism today, we need to focus not only on racist groups but also on the society from which they recruit. The mainstay of any substantial racist movement is not the pathological individual but rather a pathological vein of racism, intolerance, and bigotry in the larger population that the movement successfully mines. Racist groups recruit primarily through personal contacts, but they are able to find converts because pervasive racism continues to be tolerated in white society. Some women who come into organized racism learned in their families intensely and overtly to hate racial, religious, sexual, or political enemies. But most did not. Even mild feelings of racism and intolerance can provide a sufficient foundation on which groups can build in teaching their complex, bizarre racist sentiments.

The visible aspects of organized racism are marginalized in our society. Racist groups seeking to rally or distribute their literature in public places are almost always greeted with organized and vocal opposition. Racist groups are routinely condemned and shunned by mainstream institutions. But attacks on the root causes of organized racism, sadly, are less fervent. While Klan hoods and Nazi swastikas evoke almost universal disgust, routine practices of bigotry and intolerance do not. If we are to develop an effective strategy against organized hatred, we must do so on two levels: by countering racist groups and by fighting the racist ideas and institutions in mainstream America that ensure those groups a fertile ground for recruits.

RACIST GROUPS

Members of today's racist and anti-Semitic movement fall into four general categories: racist skinhead, Christian Identity (CI), neo-Nazi, and Ku Klux Klan. Although some groups in the militia movement overlap ideologically with racist groups, I do not include militia members in this study because their organization and pattern of recruitment are different.

Many of these racist groups are quite fluid, frequently dissolving and being resurrected under new names. Sometimes internal conflict or struggles for leadership position cause a group to collapse, even though the racist commitment of its members remains strong; sometimes leaders or members reorganize because they are seeking to evade criminal or civil charges. The resulting stream of "new" groups lends the movement an illusion of strength and rapid growth.

Some these racist groups are barely more than their names. Individuals may claim allegiance to one group—usually by wearing such group insignia as T-shirts, tattoos, or jewelry—but participate in the social and racist activities of a different group. They can identify with and act on behalf of several groups simultaneously, or remain unaffiliated with any particular group. Even well-established groups often have fuzzy boundaries. Ku Klux Klan leaders often proclaim Nazi-like sentiments. Some Klan leaders are CI preachers. Nazi skinheads appear at Klan rallies and cross burnings.

Despite a common agenda that unites anti-Semitism with hatred toward immigrants, nonwhite foreigners, nonwhites in the United States, non-Christians, the federal government, feminists, gays, lesbians, bisexuals, and other racial, religious, or sexual minorities, racist groups vary considerably. Some promote racist reconstructions of ancient Nordic religions and spiritual ideas—especially Odinism, a belief system imported from Nazi Germany that blends magic and witchcraft with white racialism and anti-Semitism;[1] others reject all spirituality and connections to religion. Some explicitly advocate racist violence, while others favor a less direct approach. Some have international ties, enacting racist rituals abroad or copying the beliefs of racist groups in foreign countries;[2] others insist on narrow isolationism and nationalism.

These differences can lead to friction in the racist movement. Leaders of intensely hierarchical Ku Klux Klan chapters often express disdain toward other groups, especially racist skinheads, that lack member accountability. Conversely, some racist activists deride those who seek to appeal to the political mainstream; thus one white supremacist assessed a rival group as "a bit timid sometimes, a little middle- to upper-class, tinged with a bit of educated snobbery." But heterogeneity in organized racism is also its strength. Some racist groups position themselves to appeal to middle-class white Christians, others to the economically marginalized. Racist skinheads draw in the young, while Christian Identity and Klan groups appeal to a broader range of ages. Such diversity allows the tentacles of organized racism to span U.S. society, luring a small but surprisingly varied group of persons into racist activism.

RACIST SKINHEADS

White power skinheads are loosely organized and transient groups of teenagers and young adults typically bound together by a culture of white power music and violent expressions of antipathy toward all African Americans, Jews, Muslims, nonwhite or non-Aryan immigrants, and those they perceive to be gay men or lesbians. (There are also antiracist skins, who adopt a similar style of clothing and street confrontation but focus their violence on racist groups or individuals.) Under such names as "romantic violence," "confederate hammer skins," and "Reich skins," white power skinheads have been accused in a number of violent assaults and murders. Most skin groups are extremely short-lived, making it impossible to determine their numbers or identify members with any precision.

Although the predatory street violence of racist skinhead groups makes them something like gangs, most skinheads reject the authoritarian leadership and internal hierarchies typically found in gangs; they are unified instead by racism and anti-Semitism. However, some white supremacist skinhead groups do claim to force members to follow behavioral rules, which can range from adherence to a set of racial or political loyalties to more mainstream demands, such as staying in school. Such talk of ideological and educational standards is no doubt exaggerated, but it suggests that a measure of organizational coherence may lurk behind the apparent chaos and anarchy of some white power skin groups.

Information about racist skinheads is difficult to obtain. Most skin groups do not publish a regular newsletter or other propaganda. Skinheads are reluctant to discuss their ideas with outsiders, and many understand little about the precepts of white supremacy or neo-Nazism that presumably direct their actions. The ideology of racist skinheads has to be pieced together from the flyers, song lyrics, racist 'zines, clothing, tattoos, insignia, and music that define skinhead life. Such evidence suggests that action and relationships among people, not ideas, are important to white power skinheads. Threats, fighting, violence, and friends sustain these groups over time. As one racist skinhead flyer proclaims, "we give white youth an alternative to weakness and submission. We refuse to be herded around like lost sheep; instead we choose to control our own fate."[3]

Many skin groups are extremely male-oriented and misogynist. The women in them—given the derogatory label "skinchicks"—play marginal roles and often are regarded by male skins as little more than sexual partners or submissive supporters of male agendas. In other white power skin groups, whose views of women are less restrictive, women may assume leadership roles and participate actively and enthusiastically in skinhead violence. Some women even have had significant influence in shaping skinhead gangs into more focused racist organizations.[4]

CHRISTIAN IDENTITY

Christian Identity (CI) is a pseudo-religious network of self-identified "churches" linked across the country by Christian Identity family Bible camps, radio shows, and other forms of mass communication.[5] Christian Identity also is associated with a network of Bible study groups and several publications, including the tabloid *Jubilee*.

The ideology of Christian Identity is extremely complex and convoluted. None of my interviewees could offer more than a superficial explanation of CI doctrine, though they expressed great commitment to its anti-Semitic and racist philosophy. It is based loosely on an eighteenth- and nineteenth-century British theology known as "British Israelism," which was imported to the United States in the 1940s. CI preaches that Jews and all persons of color are the literal offspring of Satan or his minions and that white, Anglo-Saxon Christians are the true lost tribe of Israel, the chosen people of God. According to this creed, known as the doctrine of "two seedlines," Eve was impregnated in the garden of Eden with two seeds. From Adam's seed came Abel and the white (Aryan) race; from Satan's seed came Cain, Jews, and the nonwhite races. The result is eternal racial conflict. While other anti-Semitic belief systems view Jews as allies of satanic forces, Christian Identity insists that Jews are the literal descendants, even the embodiment, of the Devil. In the words of one researcher, Christian Identity tells its members of "their golden past before the machinations of the satanic Jews robbed them of the knowledge of their covenantel birthright, and it assures them of their promised future of happiness and terrestrial power."[6]

The racist and anti-Semitic emphasis of Christian Identity is evident in a number of its practices. In its newsletters, adherents peddle tapes of Adolf Hitler's speeches and vicious tracts such as "Anne Frank Diary a Hoax" and "Interracial Marriages Forbidden by God." They denounce Catholicism as a "cult-religion" and oppose traditional Protestantism, even Christian Fundamentalism, which they regard as having given up on direct action in favor of passively waiting for God's intervention in the world. CI members support homeschooling to counteract what they perceive as the racially tolerant emphasis in public schools. Some favor outlawing racial intermarriage.[7]

The Christian Identity movement is quite decentralized, and CI members, leaders, and philosophies have been involved in other parts of the white supremacist movement. These include a network of white supremacists organized within the U.S. prison system and known as the Aryan Brotherhood; the Idaho compound "Aryan Nations," which long hosted an annual Aryan National Congress and is renowned as a gathering point for a wide range of white supremacist groups and individuals; The Order, an underground terrorist network whose members were connected to a series of violent crimes and robberies in the 1980s; and violent and terrorist acts such as the shooting at a Jewish community center day camp in Los Angeles in 1999. Christian Identity also has become increasingly influential in other segments of the white power movement, especially in some Ku Klux Klans.

Christian Identity limits women to highly subservient roles: women are to be submissive to their husbands and fathers and are to compliantly follow group dictates. One of the most influential women in Christian Identity was Cheri Peters, wife of the Colorado CI preacher Pete Peters. Her advice column, "For Women Only," drew on biblical dictates and Christian Identity philosophies to caution CI women against asserting their ideas or desires in opposition to those of male intimates or religious leaders.

NEO-NAZIS

Neo-Nazis and white supremacists make up a variety of small groups that trace their ideological lineage to Hitler and typically favor either complete separation between white Aryans and others or the extermination, quarantine, or expulsion of non-Aryans. There are still a few old-style Nazi groups that trace their legacy to the allegiances of World War II and European fascism, but these have little influence within the white supremacist movement today. More significant are so-called neo-Nazi groups that blend rituals and insignia of German Nazism (e.g., swastikas, commemoration of Adolf Hitler's birthday or death day, and denial of the Holocaust) with antagonism toward African Americans, immigrants of color, nonracist skinhead groups, and municipal authorities; they display a cultural style often based on white power music, partying, drugs and alcohol, and street violence.

Because the actions of white supremacist groups vary widely across groups and regions, they are difficult to categorize. Some groups provide support and resources (including white supremacist literature) to imprisoned racist skinheads or white supremacists, whom they see as "prisoners of war." Others seek to establish white separatist enclaves by encouraging white supremacists to move to the Pacific Northwest and buy land. Neo-Nazi group members have vandalized synagogues and desecrated Jewish cemeteries. Some sponsor phone lines with prerecorded messages of hatred aimed at racial and religious groups viewed as enemies. Others have been accused of accumulating or distributing weapons.

Women play a variety of roles in neo-Nazi and white supremacist groups. In those groups that are very male-dominated, women are seen as simply providing sexual gratification or emotional support. In others, women have taken on quasi-leadership roles. Such women have been influential in establishing the political and action agendas of their groups and in recruiting and retaining members, but they seldom act as public figureheads for their groups. There are even a few all-women white supremacist groups, though these are very small.

KU KLUX KLAN

Ku Klux Klans are a number of competing groups—many of which now find common purpose with neo-Nazis and white power skinheads—that trace their ideological heritage to the Reconstruction-era Ku Klux Klan. At any given time, there are a dozen or so Klan groups, which tend to be short-lived. Klan membership has been declining for some time, in part because of attacks from the outside: the government has infiltrated groups and prosecuted members, and antiracist groups have successfully brought civil suits resulting in the assets of several Klan groups being seized. In addition, the perception that the Klans are overly hierarchical and bound to a southern and rural political tradition has weakened them from within. Vicious internecine battles among group leaders and the Klan's longtime problem attracting committed members have led some Klan leaders to defect from the Klan or to form alliances with neo-Nazi groups. Such changes may strengthen and stabilize Klan membership or may signal future decline for the Klan movement.[8]

All Klan groups express deeply racist and anti-Semitic ideas. Most also target ethnic or sexual minorities, particularly Hispanics, Asians and Asian Americans, and gay men and lesbians. Klan chapters also promote extreme xenophobia, fighting to advance an "America first" agenda that would restrict immigration to white Europeans or would limit the civic or economic rights of legal immigrants currently living in the United States. Unlike earlier waves of the Klan, however, today's Klan groups rarely promote anti-Catholicism openly; some even claim to have Catholic members. In other respects, there is considerable variation among the different Klan groups. Some are highly organized, with leaders and members following a military model of hierarchy. Others have a much more fluid form, with unclear and shifting leadership and membership roles. Some Klans claim to have left violence behind and thus promote themselves simply as white interest groups, while others more explicitly advocate racial violence and revolutionary terrorism.

The role of women in the Ku Klux Klan is changing. Except for the 1920s, when the Klan mobilized newly enfranchised women into its crusade of anti-Catholicism, anti-Semitism, and racism, the Klan historically has restricted its membership to men, reflecting its roots as a fraternity of white male supremacy. Since the 1980s, however, most Klans have opened their doors to female members, and several have promoted a few women (generally relatives of male leaders) into middle layers of leadership. A woman now serves as a public spokesperson for at least one Klan.

METHODOLOGY

This study is based on observation of racist group events, analysis of documents published or distributed by racist groups, and in-depth, unstructured life history interviews with thirty-four women who were active members of racist groups in the United States. The women in this study are broadly representative of the range of women racial activists across the country and represent the only relatively systematic sample of racist group members in the contemporary United States. A statistically random sample of racist activists is not possible because there is no comprehensive list of racist activists or even a reliable estimate of their numbers. Except for a few public leaders, most racist activists are interested in keeping themselves hidden from the public, and the scholarly, eye. The few studies that have looked at members rather than leaders of racist groups have drawn on small numbers, generally members known personally to the researcher or referred by known members.[1] They also tend to focus on a single racist group or a single geographic area.

To create a broadly based, national sample of women racist group members, I began by collecting and reading all newsletters, magazines, flyers and recordings of music and speeches, websites, television and radio programs, videotapes, telephone and fax messages, and other communications generated or distributed by every self-proclaimed racist, anti-Semitic, white supremacist, Christian Identity, neo-Nazi, white power skinhead, and white separatist organization in the United States for a one-year period from 1993 to 1994. These were gathered from all groups that I could identify through my contacts with self-proclaimed racist activists, through citations in the primary and secondary scholarly literature, from lists maintained by major antiracist and anti-Semitic monitoring and activist organizations (including the Anti-Defamation League of B'nai B'rith, the Southern Poverty Law Center, and the Center for Democratic Renewal), from archival collections on right-wing extremism at Tulane University and the University of Kansas, and from references in the literature of other racist groups.[2]

As a result, I collected publications by more than one hundred different groups,[3] most of which issued items at least two times during that year.

I used these materials as data for a content analysis of racist literature and to determine which groups had significant numbers of women members or women in visible or leadership roles. I then selected approximately thirty groups from among those with active women members or leaders (overlap makes several of these difficult to differentiate). I selected groups that varied in their ideological emphases and form of organization so that I could assess whether these characteristics affected the recruitment and commitment of women members.

To examine whether racist groups that are remnants of racist activities in rural southern areas differ from those in other regions, I also selected groups from every region of the country, with nine from the South, ten from the West Coast, eight from the Midwest, and three from the East Coast. They were located in fifteen different states, with the greatest concentrations in Georgia (four), Oklahoma (three), Oregon (four), and Florida (four).[4] Such geographical dispersion reflects the landscape of organized racism today. Racist groups can be found in almost every area of the country, but they are particularly concentrated in the Pacific Northwest and the northern sections of the West Coast, in part because many racist group members from various parts of the country have migrated to this region in search of a pristine "white homeland."[5]

Because I first selected groups, and then selected women to interview from a sample of groups, I identify each activist according to her current group affiliation. Almost every woman identified her longest and most significant activism with her current group; but it is important to remember that many racist activists are involved in several different or differently named groups over the course of their racist careers.[6] Such mobility is particularly common among neo-Nazi and Klan groups; thus a particular neo-Nazi may have belonged earlier to a Klan group and be currently involved with Christian Identity. Few can be characterized with any precision by a single group membership, or even by a single philosophical position.

Even at a given moment, it is difficult to accurately match members with racist groups. Few racist groups maintain definitive membership lists. Many require no action to signify membership. In some groups, the process of inclusion is informal, unstructured, and gradual; new people simply join in social activities, racist actions, and ultimately discussions of group plans and strategies. In groups that are more concerned about government informants or legal vulnerability, recruits might be kept far away from the internal workings of the group during a prolonged period of informal scrutiny by existing members. In either case, the concept of "member," so integral to most understandings of social groups, can be frustratingly elusive in organized racism.

After identifying a sample of racist groups, I still faced the problem of identifying women to be interviewed. Most racist publications do not publish the actual names of members other than those who are public spokespersons for the group. Many racist activists and even some spokespersons use aliases or code names, such as "Viking Mary." Thus, finding women to be interviewed was a protracted process. I was able to contact a few women through their groups, but generally this direct approach was inadvisable: racist activists are highly suspicious of and hostile to unknown outsiders. I relied most often on a more indirect approach, using personal referrals and contacts to break through layers of evasion, deception, and political and personal posturing. To find racist women, I drew on contacts that I had established in my earlier research. I also located women racists through parole officers, correctional officials, newspaper reporters and journalists, other racist activists and former activists, federal and state task forces on gangs, attorneys, and other researchers. Although they might seem to be an unlikely source of referrals, police and criminal investigators were valuable contacts for some young racist skinheads, who both hate such authorities and find themselves occasionally dependent on them for protection from abusive peers and the dangers of life on the streets.

To ensure a variety of experiences and perspectives, I selected all the women from my target groups. This method provides a more representative look at organized racism than does a reliance on snowball samples (in which interviewees are referred by prior interviewees) or samples of convenience (in which interviewees are selected based on their accessibility to the researcher), techniques commonly used in studies of difficult-to-locate populations. Even when one interviewee was likely to know women in a group that I was interested in contacting, I rarely made use of this connection because I did not want the women to have the opportunity to slant their narratives to fit, or perhaps to contradict, stories told by earlier interviewees from related or antagonistic groups. Word of my research project spread quickly among networks of racist activists, at once putting me in the awkward position of declining to interview some women who wanted to be part of the study and helping me gain the confidence of others. The knowledge that I had interviewed someone in the past who did not immediately become the target of criminal investigation added credibility to my claim that I was not feeding information to prosecutors.[7]

In contacts and interviews, I used the same terms by which groups referred to themselves in their literature. Racist groups' preferred ways of identifying themselves and differentiating themselves from other groups are intricate. Some Klan members and groups are content to be called "racist." Others insist, against all evidence, that they are interested only in protecting the white race and are merely "white separatist," not racist. Thus I referred to members and groups as "racist," as "white power," as "white supremacist," or even as "white separatist" in line with the language of the group. In this book, however, I use the terms that I see as most accurately describing the group's agenda.

To explore whether women at different levels of racist group hierarchies vary in their racist identification or commitment, I searched for women in various positions in their groups. I selected four who were leaders known both in and outside the movement, ten who were leaders but who were not known publicly, and twenty who were rank-and-file members of racist groups. I also sought women of disparate ages in an effort to assess whether the appeal of racist groups might be understood differently by those at different ages or with different levels of family responsibilities.

The women in the study ranged in age from sixteen to ninety, with a median age of twenty-four. Reflecting the age distribution in the racist movement as a whole, the majority (twenty interviewees) were in their twenties. In general, members of the Ku Klux Klan groups were older and skinheads younger, but one adherent to racist skinhead politics was in her eighties and several Klan women were in their early twenties. Most had a boyfriend or husband, although several were divorced or never married and claimed not to be interested in a long-term relationship with a man. Despite the virulent homophobia of most racist groups, one woman identified as lesbian and several others mentioned having had short-term sexual relationships with women. About one-third were raising minor children, and the vast majority of those without children antici-pated having babies in the future.

Gathering accurate information about members of organized racist groups is difficult. Racist activists tend to be disingenuous, secretive, deliberately intim-idating, and prone to evasive or dishonest answers. Standard interviews often are unproductive, yielding little more than organizational slogans repeated as personal beliefs. Such problems have prompted many researchers to focus pri-marily on the literature produced by hate groups, but this approach provides little reliable information on people's beliefs, because it tells nothing about how people read and interpret racist propaganda and because ideas play a less im-portant role in the extreme right than in other political movements.[8] Propaganda can even be a misleading source of information on group ideologies, since it aims to shock as much as to express the group's agenda or collective beliefs.[9]

Typical interviews and questionnaires used in investigating racist activists are problematic for another reason: they collect information in a way that makes it impossible to disentangle *cause* and *effect*. For example, women racial activists often identify their boyfriend or husband as part of the racial movement, rein-forcing the perception that women are recruited into racist groups as the girl-friends or wives of male activists. Yet it is equally plausible that some intimate relationships between women and men racist activists are formed in racist groups, as women choose to become involved with men who share their ideas.[10] Standard interviews also tend to be structured on the assumption that extremist attitudes precipitate involvement in extremist politics. However, the actual causal direction may be the reverse: attitudes may become more extreme by virtue of the interviewees' association with an extremist group.

To overcome these limitations, I used a life history approach, eliciting from each woman an unstructured account of her life story rather than initially asking questions about beliefs or commitments. Life histories allow interviewees great latitude in how they talk about their lives. The open-ended interview generates personal narratives, which the sociologist Janet Hart describes as "analogous to a story with a beginning, middle and end; with a plot; with main characters, scoundrels and paragons; and with background settings."[11]

Such an approach has five advantages for the study of organized racism. First, life stories are clues to the fashioning of identity and ideology, for, as the soci-ologist Margaret Somers contends, "it is through narrativity that we come to know, understand, and make sense of the social world, and it is through nar-ratives and narrativity that we constitute our social identities."[12] Narratives by women racial activists reveal how these women "make sense" of their world and their place in that world. They tell how these women identify themselves, what they perceive as the major events and significant turning points of their lives, how they understand their own racial activism and racist beliefs, and how they define themselves in relation to political issues, to other racial or religious groups, and to the racist movement.

Second, life history narratives make it possible to understand the semantic context of individual statements. A study of how white New Zealanders talk about the Māori minority demonstrates that the content and logical flow of language of ordinary people can be part of a racist discourse, even as those people are disclaiming racist attitudes. Individual utterances or scores on attitude scales thus are problematic means of measuring racist systems of thought, both because they can vary over time and because interviewees can simultaneously disavow prejudiced intent and negatively characterize groups of people.[13] Racist understandings can be buried within speech that appears on the surface to proclaim the opposite, most obviously in declarations that "I'm not racist, but . . ." or "Some of my best friends are . . ."

In studying organized racists, we must pay attention to the *context* of talk about race. Although most racist activists do not disavow racist attitudes, they do make statements that appear to contradict principles of the racist movement—for example, proclaiming themselves to be interested in white *separatism* but not white *supremacism.*[14] Only by scrutinizing the larger pattern of discursive and political practices of racist groups can we see such distinctions as part of an effort to attract recruits from mainstream populations rather than as a reflection of underlying belief. This scrutiny rarely occurs, however, because few racist activists permit the sustained interviews or recordings of their informal talk that such contextual analysis requires.

Third, life histories string together life events in sequences, suggesting how people understand the patterning of their political and personal lives. These patterns help us untangle the causes and effects of political affiliation, making possible such judgments as whether belonging to a racist group resulted from, or precipitated, particular experiences—troubles with co-workers, imprisonment, social isolation, and so forth. The arrangement of actions and events produced in narratives also reveals the significance that a particular interviewee accords to the unfolding of larger social processes. Some told of finding their lives or racist worldviews transformed by the bombing of the Oklahoma City federal building and the subsequent federal probe into organized racism, generally in the direction of increased racist commitment; others did not mention those events. Both patterns illuminate the intersection of individual biography and social change.[15]

Fourth, life histories capture the rhythms of an activist's participation in and withdrawal from the racial movement over her or his lifetime. Scholars more often focus on how individuals become involved in political action during periods when social movements are particularly influential (e.g., in studies of women's participation in the 1970s feminist movement), but life histories, because of their breadth, provide information both on the events that crystallize political consciousness and mobilize action and on the networks and institutions that nourish (or fail to nourish) activist identities and beliefs during periods of political inactivity.[16]

Finally, a study that focuses on the events of its participants' life histories and the causes in their narrative accounts rather than on their beliefs is less likely to broadcast racist ideologies to new audiences. Life histories make it more difficult for racist activists to parrot their groups' positions when asked to relate their racial beliefs, a pronounced tendency clearly evident in media and talk show interviews in which racist activists respond to all questions with propagandistic slogans.[17]

In this study, each life history interview followed a similar format. The woman was asked to tell the story of her life, how she came to be where and who she is today. In order to observe how each woman would compose her own life story—how she would select and causally connect the events that she regarded as most significant—I intervened only to encourage a full exposition of her life, not to suggest particular directions that the narrative should take. At the conclusion of the life narratives, I asked each woman a series of open-ended but structured questions to collect comparable background data on individuals and their groups. These questions dealt with support networks, organizational policies and activities, the interviewee's personal racial practices and contacts, recruitment and entry into racist politics, role in the racist movement and in her group, education, work history, family background, religion, husbands, and intimate partners. In this part of the interview, careful attention was paid to constructing a precise chronological account of each woman's life, especially the sequence of events prior and immediately subsequent to her first contact with a racist group.

The setting of the interview was left to the discretion of the interviewee. Most were held in the woman's home or in a public setting, such as a restaurant, hotel lobby, public library, or prison. Some women were interviewed by telephone, three from the home of a prominent racist leader who arranged and scheduled the interviews and several from their own home. Interviews varied in length from two to six hours, with the initial narrative account usually taking one to two hours. All interviews were tape-recorded and transcribed in full. A few women would not permit me to interview them in person and instead completed lengthy written life histories and questionnaires.

Accounts of the past must be treated with caution, even skepticism. All interviewees slant their recollections to fit the overall impression they want to convey about their lives, and these racist women were certainly no exception. Events are highlighted or omitted, made pivotal or barely acknowledged, to reflect their importance in the plot of each life story. This feature of narrative is both revealing and concealing. It reveals how people construct their current sense of self by arranging events of their past, but it can distort actual life experiences. For this reason, I evaluate life history accounts primarily as commentaries on an interviewee's present identity and commitments rather than those of her past. I use incidents and information from the life histories as data only when these are contrary to the overall impression that a woman is trying to convey (e.g., admissions of accepting welfare support) or are supported by additional details from the structured questionnaire and chronological life account.

Since all my formal interviews were with women, I could not directly examine gender differences among racist activists; I did, however, conduct informal interviews with male racist leaders and group members and collected ethnographic data on male racists as I observed gatherings and events sponsored by racist groups. Also, I use the few secondary accounts of male racists and published autobiographies by male racist leaders that are available. Ideally, the information in this study would be set against comparable life history interview data gathered from male members of racist groups, but such information is unlikely to be available in the near future. Male racist activists tend to be more cautious about outsiders, perhaps because they are more likely to have had past run-ins with the police. Men in the racist movement also are more likely than women to hold or to aspire to formal leadership roles within their groups, making them reluctant to deviate from the party line in their views or to make admissions about their personal lives that might damage their chances at future leadership positions.

Perhaps, too, the rapport that I was able to achieve with some success with many racist women activists would be much more difficult or even impossible to win in interviews with racist men. Obviously, the intense and conflicting feelings that male racists hold about women, especially women professionals and women outside the racist movement, undermine such efforts when the researcher is female; but male scholars have had little more success. Raphael Ezekiel made remarkable connections with some racist men as he studied the social psychology of modern racists, yet his description of the emotional content of his interview with a man named Arthur resonates with the experience of other scholars of modern male racist activists: "I had been impressed mightily by the volcanic fury I felt from Arthur throughout. Even at the end he had stood with his arms folded tight, making sure we did not shake hands—which I didn't begin to offer."[18] Racist women, despite the manifold difficulties they pose to interviewers, are less likely than men to try to maintain an emotional facade to safeguard their status with the racist movement. Moreover, they share the propensity widely noted in women to willingly disclose information in interviews.[19]

ANTIRACIST ORGANIZATIONS

Many national and local groups monitor and oppose organized racism in the United States; some of the major ones are listed below. Each can provide current information on particular racist groups, on national and international trends in the racist movement, and on effective strategies to combat organizing by racist groups. Financial contributions to these groups will help stop the spread of organized hatred and bigotry.

American Jewish Committee
The Jacob Blaustein Building
165 East 56th Street
New York, NY 10022

Anti-Defamation League of B'nai B'rith
823 United Nations Plaza
New York, NY 10017

Center for Democratic Renewal
P.O. Box 50469
Atlanta, GA 30302

Center for New Community
6429 West North Avenue, Suite 101
Oak Park, IL 60302

Northwest Coalition for Human Dignity
P.O. Box 21428
Seattle, WA 98111

Public Research Associates
1310 Broadway, Suite 201
Somerville, MA 02144

Simon Wiesenthal Center
1390 South Roxbury Drive
Los Angeles, CA 90035

Southern Poverty Law Center
400 Washington Avenue
Montgomery, AL 36104

■

NOTES

INTRODUCTION: CROSSING A BOUNDARY

1. Most credible scholarship and data on organized racism are produced by individuals and groups stridently opposed to racist agendas. Although valuable in providing information on hard-to-study groups, much of this work is descriptive rather than analytical. These studies focus not on scholarly but on political concerns, and their great range of definitions and understandings of organized racism result in conflicting conclusions about the nature of these groups, their ideologies, and the extent to which they form a national or international racist movement. Similar observations about European scholarship are made in Cas Mudde, "The War of Words Defining the Extreme Right Party Family," *West European Politics* 19 (1996): 225–49.

2. For similar observations, see Friedhelm Neidhardt, "Left-Wing and Right-Wing Terrorist Groups: A Comparison for the German Case," in *International Social Movement Research,* vol. 4, *Social Movements and Violence: Participation in Underground Organizations,* ed. Donatella della Porta (London: JAI Press, 1992), 218.

3. Elias's observation is cited in Roy Rosenzweig and David Thelen, *The Presence of the Past: Popular Uses of History in American Life* (New York: Columbia University Press, 1998), 199–200.

4. A brilliant effort in analyzing the pageantry of right-wing politics is Mabel Berezin, *Making the Fascist Self: The Political Culture of Interwar Italy* (Ithaca, N.Y.: Cornell University Press, 1997). See also Michael Barkun, "Introduction: Understanding Millennialism," in *Millennialism and Violence,* ed. Michael Barkun (London: Frank Cass, 1996), 1–9.

5. Donatella della Porta, *Social Movements, Political Violence, and the State: A Comparative Analysis of Italy and Germany* (Cambridge: Cambridge University Press, 1995). The discussion of anti-Semitism in Michel Wieviorka, *The*

Arena of Racism, trans. Chris Turner (London: Sage, 1994), xiv, illustrates the advantage of understanding racism as a social movement. Viewing white racism as a social movement also reduces the tendency to consider whiteness as normative and racial minorities as mounting challenger movements. In some ways, the racist movement resembles a "community of challengers," though its tactics of disruption distinguish it from movements that seek inclusion in state power. See Clarence Y. H. Lo, "Communities of Challengers in Social Movement Theory," in *Frontiers in Social Movement Theory,* ed. Aldon D. Morris and Carol McClurg Mueller (New Haven: Yale University Press, 1992), 224–47.

6. Alberto Melucci, "A Strange Kind of Newness: What's 'New' in New Social Movements?" in *New Social Movements: From Ideology to Identity,* ed. Enrique Laraña, Hank Johnston, and Joseph R. Gusfield (Philadelphia: Temple University Press, 1994), 103. See also Hank Johnston, Enrique Laraña, and Joseph R. Gusfield, "Identities, Grievances, and New Social Movements," in ibid., 3–35; they explicitly suggest that concepts of "new social movement" theory may be applicable to extremist right-wing youth movements.

7. Several scholars have analyzed emotions as communicative expressions between people rather than as purely psychological phenomenon. See Ian Burkitt, "Social Relationships and Emotions," *Sociology* 31 (1997): 40, 41; Gary Alan Fine, "Public Narration and Group Culture," in *Social Movements and Culture,* ed. Hank Johnston and Bert Klandermans (Minneapolis: University of Minnesota Press, 1995), 127–43; Brian Parkinson, "Emotions Are Social," *British Journal of Psychology* 87 (1996): 663–84; and Arlie Hochschild, *The Managed Heart: Commercialization of Human Feeling* (Berkeley: University of California Press, 1983). In this sense, emotion, like informal organization networks, is one of the "platform[s] from which movement formation occurs" (Johnston, Laraña, and Gusfield, "Identities," 24). See also Doug McAdam, *Freedom Summer* (New York: Oxford University Press, 1988), and Aldon Morris, *The Origins of the Civil Rights Movement* (New York: Free Press, 1984).

8. Paying proper attention to the emotional dimensions of organized racism can be tricky. Studies of women in extremist groups often unduly emphasize emotions to explain their participation, while that of men is seen as purposeful and strategic. See Myra M. Ferree, "The Political Context of Rationality: Rational Choice Theory and Resource Mobilization," in Morris and Mueller, *Frontiers in Social Movement Theory,* 29–52; Catherine A. Lutz, "Engendered Emotion: Gender, Power, and the Rhetoric of Emotional Control in American Discourse," in *Language and the Politics of Emotion,* ed. Catherine A. Lutz and Lila Abu-Lughod (Cambridge: Cambridge University Press, 1990), 69–91; Sandra Morgen, " 'It Was the Best of Times, It Was the Worst of Times': Emotional Discourse in the Work Cultures of Feminist Health Clinics," in *Feminist Organizations: Harvest of the New Women's Movement,* ed. Myra M. Ferree and Patricia Y. Martin (Philadelphia: Temple University Press, 1995), 234–47; James A. Aho, *This Thing of Darkness: A Sociology of the Enemy* (Seattle: University of Washington Press, 1994); William A. Gamson, "Constructing Social Protest," in Johnston and Klandermans, *Social Movements and Culture,* 85–106; Julian M. Groves, "Learning to Feel: The Neglected Sociology of Social Movements,"

Sociological Review 43 (1995): 435–61; Alberto Melucci, "The Process of Collective Identity," in Johnston and Klandermans, *Social Movements and Culture,* 41–63; Verta Taylor, *Rock-a-by Baby: Feminism, Self-Help, and Postpartum Depression* (New York: Routledge, 1996); and Verta Taylor and Nancy Whittier, "Analytic Approaches to Social Movement Culture: The Culture of the Women's Movement," in Johnston and Klandermans, *Social Movements and Culture,* 163–87.

9. Studies differ about whether only psychologically impaired persons are drawn to right-wing extremism. Such groups may attract a disproportionate number of persons with inflexible or intolerant personalities, but there is little evidence that they draw largely on the ranks of the clinically abnormal. See James Aho, *The Politics of Righteousness: Idaho Christian Patriotism* (Seattle: University of Washington Press, 1990); Maxwell Taylor and Ethel Quayle, *Terrorist Lives* (London: Brassey's, 1994), esp. 13; and Raphael S. Ezekiel, *The Racist Mind: Portraits of American Neo-Nazis and Klansmen* (New York: Viking, 1995). In a study of right-wing terrorist groups, Neidhardt notes the variety of character traits within these groups but also observes that social "loaners" and "floaters" tend to be attracted to the far right ("Left-Wing and Right-Wing Terrorist Groups"). Other scholars also argue that extremist groups appeal to persons who are rigid or intolerant. See Dick Anthony and Thomas Robbins, "Religious Totalism, Violence, and Exemplary Dualism: Beyond the Extrinsic Model," in Barkun, *Millennialism and Violence,* 10–50. How the emotional dynamics of social movements can be examined as products of rational social actions rather than as outcomes of irrational collective behavior is explored in Groves, "Learning to Feel," and in Verta Taylor, "Watching for Vibes: Bringing Emotions into the Study of Feminist Organizations," in Ferree and Martin, *Feminist Organizations,* 223–33.

10. Berezin, *Making the Fascist Self,* 29.

11. Floyd Cochran, a prominent antiracist activist quoted in Linda Yglesias, untitled article in *New York Daily News,* July 27, 1993; clipping in "Aryan Action Line" folder, Anti-Defamation League of B'nai B'rith, New York.

12. Indeed, many theories presume that all racists are men—for example, the psychoanalytic explanation of extreme racism as an "incapacity to cope with the resemblance with the Other, the foreigner and, also, women" (Wieviorka, *Arena of Racism,* 23). See also Tore Bjørgo, introduction to *Terror from the Extreme Right,* ed. Tore Bjørgo (London: Frank Cass, 1995), 11.

13. Aho also refutes the stereotypical association of poverty with racism in his study of the Christian Patriot movement of the 1980s, *The Politics of Righteousness.* Within many segments of organized racism, the occupations of members and leaders vary widely and include professional and executive positions, at least before the individuals enlist in the racist movement. See "Bigotry or Brotherhood?" a special report by the *Spokane Spokesman Review–Spokesman Chronicle,* December 31, 1986.

14. For example, in his study of a racist group in Detroit, *The Racist Mind,* Ezekiel finds family problems and trauma in the background of many of the racist men he interviewed

15. On "bearing witness," see Virginia Lieson Brereton, *From Sin to Sal-*

vation: Stories of Women's Conversion, 1800 to the Present (Bloomington: Indiana University Press, 1991). On the perception of researchers as "naive sympathizers," see Richard G. Mitchell, *Secrecy and Fieldwork* (Newbury Park, Calif.: Sage, 1993), 14.

16. On approaching interviewees, see Nigel G. Fielding, "Mediating the Message: Affinity and Hostility in Research on Sensitive Topics," in *Researching Sensitive Topics,* ed. Claire M. Renzetti and Raymond M. Lee (Newbury Park, Calif.: Sage, 1993), 146–80; Erich Goode, "The Ethics of Deception in Social Research: A Case Study," *Qualitative Sociology* 19 (1996): 11–33; Raymond M. Lee, *Dangerous Fieldwork* (Newbury Park, Calif.: Sage, 1995); and Melvin Pollner and Robert M. Emerson, "The Dynamics of Inclusion and Distance in Fieldwork Relations," in *Contemporary Field Research: A Collection of Readings,* ed. Robert M. Emerson (Prospect Heights, Ill.: Waveland, 1983), 235–52.

17. In my earlier research on the 1920s Ku Klux Klan—a racist, anti-Semitic, and anti-Catholic movement whose large membership made it nearly normative in many communities dominated by white native-born Protestants—I found that those interviewees, too, had little interest in my political disagreements with the Klan, but for a different reason; see *Women of the Klan: Racism and Gender in the 1920s* (Berkeley: University of California Press, 1991). These elderly former Klan members, remembering the wide acceptance of the Klan in the 1920s and living in racially and religiously homogeneous communities, believed that a white person like me must secretly share the racial agenda of the Klan, despite any public pronouncements to the contrary.

18. See Kathleen M. Blee, "Evidence, Empathy, and Ethics: Lessons from Oral Histories of the Klan," *Journal of American History* 80 (1993): 596–606; Nigel Fielding, "Observational Research on the National Front," in *Social Research Ethics: An Examination of the Merits of Covert Participant Observation,* ed. Martin Blumer (London: Macmillan, 1982), 80–104; Aída Hurtado and Abigail J. Stewart, "Through the Looking Glass: Implications of Studying Whiteness for Feminist Methods," unpublished photocopy (n.d.); Antonius C. G. M. Robben, "The Politics of Truth and Emotion among Victims and Perpetrators of Violence," in *Fieldwork under Fire: Contemporary Studies of Violence and Survival,* ed. Carolyn Nordstrom and Antonius C. G. M. Robben (Berkeley: University of California Press, 1995), 81–104.

19. No pseudonyms are used in references to the written propaganda of racist groups.

20. Nigel G. Fielding, "Mediating the Message: Affinity and Hostility in Research on Sensitive Topics," in Renzetti and Lee, *Researching Sensitive Topics,* 148; see also Lee, *Dangerous Fieldwork.*

21. Fielding, "Mediating the Message," 148. Feminist scholars' emphasis on authenticity, empathy, and trust in research practice often assumes some ideological compatibility between the scholar and those being studied. Moreover, the rapport nurtured in the course of interviewing may give interviewees an exaggerated sense of their control over how their lives are presented and interpreted by scholars, thereby inadvertently heightening their exploitation. See Blee, "Evidence, Empathy, and Ethics"; the essays in Diane L. Wolf, ed., *Feminist Dilemmas in Fieldwork* (Boulder, Colo.: Westview, 1996), especially those

by Günseli Berik, "Understanding the Gender System in Rural Turkey: Field-work Dilemmas of Conforming and Intervention" (56–71), and Jaytai Lal, "Sit-uating Locations: The Politics of Self, Identity, and 'Other' in Living and Writing the Text" (185–214); and the essays in Sherna Berger Gluck and Daphne Patai, eds., *Women's Words: The Feminist Practice of Oral History* (New York: Rout-ledge, 1991), especially Daphne Patai, "U.S. Academics and Third World Women: Is Ethical Research Possible?" (137–53); Judith Stacey, "Can There Be a Feminist Ethnography?" (111–19); and Katherine Borland, "'That's Not What I Said': Interpretive Conflict in Oral Narrative Research" (63–75). See also Ros-alind Edwards, "An Education in Interviewing: Placing the Researcher and the Research," in Renzetti and Lee, *Researching Sensitive Topics,* 181–96, and Fred-die R. Obligacion, "Managing Perceived Deception among Respondents: A Traveler's Tale," *Journal of Contemporary Ethnography* 23 (1994): 29–50.

22. A successful interview requires that the initial distance between inter-viewer and respondent be lessened; a fairly close relationship—the so-called dyadic connection—is particularly critical when the researcher is seeking a life history narrative that is accurate, richly detailed, and comprehensive in scope. Hanspeter Kriesi explores the need for some measure of empathy and rapport to produce valid explanations in "The Rebellion of the Research 'Objects,'" in *Studying Collective Action,* ed. Mario Diani and Ron Eyerman (London: Sage, 1992), 194–216. The difficulty of moving between rapport and distance when the subjects are unsympathetic is analyzed skillfully in Johanna Esseveld and Ron Eyerman, "Which Side Are You On? Reflections on Methodological Issues in the Study of 'Distasteful' Social Movements," in ibid., 217–37.

23. Researchers often must repeatedly win the trust of interviewees over the course of fieldwork. See J. D. Brewer, "Sensitivity as a Problem in Field Re-search: A Study of Routine Policing in Northern Ireland," in Renzetti and Lee, *Researching Sensitive Topics,* 125–45.

24. On establishing rapport through verbal connection, see Molly Andrews, *Lifetimes of Commitment: Aging, Politics, Psychology* (Cambridge: Cambridge University Press, 1991), 56.

25. See also Carolyn Ellis, "Emotional and Ethical Quagmires in Returning to the Field," *Journal of Contemporary Ethnography* 24 (1995): 68–98; Sherryl Kleinman and Martha A. Copp, *Emotions and Fieldwork* (Newbury Park, Calif.: Sage, 1993); Ted Swedenburg, "With Genet in the Palestinian Field," in Nordstrom and Robben, *Fieldwork under Fire,* 25–60; and Jerome Himmel-stein, "All But Sleeping with the Enemy," paper presented at the American So-ciological Association annual meeting, San Francisco, August 1998.

26. Barrie Thorne, "Political Activist as Participant Observer: Conflicts of Commitment in a Study of the Draft Resistance Movement of the 1960s," in Emerson, *Contemporary Field Research,* 225.

27. Robben, "Politics of Truth and Emotion," 85.

28. See Claudia Koonz, *Mothers in the Fatherland: Women, Family Life, and Nazi Politics* (New York: St. Martin's, 1987), and Robben, "Politics of Truth and Emotion."

29. In anthropology, scholarly reflection on the emotional side of doing field-work is generally accepted as part of the discourse of the discipline, but soci-

ology's traditional emphasis on distancing researcher and subject has made such discussions much more exceptional.

30. Few researchers have explored the gendered nature of safety in field research. For example, Susan Phillips's otherwise excellent ethnography, *Wallbangin': Graffiti and Gangs in Los Angeles* (Chicago: University of Chicago Press, 1999), pays little attention to how being a woman researcher affected her relationships with male gang members.

31. For examples of the use of music to spread hate, see Devin Burghart, ed., *Soundtracks to the White Revolution: White Supremacist Assaults on Youth Music Subcultures* (Chicago: Center for New Community, 1999), 102.

32. Oliver Sacks, *A Leg to Stand On* (New York: Simon and Schuster, 1984),156–57. I am grateful to Sharon Betcher for pointing me to this example.

33. I draw on Arlie Hochschild's ideas of emotional labor here, although she focuses on the emotional work done by individuals; see *Managed Heart*.

34. See Blee, "Evidence, Empathy, and Ethics," and Kum-Kum Bhavnani, "Empowerment and Social Research: Some Comments," *Text* 8.1–2 (1988): 47–49.

35. See Berezin, *Making the Fascist Self,* 9.

CHAPTER 1: THE RACIST SELF

1. The evidence on the relationship of self-interest to racial attitudes is mixed even in the mainstream population. See Steven A. Tuch and Michael Hughes, "Whites' Racial Policy Attitudes," *Social Science Quarterly* 77 (1996): 723–45; see also Mary R. Jackman, "Individualism, Self-Interest, and White Racism," *Social Science Quarterly* 77 (1996): 760–67.

2. Ingo Hasselbach, with Tom Reiss, *Führer-Ex: Memoirs of a Former Neo-Nazi* (New York: Random House, 1996), 242–43.

3. On recruitment through personal ties, see David A. Snow, Louis A. Zurcher Jr., and Sheldon Ekland-Olson, "Social Networks and Social Movements: A Microstructural Approach to Differential Recruitment," *American Sociological Review* 45 (1980): 787–801; Donatella della Porta, *Social Movements, Political Violence, and the State: A Comparative Analysis of Italy and Germany* (Cambridge: Cambridge University Press, 1995), 202; and Leila J. Rupp and Verta Taylor, *Survival in the Doldrums: The American Women's Rights Movement, 1945 to the 1960s* (Columbus: Ohio State University Press, 1990), 133.

4. James Aho describes Christian Patriots as undergoing a "multi-step" process of mobilization as they are recruited through personal ties to significant members of local social groups; see *The Politics of Righteousness: Idaho Christian Patriotism* (Seattle: University of Washington Press, 1990), 186. For non-racist groups, see William A. Gamson, *Talking Politics* (New York: Cambridge University Press, 1992).

5. Kevin Flynn and Gary Gerhardt, *The Silent Brotherhood: Inside America's Racist Underground* (New York: Signet/Penguin, 1990), 107–8.

6. Aho, *Politics of Righteousness,* 190.

7. Converts often explain their turning points passively but later reveal that more active tactics were employed; see Roger Straus, "A Situation of Desired Self-Change and Strategies of Self-Transcendence," in *Doing Social Life: The Qualitative Study of Human Interaction in Natural Settings,* ed. John Lofland (New York: John Wiley and Sons, 1976), 252–73.

8. Earlier, social science theories described commitment to racist, fascist, and right-wing extremist groups as the result of the psychological deficits or pathologies of their members. The simplistic and conspiratorial ideas of right-wing extremism were considered attractive to those with low tolerance for ambiguity and a high need for rigid, stereotyped views (i.e., "authoritarian personalities"), or those (in a later characterization) who exhibit a "paranoid style" in their politics. These theories are responsible for our familiar understandings of adherence to extremist right-wing movements as the outgrowth of authoritarian parenting, lack of education, ignorance, or irrational prejudices and of participants in rightist politics as unbalanced, frustrated, or deluded. See Theodor Adorno et al., *The Authoritarian Personality* (1950; reprint, New York: W. W. Norton, 1969); Richard Hofstadter, *The Paranoid Style in American Politics* (New York: Alfred A. Knopf, 1966); and Seymour Martin Lipset and Earl Raab, *The Politics of Unreason* (New York: Harper and Row, 1970). An excellent critique of this literature is offered by Alan Brinkley, "The Problem of American Conservatism," paper presented at the Organization of American Historians annual meeting, Anaheim, Calif., May 1993. See also Dick Anthony and Thomas Robbins, "Religious Totalism, Violence and Exemplary Dualism: Beyond the Extrinsic Model," in *Millennialism and Violence,* ed. Michael Barkun (London: Frank Cass, 1996), 10–50. In *Fascists: A Social Psychological View of the National Front* (London: Academic Press, 1978), Michael Billig presents a more sophisticated analysis of the personality thesis, arguing that while fascist personality types are persistently attracted to fascism, others are attracted for a variety of reasons when the social conditions are favorable to fascism. Raphael S. Ezekiel, in *The Racist Mind: Portraits of American Neo-Nazis and Klansmen* (New York: Viking, 1995), makes use of psychological arguments (as does Billig); but nonpsychological explanations predominate in contemporary historiography of right-wing movements, in part because the assumption that racists are crazy cannot explain historical fluctuations in the number of people in racist movements. See David Bennett, *The Party of Fear: From Nativist Movements to the New Right in American History* (Chapel Hill: University of North Carolina Press, 1988), and David M. Chalmers, *Hooded Americanism: The History of the Ku Klux Klan* (Durham, N.C.: Duke University Press, 1981).

9. Interest-based accounts have shed valuable light on the considerations of social status that underlie right-wing social movements against legalized abortion, vice, or women's rights and on the hope for material benefits that has bolstered many fascist movements. Scholars have argued, from a variety of political and theoretical stances, that right-wing political actions result from status threats or the projection of status anxieties. Such arguments can be found in conventional studies of the right, exemplified by Daniel Bell, "The Dispossessed," and Seymour Martin Lipset, "The Sources of the Radical Right—

1955," both in *The Radical Right,* ed. Daniel Bell (New York: Anchor, 1964), 1–45, 307–71, and, to a lesser extent, in Glen Jeansonne, *Women of the Far Right: The Mother's Movement and World War II* (Chicago: University of Chicago Press, 1996). A much more nuanced version, situated in a feminist framework, appears in Pamela Conover and Virginia Gray, *Feminism and the New Right: Conflict over the American Family* (Westport, Conn.: Praeger, 1984); Rosalind Pollack Petchesky, "Antiabortion, Antifeminism, and the Rise of the New Right," *Feminist Studies* 7 (1981): 206–46; Kristin Luker, *Abortion and the Politics of Motherhood* (Berkeley: University of California Press, 1984); Faye Ginsburg, "Procreation Stories: Reproduction, Nurturance, and Procreation in Life Narratives of Abortion Activists," *American Ethnologist* 14 (1987): 623–36; Susan Marshall, "In Defense of Separate Spheres: Class and Status Politics in the Antisuffrage Movement," *Social Forces* 65 (1986): 327–51; Susan Marshall, "Rattle on the Right: Bridge Labor in Antifeminist Organizations," in *No Middle Ground: Women and Radical Protest,* ed. Kathleen M. Blee (New York: New York University Press, 1998), 155–79; Rebecca E. Klatch, *Women of the New Right* (Philadelphia: Temple University Press, 1987); and Nicola Beisel, *Imperiled Innocents: Anthony Comstock and Family Reproduction in Victorian America* (Princeton: Princeton University Press, 1997). Studies of the far right that draw on the perspective of rational choice include William Brustein, "The 'Red Menace' and the Rise of Italian Fascism," *American Sociological Review* 56 (1991): 652–64, and William Brustein and Barry Markovsky, "The Rational Fascist: Interwar Fascist Party Membership in Italy and Germany," *Journal of Political and Military Sociology* 17 (1989): 177–202.

10. Such explanations continue to appear in studies of women's participation in marginal and extremist groups; see the analysis of women joining urban gangs in order to meet people in Martín Sánchez Jankowski, *Islands in the Street: Gangs and American Urban Society* (Berkeley: University of California Press, 1991).

11. The scholarship on the dynamic relationships between political parties or political movements and their adherents, though extensive, generally assumes that parties and movements adjust their appeals to match the presumed interests of their recruits, not that members dynamically construct their sense of self-interest.

12. In his study of Northern Ireland, "Political Violence by the Nonaggrieved: Explaining the Political Participation of Those with No Apparent Grievances" (in *International Social Movement Research,* vol. 4, *Social Movements and Violence: Participation in Underground Organizations,* ed. Donatella della Porta [London: JAI Press, 1992], 79–103), Robert White asks why people who lack apparent, immediate grievances become involved in social movements. He concludes that participants generally had little specific knowledge about the situation but that they shared a general sense, based in family and social networks, that Ireland should have self-determination. See also Hans-Georg Betz, *Radical Right-Wing Populism in Western Europe* (New York: St. Martin's, 1994); Mark S. Hamm, *American Skinheads: The Criminology and Control of Hate Crimes* (Westport, Conn.: Praeger, 1994); Nancy McLean, *Behind the Mask of Chivalry: The Making of the Second Ku Klux Klan* (New York: Oxford

University Press, 1994); and Leonard Weinberg, "The American Radical Right: Exit, Voice and Violence," in *Encounters with the Radical Right,* ed. Peter H. Merkl and Leonard Weinberg (Boulder, Colo.: Westview, 1993), 185–203.

13. This notion that self-interest is influenced by social interaction builds on the idea of grievances as socially constructed, described in Bert Klandermans and Dirk Oegema, "Potential, Networks, Motivations, and Barriers: Steps toward Participation in Social Movements," *American Sociological Review* 52 (1987): 521–31. See also Margaret Wetherell and Jonathan Potter, *Mapping the Language of Racism: Discourse and the Legitimation of Exploitation* (New York: Columbia University Press, 1992), and R. W. Connell, *Gender and Power: Society, the Person, and Sexual Politics* (Stanford: Stanford University Press, 1987).

14. John Lofland and Norman Skonovd, "Conversion Motifs," *Journal for the Scientific Study of Religion* 20 (1981): 378.

15. Fashioning an identity for the self is theorized very well in Arlene Stein, *Sex and Sensibility: Stories of a Lesbian Generation* (Berkeley: University of California Press, 1997). See also Arno L. Mayer, "Memory and History: On the Poverty of Remembering and Forgetting the Judeocide," *Radical History Review,* no. 56 (spring 1993): 5–20, and David A. Snow, E. Burke Rochford, Steven K. Worden, and Robert D. Benford, "Frame Alignment Processes, Micromobilization, and Movement Participation," *American Sociological Review* 51 (1986): 464–81.

16. C. Wright Mills, "Situated Actions and Vocabularies of Motive," *American Sociological Review* 5 (1940): 404–13, cited in Snow, Zurcher, and Ekland-Olson, "Social Networks," 795. See also David A. Snow and Richard Machalek, "The Sociology of Conversion," *Annual Review of Sociology* 10 (1984): 173.

17. Snow and Machalek, "Sociology of Conversion," 173.

18. Margaret Somers, "The Narrative Constitution of Identity: A Relational and Network Approach," *Theory and Society* 23 (1994): 606, 618; Margaret Wetherell, "Life Histories/Social Histories," in *Identities, Groups and Social Issues,* ed. Margaret Wetherell (London: Sage, 1996), 305. See also Nigel Fielding, *The National Front* (London: Routledge and Kegan Paul, 1981), esp. 10; Janet Hart, "Cracking the Code: Narrative and Political Mobilization in the Greek Resistance," *Social Science History* 16 (1992): 634; Jerome Bruner, "The Narrative Construction of Reality," *Critical Inquiry* 18 (1991): 1–21; and Verta Taylor and Nancy Whittier, "Theoretical Approaches to Social Movement Culture," paper presented at the American Sociological Association's Workshop on Culture and Social Movements, San Diego, August 1992.

19. See William C. Tremmel, "The Converting Choice," *Journal for the Scientific Study of Religion* 10 (1971):17–25; Peter Bearman and Katherine Stovel, "Becoming a Nazi: Models of Identity Formation," paper presented at the American Sociological Association annual meeting, Miami, August 1993; Virginia Lieson Brereton, *From Sin to Salvation: Stories of Women's Conversion, 1800 to the Present* (Bloomington: Indiana University Press, 1991); Carole Cain, "Personal Stories: Identity Acquisition and Self-Understanding in Alcoholics Anonymous," *Ethos* 19 (1991): 210–53; David Theo Goldberg, introduction to *Anat-*

omy of Racism, ed. David Theo Goldberg (Minneapolis: University of Minnesota Press, 1990), xi–xxiii; and Hart, "Cracking the Code."

20. Billig, *Fascists,* 236.

21. Max Heirich, "Change of Heart: A Test of Some Widely Held Theories about Religious Conversion," *American Journal of Sociology* 83 (1977): 673–75, cited in Snow and Machalek, "Sociology of Conversion," 170. For a similar pattern in religious conversions, see Roger A. Straus, "Religious Conversion as a Personal and Collective Accomplishment," *Sociological Analysis* 40 (1979): 158–65.

22. Snow and Machalek's assessment of the "rhetorical indicators" of conversion as reconstruction of one's autobiography, adoption of a new causal scheme, and embrace of the convert role, together with their discussion of the "alignment process" in conversion, is particularly useful here ("Sociology of Conversion," 176).

23. Brereton, *From Sin to Salvation,* xiii.

24. Brereton, *From Sin to Salvation,* 72, 71.

25. See Lofland and Skonovd, "Conversion Motifs."

26. On a collective level, what Edward Walsh describes as "suddenly imposed grievances" may mobilize large numbers of persons into social movements by increasing public recognition of a social phenomenon ("Resource Mobilization and Citizen Protest in Communities around Three Mile Island," *Social Problems* 29 [1981]: 1–21). See Doug McAdam, "Culture and Social Movements," in *New Social Movements: From Ideology to Identity,* ed. Enrique Laraña, Hank Johnston, and Joseph R. Gusfield (Philadelphia: Temple University Press, 1994), 36–57. For a valuable discussion of the role of crisis in stimulating participation in social movements, see Caroline Kelly and Sara Breinlinger, *The Social Psychology of Collective Action: Identity, Injustice, and Gender* (London: Taylor and Francis, 1996), esp. 108.

27. Maxwell Taylor and Ethel Quayle, *Terrorist Lives* (London: Brassey's, 1994), 44.

28. See Albert Bandura, "The Psychology of Chance Encounters and Life Paths," *American Psychologist* 37 (1982): 747–55.

29. Aho, *Politics of Righteousness,* 183, 187; see also Ezekiel, *Racist Mind,* 62. The priority of social bonding is also observed in other violent groups, such as gangs. See Mary G. Harris, *Cholas: Latino Girls and Gangs* (New York: AMS Press, 1988).

30. See Gabriele Rosenthal, "German War Memories: Narrability and the Biographical and Social Functions of Remembering," *Oral History* 19.2 (1991): 36.

31. Straus, "Situation of Desired Self-Change."

32. Ezekiel, *Racist Mind,* 64.

33. Straus, in "Situation of Desired Self-Change," argues that individuals are more active in the process of self-transformation than their passive accounts would suggest.

34. This feeling expressed by the women I interviewed is similar, in a perverse way, to W. E. B. Du Bois's concept of blacks' "double consciousness": for those who are dominated, having to see things both as they are and through the

eyes of the dominators creates pain. See also Billig, *Fascists;* Hasselbach, *Führer-Ex;* Elmer Luchterhand and Norbert Wieland, "The Focused Life History in Studying Involvement in a Genocidal Situation in Nazi Germany," in *Biography and Society: The Life History Approach in the Social Sciences,* ed. Daniel Bertaux (Beverly Hills, Calif.: Sage, 1981), 267–87.

35. Harris's study of girls in gangs (*Cholas*) found a similar dreamlike quality to how the girls related events to the researcher, as did Luisa Passerini's study of women in Italy's underground; see "Lacerations in the Memory: Women in the Italian Underground Organizations," in della Porta, *Social Movements and Violence,* 161–212.

36. Billig, *Fascists,* 226–27.

37. Rosenthal, "German War Memories," 39.

38. Interviewed by Hamm in *American Skinheads,* 117.

39. Two of the men's statements that I cite predate my interviews of women, but all come from the modern (post-1960) racist movement. The men's autobiographies are written propaganda by racist leaders; their agenda and tone differ from those of the women's stories, drawn both from leaders and rank-and-file members of the movement.

40. Karl R. Allen, "Why I Joined the Nazi Party," *Stormtrooper,* March–April 1963, 12–13, 17, 21; in Special Collections, Howard-Tilton Memorial Library, Tulane University, New Orleans, "American Nazi Party–Phoenix" file.

41. John Gerhard, "Leadership to Victory," *American White Nationalist Party* 1.11 (1971–72): 3; in "American White Nationalist Party, Toledo" file, in Special Collections, Howard-Tilton Memorial Library, Tulane University.

42. "Order Member David Tate Speaks," *WAR* 12 (April 1993): 9.

CHAPTER 2: WHITENESS

1. The insistence that pure whiteness has Nordic roots is explored in Geoffrey G. Field, "Nordic Racism," *Journal of the History of Ideas* 38 (1977): 523–40.

2. On the achieved and transient nature of collective identity, see Bert Klandermans, "Transient Identities? Membership Patterns in the Dutch Peace Movement," in *New Social Movements: From Ideology to Identity,* ed. Enrique Laraña, Hank Johnston, and Joseph Gusfield (Philadelphia: Temple University Press, 1994), 68–84, and Alberto Melucci, "Frontier Land: Collective Action between Actors and Systems," in *Studying Collective Action,* ed. Mario Diani and Ron Eyerman (London: Sage, 1992), 238–58.

3. Toni Morrison, *Playing in the Dark: Whiteness and the Literary Imagination* (New York: Vintage, 1992), 72. My thanks to Jean Ferguson Carr for tracking down this citation.

4. Ruth Frankenberg, *White Women, Race Matters: The Social Construction of Whiteness* (Minneapolis: University of Minnesota Press, 1993), 196, 191. See also the excellent discussion of racialized identity in Caroline Knowles, "Race, Identities, and Lives," *Sociological Review* 47 (1999): 110.

5. Cheri Peters, "Whoredom in America" and "For Women Only," *Scriptures for America* 1 (1991): 3–6.

6. My decision to include racially offensive words in their entirety is influenced by the thoughtful discussion in Michael Billig, "Humor and Hatred: The Racist Jokes of the Ku Klux Klan," *Discourse and Society* 12 (2001): 296.

7. Frankenberg, *White Women, Race Matters,* 231; Micaela di Leonardo, "Habits of the Cumbered Heart: Ethnic Community and Women's Culture as American invented Traditions," in *Golden Ages, Dark Ages: Imagining the Past in Anthropology and History,* ed. Jay O'Brien and William Roseberry (Berkeley: University of California Press, 1991), 234–52. See also Noel Ignatiev, *How the Irish Became White* (New York: Routledge, 1995).

8. Cheryl I. Harris, "Whiteness as Property," *Harvard Law Review* 106 (1993): 1736. Ann Laura Stoler, in "Carnal Knowledge and Imperial Power: Gender, Race, and Morality in Colonial Asia" (in *Gender at the Crossroads of Knowledge: Feminist Anthropology in the Postmodern Era,* ed. Micaela di Leonardo [Berkeley: University of California Press, 1991], 75), makes an important point: the "politics of exclusion" practiced by white Europeans in early-twentieth-century colonial communities entailed the internal policing of members to exclude the colonized. See also Ignatiev, *How the Irish Became White.* A fascinating study of the negotiation of race in a situation of interracial proximity is found in Glenda Elizabeth Gilmore, *Gender and Jim Crow: Women and the Politics of White Supremacy in North Carolina, 1896–1920* (Chapel Hill: University of North Carolina Press, 1996), esp. 74.

9. See Aída Hurtado and Abigail J. Stewart, "Through the Looking Glass: Implications of Studying Whiteness for Feminist Methods," unpublished photocopy, n.d. On the distinction between white supremacism as a system of beliefs and as a political program, see also Barbara J. Fields, "Ideology and Race in American History," in *Region, Race, and Reconstruction,* ed. D. Morgan Kousser and James M. McPherson (New York: Oxford University Press, 1982), 143–77.

10. Ignatiev, *How the Irish Became White;* Karen Brodkin, *How Jews Became White Folks and What That Says about Race in America* (New Brunswick, N.J.: Rutgers University Press, 1998); and Tomás Almaguer, *Racial Fault Lines: The Historical Origins of White Supremacy in California* (Berkeley: University of California Press, 1994).

11. See Leonardo, "Habits of the Cumbered Heart."

12. Harris, "Whiteness as Property"; see also Ignatiev, *How the Irish Became White.*

13. See Benedict Anderson, *Imagined Communities: Reflections on the Origin and Spread of Nationalism,* rev. ed. (London: Verso, 1991), 19.

14. Like Stoler, who describes the efforts to establish transnational colonialist projects ("Carnal Knowledge and Imperial Power," 74), Anderson perceptively argues that because racism reflects class rather than national aspirations, it does not necessarily rest on nationalistic antagonisms (*Imagined Communities,* 149–50). In several European nations, such as Great Britain and Germany, however, race and nation tend to be conflated. See Nigel Fielding, *The National Front* (London: Routledge and Kegan Paul, 1981). The effort to establish a Pan-

Aryan movement is likely to falter for many reasons, including the Christian Identity orientation of many U.S. racist groups, which is less influential in the European far right.

15. See Robert F. Berkhofer, *The White Man's Indian: Images of the American Indian from Columbus to the Present* (New York: Knopf, 1978).

16. Anderson, *Imagined Communities*, 77.

17. For a useful presentation of how the "illusion of collective identity" can be created through staged spectacle, see Anne McClintock, "Family Feuds: Gender, Nationalism, and the Family," *Feminist Review*, no. 44 (summer 1993): 70. See also David Theo Goldberg, "The Social Formation of Racist Discourse," in *Anatomy of Racism*, ed. David Theo Goldberg (Minneapolis: University of Minnesota Press, 1990), 311.

18. Goldberg, "Social Formation of Racist Discourse," 309. Paul Gilroy also perceptively traces racism to collective identities rooted in tradition in his book *"There Ain't No Black in the Union Jack": The Cultural Politics of Race and Nation* (Chicago: University of Chicago Press, 1991). An interesting discussion of how white Americans frame the past is found in Roy Rosenzweig and David Thelen, *The Presence of the Past: Popular Uses of History in American Life* (New York: Columbia University Press, 1998).

19. For example, see David Edgar, "Racism, Fascism, and the Politics of the National Front," *Race and Class* 19 (1977): 111–31.

20. Marilyn Frye, "On Being White: Thinking toward a Feminist Understanding of Race and Race Supremacy," in *The Politics of Reality: Essays in Feminist Theory* (Trumansburg, N.Y.: Crossing Press, 1983), 117.

21. Frankenberg, *White Women, Race Matters*, 188. Dan T. Carter's *Politics of Rage: George Wallace, the Origins of the New Conservatism, and the Transformation of American Politics* (New York: Simon and Schuster, 1995) is an excellent case study of the strategic employment of racist rhetoric.

22. Michael Omi and Howard Winant, *Racial Formation in the United States: From the 1960s to the 1990s*, 2nd ed. (New York: Routledge, 1994). The complexity of white supremacist thinking is underanalyzed in the works by Abby Ferber (see "Of Mongrels and Jews: The Deconstruction of Racialized Identities in White Supremacist Discourse," *Social Identities* 3 [1997]: 193–208) and, particularly, Jessie Daniels. Daniels's analysis in *White Lies: Race, Class, Gender, and Sexuality in White Supremacist Discourse* (New York: Routledge, 1997) is especially problematic; she argues that whiteness and blackness are simply "taken for granted" in supremacist propaganda (73), despite giving examples of whites who, because they have engaged in interracial sex, are no longer considered white. Gilmore offers a particularly insightful look at how stigmatized behavior can read white persons out of the white race in her discussion of white prostitutes (*Gender and Jim Crow*, 72).

23. White Aryan Resistance, hate line transcription, October 10, 1989; in files of the Anti-Defamation League of B'nai B'rith, New York.

24. Elizabeth Sherry, "Skin Traitor," *WAR* 7.3 (1988): 4.

25. David Lane, *White Genocide Manifesto* (St. Maries, Idaho: 14 Word Press, [ca. 1995]), n.p.

26. In part, their inference rested on the assumption that only whites would willingly risk meeting racist activists. Expectations about my race also reflected the overwhelming assumption—shared within the racist movement and throughout much of mainstream U.S. culture—that anyone not identified to the contrary must be white. Marking myself as a university professor further increased expectations that I would be white. My analysis is guided by Marjorie DeVault's important insight that race and ethnicity are often relevant in the research enterprise, even when not made explicit. She argues that "'hearing' race and ethnicity in our talk with informants requires active attention and analysis"; see "Ethnicity and Expertise: Racial-Ethnic Knowledge in Sociological Research," *Gender and Society* 9 (1995): 613. As others have found while doing research in societies that are both similar and different from their own, the location of a researcher both inside and outside the meaning structure of those being studied is potentially revelatory, even as it poses methodological difficulties. See Patricia Zavella, "Feminist Insider Dilemmas: Constructing Ethnic Identity with 'Chicana' Informants," *Frontiers* 8.3 (1993): 53–76; Rosalind Edwards, "Connecting Method and Epistemology: A White Woman Interviewing Black Women," *Women's Studies International Forum* 13 (1990): 477–90; and Josephine Beoku-Betts, "When Black Is Not Enough: Doing Field Research among Gullah Women," *NWSA Journal* 6 (1994): 413–33.

27. Hank Johnston, Enrique Laraña, and Joseph R. Gusfield, in "Identities, Grievances, and New Social Movements," in Johnston, Laraña, and Gusfield, *New Social Movements,* label the provision of identities by organizations in a top-down fashion a "strategic constructionist perspective" (18).

28. Aryan Women's League hate line transcription, June 11, 1990, in files of Anti-Defamation League.

29. Heléne Lööw, "The Cult of Violence: The Swedish Racist Counterculture," in *Racist Violence in Europe,* ed. Tore Bjørgo and Rob White (New York: St. Martin's, 1993), 69.

30. AWL transcription, February 2, 1992, in files of Anti-Defamation League; also "Race and Reason" (ca. 1993), in "Aryan Women's League" files, Anti-Defamation League.

31. Luisella de Cataldo Neuburger and Tiziana Valentini, *Women and Terrorism,* trans. Leo Michael Hughes (New York: St. Martin's, 1998), 85.

32. See the flyer distributed by White Sisters under the title "Martyrs and Political Prisoners: Remember Kathy Ainsworth" (ca. 1994), claimed to be a reprint from the *Los Angeles Times,* February 13, 1970.

33. To some extent, recourse to principle is not unusual among members of extremist groups. Research on other terrorists also finds that they are likely to justify their actions as motivated by altruism rather than personal gain. Social psychologists refer to such presentation and understanding of nefarious behavior as honorable as "cognitive restructuring." See Maxwell Taylor and Ethel Quayle, *Terrorist Lives* (London: Brassey's, 1994), 9, and Donatella della Porta, *Social Movements, Political Violence, and the State: A Comparative Analysis of Italy and Germany* (Cambridge: Cambridge University Press, 1995), 113–64.

34. Gilmore, *Gender and Jim Crow,* 92.

CHAPTER 3: ENEMIES

1. "Hate Groups Face Sweeps by Police," *Sacramento Bee*, July 12, 1999.

2. In *Understanding Everyday Racism: An Interdisciplinary Theory* (Newbury Park, Calif.: Sage, 1991), Philomena Essed defines "everyday racism" as "systematic, recurrent, familiar practices" that connect "structural forces of racism with routine situations in everyday life" (3, 2). However, terms like *racism* can mask as well as disclose the ideas and practices that construct groups of people as racial adversaries. This masking is illustrated in Ronald P. Formisano's *Boston against Busing: Race, Class, and Ethnicity in the 1960s and 1970s* (Chapel Hill: University of North Carolina Press, 1991), which shows the complexities of motive and rhetoric that can be obscured under the label *racism*.

3. Michael Billig, in *Fascists: A Social Psychological View of the National Front* (London: Academic Press, 1978, 190), makes the important point that "racialist beliefs are not in themselves sufficient to form an articulated ideology [but] need to be integrated into a system of thought." In "'Race Stereotypes' and Racist Discourse," *Text* 8.1–2 (1988): 73, Susan Condor observes that the rhetoric of the fascistic British National Front distinguishes "racialism," the recognition of racial difference, from "racism," the promotion of hatred.

4. The unification of organized racism by a set of common beliefs is discussed in Margaret Wetherell and Jonathan Potter, *Mapping the Language of Racism: Discourse and the Legitimation of Exploitation* (New York: Columbia University Press, 1992). See also Nigel Fielding, *The National Front* (London: Routledge and Kegan Paul, 1981), 60.

5. *WAR*, August 1994, in "Aryan Women's League" file, Anti-Defamation League of B'nai B'rith, New York.

6. Aryan Women's League, hate line transcription, June 11, 1990, in the collection of the Anti-Defamation League.

7. Aryan Women's League, "Countdown to 1995," *WAR* 12.1 (1994): 7.

8. A classic study of ideological conversion is John Lofland and Rodney Stark, "Becoming a World-Saver: A Theory of Conversion to a Deviant Perspective," *American Sociological Review* 30 (1965): 862–75. An example of racist learning is the coaching provided by Matt Hale, head of the World Church of the Creator (WCOTC), described in an interview with a female member of WCOTC after Benjamin Smith's violent rampage against Jews, blacks, and Asians in the Midwest in June 1999 that is excerpted in Kirsten Scharnberg, "A Gospel of Hatred," *Chicago Tribune*, July 11, 1999.

9. "Prosecutor Assesses Homogenized Racists," *Palos Verdes (Calif.) Peninsula News*, October 25, 1986.

10. David Norman Smith, "The Social Construction of Enemies: Jews and the Representation of Evil," *Sociological Theory* 14 (1996): 211. For an excellent history of anti-Semitism, see H. H. Ben-Sasso, *A History of the Jewish People* (Cambridge, Mass.: Harvard University Press, 1976). See also James H. Robb, *Working-Class Anti-Semite: A Psychological Study in a London Borough* (London: Tavistock, 1954); Thomas C. Wilson, "Compliments Will Get You Nowhere: Benign Stereotypes, Prejudice, and Anti-Semitism," *Sociological*

Quarterly 37 (1996): 465–79; and Paul Hockenos, *Free to Hate: The Rise of the Right in Post-Communist Eastern Europe* (New York: Routledge, 1993), 273.

11. See Evelyn Brooks Higginbotham, "African-American Women's History and the Metalanguage of Race," *Signs* 17 (1992): 251–74; George L. Mosse, *Nationalism and Sexuality: Middle-Class Morality and Sexual Norms in Modern Europe* (Madison: University of Wisconsin Press, 1985), 10, 42, 132, 136; and Sander L. Gilman, *Difference and Pathology: Stereotypes of Sexuality, Race, and Madness* (Ithaca, N.Y.: Cornell University Press, 1985), esp. 23.

12. Henry Louis Gates Jr., quoted in Higginbotham, "African-American Women's History," 258.

13. Paul Gilroy, *The Black Atlantic: Modernity and Double Consciousness* (Cambridge, Mass.: Harvard University Press, 1993), 45; see also Paul Gilroy, *"There Ain't No Black in the Union Jack": The Cultural Politics of Race and Nation* (Chicago: University of Chicago Press, 1991), 86, 109. Scholars commonly distinguish between "new racism" and "classical racism": the former locates racial differences in culture rather than biology and the latter emphasizes nation and biological definitions of race. A slightly more complex taxonomy of racism distinguishes "racialism" (beliefs that racial characteristics are essential) both from "extrinsic racism" (beliefs that persons of different races merit different social treatment) and from "intrinsic racism" (beliefs that the races differ in their moral worth). See David Theo Goldberg, introduction to *Anatomy of Racism,* ed. David Theo Goldberg (Minneapolis: University of Minnesota Press, 1990), xi–xxiii. However, the views expressed by racist groups move across these categories, depending on the particular aim and audience of specific propaganda. See John Solomon and Les Bac, "Conceptualising Racisms: Social Theory, Politics, and Research," *Sociology* 28 (1994): 143–62, and Cas Mudde, "Right-Wing Extremism Analyzed: A Comparative Analysis of the Ideologies of Three Alleged Right-Wing Extremist Parties (NPD, NSP, CP '86)," *European Journal of Political Research* 27 (February 1995): 211.

14. Beliefs and values that are not explicitly racist also underlie the ideology of racial threat. For example, the emphasis on security is nested within general ideas of valuing persons according to their economic productivity or financial position, of stressing personal safety and protection from bodily harm by strangers, and of viewing economic opportunity in American society as meritocractic. It also draws on more clearly racial principles held by many whites, such as the disapproval of interracial bodily contact, particularly if initiated by members of racial minorities. A useful discussion of how commonsense ideas are incorporated into right-wing ideology and how right-wing attitudes can vary is found in Michael Billig, "Imagining Nationhood," in *Social Movements and Culture,* ed. Hank Johnston and Bert Klandermans (Minneapolis: University of Minnesota Press, 1995), 66. See also Wetherell and Potter, *Mapping the Language of Racism.*

15. Less often, minority women also appear threatening by virtue of their physical size or their numbers. A powerful discussion of this apparent threat in schools undergoing racial desegregation appears in Beth Roy, "Goody Two-

Shoes and Hell-Raisers: Women's Activism, Women's Reputations in Little Rock," in *No Middle Ground: Women and Radical Protest*, ed. Kathleen M. Blee (New York: New York University Press, 1998), 96–132.

16. On the general tendency of social movements to use frameworks already existing in the culture, see Doug McAdam, "Culture and Social Movements," in *New Social Movements: From Ideology to Identity*, ed. Enrique Laraña, Hank Johnston, and Joseph R. Gusfield (Philadelphia: Temple University Press, 1994), 36–57. On the specific relevance to the white supremacist movement, see Mitch Berbrier, "'Half the Battle': Cultural Resonance, Framing Processes, and Ethnic Affectations in Contemporary White Supremacist Rhetoric," *Social Problems* 45 (1998): 431–50.

17. In a study of the contemporary racist movement, Betty Dobratz argues that assertions of white separatism rather than white supremacism in the speeches and writings of racist leaders should be taken at face value ("The White Separatist Movement in the U.S.: A Look at Their Ideology," paper presented at the American Sociological Association annual meeting, Toronto, August 1997), but my interviews suggest that a focus on propaganda obscures the extent to which these views overlap. Perhaps a more important distinction is that made by Etienne Balibar in "Racism and Nationalism" (in *Race, Nation, Class: Ambiguous Identities*, ed. Etienne Balibar and Immanuel Wallerstein, trans. Chris Turner [London: Verso, 1991], 37–65) between systems of belief that are "auto-referential" (based in a conviction that one's own race is superior) and those that are "hetero-referential" (based in a conviction that others belong to inferior or evil races). Although some racist activists see all whites as superior to all nonwhites and others see only those whites engaged in racially conscious actions as superior, all embrace the notion that persons of other races are deficient, malevolent, or both.

18. Finding such unlikely allies is not new. See Philip Jenkins's discussion of the alliance of the Christian Front with some black anti-Semites in the late 1930s in *Hoods and Shirts: The Extreme Right in Pennsylvania, 1925–1950* (Chapel Hill: University of North Carolina Press, 1997), 183.

19. See Fielding, *National Front*, 61, and Ruth Frankenberg, *White Women, Race Matters: The Social Construction of Whiteness* (Minneapolis: University of Minnesota Press, 1993), 80.

20. My interviewees had only vague notions of Jews; in contrast, the English anti-Semites interviewed by Robb and analyzed in *Working-Class Anti-Semite* were very specific in their negative characterizations of Jews. My findings are consistent with the conclusion that Theodore Abel reached in 1938 after studying the autobiographical statements that six hundred German Nazis had submitted for a prize competition. Abel argued that the average Nazi follower "was strongly dissatisfied with the republican regime in Germany, but had no specific anti-Semitic bias"; see *Why Hitler Came to Power: An Answer Based in the Original Life Stories of Six Hundred of His Followers* (New York: Prentice-Hall, 1938), 6. Such contentions about Germans are now hotly debated; see especially Daniel J. Goldhagen's study of longtime German anti-Semitism, *Hitler's Willing Executioners: Germans and the Holocaust* (New York: Random

House, 1996). For one strident but informed critique of Goldhagen, see Norman G. Finkelstein and Rut Bettina Birn, *A Nation on Trial: The Goldhagen Thesis and Historical Truth* (New York: Henry Holt, 1998).

21. Ingo Hasselbach, with Tom Reiss, *Führer-Ex: Memoirs of a Former Neo-Nazi* (New York: Random House, 1998), 243–44.

22. Conspiratorial thinking is widely shared across the racist right, even among groups not generally regarded as conspiracy-based. Sometimes belief in Jewish conspiracies by those in organized racism is linked to other forms of what the historian Michael Barkun refers to as "stigmatized knowledge" (e.g., beliefs in the anti-Christ, the occult, and other conspiracy theories), causing racist activists over time to drift ever further from mainstream ways of thinking. See Barkun, "Conspiracy Theories as Stigmatized Knowledge: The Basis for a New Age Racism?" in *Nation and Race: The Developing Euro-American Racist Subculture,* ed. Jeffrey Kaplan and Tore Bjørgo (Boston: Northeastern University Press, 1998), 58–71.

23. Glenda Elizabeth Gilmore, *Gender and Jim Crow: Women and the Politics of White Supremacy in North Carolina, 1896–1920* (Chapel Hill: University of North Carolina Press, 1996), 99.

24. Aryan Women's League, hate line transcription, June 11, 1990.

25. An interesting discussion of how fascist party members believe that the "real" facts of history are ignored is found in Billig, *Fascists.*

26. Quoted in Stephen Singular, *Talked to Death: The Life and Murder of Alan Berg* (New York: William Morrow, 1987), 109.

27. Fielding, *National Front,* esp. 133, 135, 150–51.

28. In the Norwegian far right, Katrine Fangen concludes, ZOG is similarly understood as "a world with its own logic, acting behind the real world"; see "Living Out Our Ethnic Instincts: Ideological Beliefs among Right-Wing Activists in Norway," in Kaplan and Bjørgo, *Nation and Race,* 225.

29. Message quoted in "Dial-A-Nazi Phone Line Sparks Cries of Outrage," *New York Post,* April 30, 1993.

30. Smith, "Social Construction of Enemies," 234.

31. A 1979 letter, in "Church of Jesus Christ-Christian/Aryan Nations" file, in Special Collections, Howard-Tilton Memorial Library, Tulane University, New Orleans.

32. A novel outlining an Aryan supremacist blueprint for the future; it allegedly inspired Timothy McVeigh's bombing of the Alfred P. Murrah Federal Building in Oklahoma City.

33. Gill Seidel, *The Holocaust Denial: Anti-Semitism, Racism, and the New Right* (Leeds, England: Beyond the Pale Collective, 1986).

34. *The True History of "The Holocaust"* (Uckfield, England: Historical Review Press, n.d.), 1.

35. Deborah E. Lipstadt, *Denying the Holocaust: The Growing Assault on Truth and Memory* (New York: Free Press, 1993).

36. Raphael S. Ezekiel, *The Racist Mind: Portraits of American Neo-Nazis and Klansmen* (New York: Viking, 1995), xxv.

37. See Tore Bjørgo, introduction to *Terror from the Extreme Right,* ed. Tore Bjørgo (London: Frank Cass, 1995), 1–16.

38. Gonaro C. Armas, "Being Prepared, Millennium Style," Associated Press story, June 12, 1999.

39. See Tore Bjørgo, "Role of the Media in Racist Violence," in *Racist Violence in Europe*, ed. Tore Bjørgo and Rob White (New York: St. Martin's, 1993), 96–112.

40. See "Geraldo Again!" and "Slater on King" in *White Patriot*, no. 90 (1992), a publication of the Knights of the Ku Klux Klan, Harrison, Arkansas; in Wilcox Collection, Kenneth Spencer Research Library, University of Kansas, Lawrence. A perceptive analysis of the complicated dynamics among talk show producers, guests, and audiences is offered in Joshua Gamson, *Freaks Talk Back: Tabloid Talk Shows and Sexual Nonconformity* (Chicago: University of Chicago Press, 1998).

41. Kristina, "The Government and Its Control of Our Children," *WAR*, October 1993, in "Aryan Women's League" file, Anti-Defamation League.

42. Michael Barkun, "Introduction: Understanding Millennialism," in *Millennialism and Violence*, ed. Michael Barkun (London: Frank Cass, 1996), 5.

43. Dick Anthony and Thomas Robbins, "Religious Totalism, Violence and Exemplary Dualism: Beyond the Extrinsic Model," in Barkun, *Millennialism and Violence*, 19. Because they lack the millennialists' certainty in the triumph of goodness, white supremacists reject other characteristics of violent millennial movements, such as the push toward what Reinaldo L. Román describes as "provocation and self-immolation as a means of martyrdom" (see "Christian Themes: Mainstream Traditions and Millenarian Violence," in ibid., 52–82; quotation, 57); they project their violence instead outward onto designated racial enemies.

44. Standard interview formats are unlikely to elicit such ambivalent statements. One partial explanation for the women's equivocation might be a desire to appear less extreme in front of me, an outsider; this dynamic is discussed in Michael Billig, "The Notion of 'Prejudice': Some Rhetorical and Ideological Aspects," *Text* 8.1–2 (1988): 91–110, esp. 94, 100. But similar contradictions also pervaded informal conversations among racist women in group settings, suggesting that there is an actual gap between private sentiment and public propaganda in organized racism. In addition, at least some interviewees seemed determined to present themselves to me as not less but more extreme than they in fact were. Racist propaganda targeted to potential and new recruits is usually more tempered than that circulated among committed and longtime members, reflecting what Billig terms the distinction between surface and core ideas in racist extremism (*Fascists*, 191), which may account for some differences in how women express and practice extraordinary racism. As already noted, however, I found ambivalence among committed as well as more peripheral racist group members; thus this second explanation can be no more than partial.

45. See also the discussion of the discrepancy between group ideology and individual belief in Billig, *Fascists*, 237.

46. Raymond Cochrane and Michael Billig found similar contradictions between public positions and private actions of avowed racists; see "I'm Not National Front Myself, But . . . ," *New Society*, May 17, 1984, 255–58.

47. Such connections to outsiders should not be confused with the fraudu-

lent expressions of affinity for victims that are frequently voiced by those looking back on wars or other violent activity. See Elmer Luchterhand and Norbert Wieland, "The Focused Life History in Studying Involvement in a Genocidal Situation in Nazi Germany," in *Biography and Society: The Life History Approach in the Social Sciences,* ed. Daniel Bertaux (Beverly Hills, Calif.: Sage, 1981), 281.

48. William A. Gamson, *Talking Politics* (New York: Cambridge University Press, 1992), 84.

49. Hank Johnston, Enrique Laraña, and Joseph R. Gusfield, "Identities, Grievances, and New Social Movements," in Laraña, Johnston, and Gusfield, *New Social Movements,* 24.

50. Ezekiel, *Racist Mind,* 119.

51. In contrast, dissent in Germany within the tightly organized Nazi Party after the mid-1930s was possible only among intimate groups, if at all. See Detlev J. K. Peukert, *Inside Nazi Germany: Conformity, Opposition, and Racism in Everyday Life,* trans. Richard Deveson (New Haven: Yale University Press, 1987), 77. Billig notes the discrepancies between official ideologies and personal beliefs in British fascism and suggests that some members seek in fascist groups support for their own crude racial beliefs without accepting the groups' overarching conspiracy theories (*Fascists,* 319).

52. As Balibar cautions in "Racism and Nationalism," the idea that racism is coterminous with nationalism can be problematic if taken to imply that racism is invariant and inevitable in modern societies structured by national loyalties. See also Gilroy, *"Ain't No Black in the Union Jack";* Mudde, "Right-Wing Extremism Analyzed"; and Nancy McLean, *Behind the Mask of Chivalry: The Making of the Second Ku Klux Klan* (New York: Oxford University Press, 1994). On patriarchy and women's rights in right-wing extremist movements, see Kathleen M. Blee, *Women of the Klan: Racism and Gender in the 1920s* (Berkeley: University of California Press, 1991), and Martin Durham, *Women and Fascism* (London: Routledge, 1998).

53. William Achordate, "The Values of Fascism," *Journal of Social Issues* 24 (1968): 89–104.

54. Balibar, "Racism and Nationalism," 40. Balibar's description applies better to the ideological variability of modern racist movements than does the more common assumption, found in Ezekiel's social psychology of modern racists, that "agreement on basic ideas is the glue that holds the movement together, that the ideas are important to the members" (*Racist Mind,* xxix). See also David Theo Goldberg, *Racist Culture: Philosophy and the Politics of Meaning* (Cambridge, Mass.: Blackwell, 1993), and Billig, *Fascists.*

55. For one example, see the brilliant dissection of Soviet Stalinist political art in Victoria E. Bonnell, "The Peasant Woman in Stalinist Political Art of the 1930s," *American Historical Review* 98 (1993): 55–82. See also Francesca Polletta, "'It Was Like a Fever . . . ': Narrative and Identity in Social Protest," *Social Problems* 45 (1998): 137–59.

56. Discussed in Billig, "Imagining Nationhood." See also Wetherell and Potter, *Mapping the Language of Racism.*

CHAPTER 4: THE PLACE OF WOMEN

1. "White Women Practice Unity," *Aryan Action Line,* no. 2 (winter 1992): 1.

2. Untitled item in "Aryan Women's League" file, Anti-Defamation League of B'nai B'rith, New York.

3. The classic discussion of maternalism in politics is Sara Ruddick, *Maternal Thinking: Toward a Politics of Peace* (New York: Ballantine, 1989); see esp. 231. The essays in Alexis Jetter, Annelise Orleck, and Diana Taylor, eds., *The Politics of Motherhood: Activist Voices from Left to Right* (Hanover, N.H.: University Press of New England, 1997), broaden the treatment of maternalist political practices. See also Virginia Shapiro, *The Political Integration of Women: Roles, Socialization, and Politics* (Urbana: University of Illinois Press, 1984), 152, 182.

4. Joan Scott, "Gender: A Useful Category of Historical Analysis," *American Historical Review* 91 (1986): 1070.

5. Scholars have demonstrated that race and gender are conceptually entangled in modern Western societies: gender is implicated in the construction of race and race in the construction of gender. As Vron Ware notes, "ideas about what it means to be white . . . defined against the racialized 'other,' are also implicated in the social construction of gender"; see "Island Racism: Gender, Place, and White Power," *Feminist Review,* no. 54 (autumn 1996): 65. Although the relationship between *race* and gender has been intensely scrutinized in recent years, scant attention has been paid to the relationship between *racism* and gender. The little scholarship that exists focuses almost exclusively on racist appeals directed to men. See Nancy Leys Stephan, "Race and Gender: The Role of Analogy in Science," in *Anatomy of Racism,* ed. David Theo Goldberg (Minneapolis: University of Minnesota Press, 1990), 38–57, and Sandra Harding, ed., *The "Racial" Economy of Science: Toward a Democratic Future* (Bloomington: Indiana University Press, 1993).

6. See Nancy McLean, *Behind the Mask of Chivalry: The Making of the Second Ku Klux Klan* (New York: Oxford University Press, 1994). On the broader scope of "masculinities" in modern society, see R. W. Connell, *Masculinities* (Berkeley: University of California Press, 1995). Although gay men and lesbians are almost universally *victims* of rather than *participants* in organized racism, the rare phenomenon of gay male Nazis and racist skinheads reflects a complex interplay of gender, sexuality, and racism. In a study of British gay neo-Nazis, Murray Healy points out that Nazi and skinhead images can also be eroticized within gay male subcultures, noting that "gay skinheads shouldn't exist, *but they do*"; see *Gay Skins: Class, Masculinity, and Queer Appropriation* (London: Cassell, 1996) 4, 39, 60. Thus in the personals in a gay Nazi publication we find a "young rightist [who] wishes to meet others"; *NS Kampfruf* 1.5–6 (July–August 1974). See also the advertisements in *NS Mobilizer* 1.11, 12, 14 (January–March 1975); both in the Wilcox Collection, Kenneth Spencer Research Library, University of Kansas, Lawrence. A description of publications that appeal to right-wing extremists who are seeking a sexually

open racist group is found in "NSL [National Socialist League] Gives Gays Political Alternative," *Dixon Line-Reason,* July–August 1975, 9. Against all logic, an advertisement by a self-styled Nazi "master-at-arms" claims that Jews are the persecutors of gays and Nazis their saviors, and he implores "you Thai boys, you Japanese, Filipinos, Chinese, Indonesians, Vietnamese and Malays . . . all you dear boys from the other side of the world, come to the old master-at-arms shack under the banner of the Swastika. The super-rich Jew is out to destroy you [considering] you merely so much excess population to be eliminated . . . and trying to murder most of your race and enslave the rest of you under their symbol, the triangle." Though we should not overlook this subculture, overstating its size or importance may be more dangerous, especially given the effort by leaders of the U.S. Christian right to equate Nazism with male homosexuality. See "Homophobia and the Christian Right," *Dignity Report* 6.1 (spring 1999), published by the Coalition for Human Dignity, Seattle. For a historical assessment of the link between homosexuality and German Nazism, see George L. Mosse, *Nationalism and Sexuality: Middle-Class Morality and Sexual Norms in Modern Europe* (Madison: University of Wisconsin Press, 1985), 42, 176.

7. Raphael S. Ezekiel, *The Racist Mind: Portraits of American Neo-Nazis and Klansmen* (New York: Viking, 1995), 317; Stephen Baron, "The Canadian West Coast Punk Subculture: A Field Study," *Canadian Journal of Sociology* 14 (1989): 289–316; Friedhelm Neidhardt, "Left-Wing and Right-Wing Terrorist Groups: A Comparison for the German Case," in *International Social Movement Research,* vol. 4, *Social Movements and Violence: Participation in Underground Organizations,* ed. Donatella della Porta (London: JAI Press, 1992), 218.

8. *Resistance,* no. 4 (spring 1995), cover and inside cover.

9. See the discussion of the exclusion of women from organized crime in Renate Siebert, *Secrets of Life and Death: Women and the Mafia* (London: Verso, 1996), 7, and the insights about gender and fascism in Klaus Theweleit, *Male Fantasies,* vol. 1, *Women, Floods, Bodies, History,* trans. Stephan Conway with Erica Carter and Chris Turner (Minneapolis: University of Minnesota Press, 1987), 63.

10. Martin Durham, "Women and the British Extreme Right," in *The Far Right in Western and Eastern Europe,* ed. Luciano Cheles, Ronnie Ferguson, and Michalina Vaughan, 2nd ed. (New York: Longman, 1995), 277.

11. Cheri Peters, "For Women Only," *Scriptures for America,* no. 3 (1989); Debbie Villier, "Young Women Should Marry and Be Homemakers Much Earlier Than Now. Be Fruitful and Multiply. Be Happy," *All the Way: The Fighting Journal of the Nationalist Movement* 8.11 (November 1994): 3.

12. Mosse, *Nationalism and Sexuality,* 134.

13. For examples of varied ideas about women, see the cases of the 1920s Ku Klux Klan, the German Nazi Party, and Italian fascism during World War II, analyzed in Kathleen M. Blee, *Women of the Klan: Racism and Gender in the 1920s* (Berkeley: University of California Press, 1992); Claudia Koonz, *Mothers in the Fatherland: Women, the Family, and Nazi Politics* (New York: St. Martin's, 1987); and Victoria de Grazia, *How Fascism Ruled Women: Italy, 1922–1945* (Berkeley: University of California Press, 1992).

14. Mosse, *Nationalism and Sexuality*, 17.

15. Ware, "Island Racism," 79. For a fascinatingly similar discussion of women depicted as racial victims, see Jane Helleiner's study of male Irish Travellers, who were characterized as brutish threats to rural Irish women: "'Women of the Itinerant Class': Gender and Anti-Traveller Racism in Ireland," *Women's Studies International Forum* 20 (1997): 275–87.

16. For an excellent discussion of the role of sexual and gender imagery in another right-wing extremist movement, see Paola Bacchetta, "Communal Property/Sexual Property: On Representations of Muslim Women in a Hindu Nationalist Discourse," in *Forging Identities: Gender, Communities, and the State in India*, ed. Zoya Hasan (Boulder, Colo.: Westview, 1994), 188–225.

17. "The Aryan That Made a MAN out of 'Mac,'" *WAR* 13 (August 1994): 5.

18. *White Sisters*, no. 1 (spring 1990), published by the Aryan's Women's League.

19. Glenda Elizabeth Gilmore, *Gender and Jim Crow: Women and the Politics of White Supremacy in North Carolina, 1896–1920* (Chapel Hill: University of North Carolina Press 1996), 93.

20. "A Challenge to White People" (published and distributed by the Aryan Women's League in San Francisco, 1989).

21. Richard Butler is quoted in Ezekiel, *Racist Mind*, 138.

22. "Is Nordic Womanhood Worth Saving?" *Instauration* 16.4 (March 1991): 7.

23. "The Saddest Story Ever Told" (distributed by NSWAP [National Socialist White American's Party], ca. 1996).

24. Durham, "Women and the British Extreme Right," 278–79.

25. Rudolf M. Dekker, "Women in Revolt," *Theory and Society* 16 (1987): 337–62. The notion that right-wing extremist women are irrational and hysterical, and thus not fully accountable for their politics, is common in mainstream writings as well. For example, one contemporary journalist wrote of the American fascist Elizabeth Dilling that, in her, "hysteria is combined with complete sincerity and superficial plausibility"; Milton S. Mayer, "Mrs. Dilling: Lady of *The Red Network*," *American Mercury*, July 1939, 294.

26. The participants in interracial relationships are usually assumed to be white women and nonwhite men, though charges that President Bill Clinton was sexually involved with nonwhite women surfaced in the racist press. See Robert Fountain, "President Clinton Fathers Illegitimate Mulatto Boy," *War Eagle: A Voice and Forum for Revolutionary Pan-Aryanism* 2.1 (1994): 1.

27. Aryan Women's League, hate line transcription, June 11, 1990; in files of the Anti-Defamation League.

28. For an example of this speculation, see Bill Stanton, *Klanwatch: Bringing the Ku Klux Klan to Justice* (New York: Grove Weidenfeld, 1991), 213.

29. See Blee, *Women of the Klan;* see also McLean, *Behind the Mask.*

30. "The Death of the White Race" (flyer distributed by Aryan Nations, ca. 1994).

31. White Aryan Resistance, hate line transcription, October 10, 1989; in files of the Anti-Defamation League.

32. Claudie Lesselier, "The Women's Movement and the Extreme Right in France," in *The Nature of the Right: A Feminist Analysis of Order Patterns,* ed. Gill Seidel (Amsterdam: John Benjamin, 1988), 173–85.

33. De Grazia, *How Fascism Ruled Women,* 70.

34. White Aryan Resistance, hate line transcription, October 10, 1989.

35. Kenneth S. Stern, *A Force upon the Plain: The American Militia Movement and the Politics of Hate* (New York: Simon and Schuster, 1996), 26. See also Kristina, "The Government and Its Control of Our Children," *WAR,* October 1993, in "Aryan Women's League" file, Anti-Defamation League.

36. *White Sisters,* no. 2 (winter 1991).

37. "Warrior Breed" (flyer from Warrior Breed, n.d.).

38. See "The Lifegiving Delights of the Aryan Woman's Bosom" (pamphlet distributed by the America First Committee, 1994).

39. "Why I Love and Why I Hate," *WAR* 12 (May 1993): 6.

40. Ivy Rolfsdottir, "Poem for a Norse Man" (flyer distributed by the White Raven, ca. 1993).

41. "Mary Snell . . . A Woman of Valor," *Jubilee,* May–June 1995, 16.

42. Women widowed in feuds can provide similar functions, as Dwight B. Billings and Kathleen M. Blee described in *The Road to Poverty: The Making of Wealth and Hardship in Appalachia* (New York: Cambridge University Press, 2000), 309–10. On the phenomenon of Nazi widows, see Claudia Koonz, "The Competition for a Woman's Lebensraum," in *When Biology Became Destiny: Women in Weimar and Nazi Germany,* ed. Renate Bridenthal, Atina Grossmann, and Marion Kaplan (New York: Monthly Review, 1984), 227. In his memoir, a German former neo-Nazi recalls an assistance program for imprisoned neo-Nazis run by old Nazi widows, whom he describes as "actually more ideologically harder and more ruthless than most neo-Nazis of my generation"; Ingo Hasselbach, with Tom Reiss, *Führer-Ex: Memoirs of a Former Neo-Nazi* (New York: Random House, 1998), 149.

43. American Nationalist Party, *Bulletin* 69 (1978); see also a speech by Charles White, head of the American Nationalist Party, excerpted in *Low Country (Charleston, S.C.) News and Review,* December 6, 1977. Both clippings are in Special Collections, Howard-Tilton Memorial Library, Tulane University, New Orleans.

44. The new openness to women in white racist groups is in some ways similar to ambiguous ideas about gender in Christian right-wing groups like the Promise Keepers—to what Mary Stewart Van Leeuwen terms a "rhetoric of soft patriarchy"; see "Servanthood or Soft Patriarchy? A Christian Feminist Looks at the Promise Keepers Movement," *Journal of Men's Studies* 5 (1997): 233–62.

45. Hammerbringer/Baxter the Pagan, "From a Man's Point of View," *WAR* 8.4 (1989): 14.

46. "White Aryan Resistance Positions," *WAR* 13, August 1994, 12.

47. Untitled flyer; also in White Aryan Resistance, hate line transcription, October 10, 1989.

48. White Aryan Resistance, hate line transcription, October 10, 1989.

49. *White Sisters,* 22.4 (ca. 1994): 11.

50. "Attention White Women: An Introduction to the Aryan Women's League" (flyer distributed by the Aryan Women's League, n.d.).

51. "Stand By Your Man," *A.W.L. Newsletter* 3.2 (ca. 1994): 14; "Margaret Sanger: Eugenics Visionary and Founder of Planned Parenthood," in "White Sisters," a special feature of *WAR* 12.4 (1993): 7; "Mary Bacon: A Woman of Courage," *WAR* 11.5 (1992): 12.

52. See Bill Wallace, "Five More Neo-Nazis Get Prison for Crime Wave," *San Francisco Chronicle,* February 8, 1986; Stephen Singular, *Talked to Death: The Life and Murder of Alan Berg* (New York: William Morrow, 1987); Michael Barkun, *Religion and the Racist Right: The Origins of the Christian Identity Movement* (Chapel Hill: University of North Carolina Press, 1994); and Kevin Flynn and Gary Gerhardt, *The Silent Brotherhood: Inside America's Racist Underground* (New York: Signet/Penguin, 1990).

53. Feminist scholars have argued that a number of social movements organize women on the basis of a "female consciousness" grounded not in feminism but in the commonality of women's tasks. See Temma Kaplan, "Female Consciousness and Collective Action: The Case of Barcelona, 1910–1918," *Signs* 7 (1982): 545–66; see also Nancy F. Cott, "What's in a Name? The Limits of 'Social Feminism'; or, Expanding the Vocabulary of Women's History," *Journal of American History* 76 (1989): 809–29.

54. Robert Miles is quoted in "Bigotry or Brotherhood?" a special report by the *Spokane Spokesman Review–Spokesman Chronicle,* December 31, 1986.

55. Mabel Berezin, *Making the Fascist Self: The Political Culture of Interwar Italy* (Ithaca, N.Y.: Cornell University Press, 1997), 69.

56. Conflicting stances toward families and family life have also characterized extremist right-wing movements of the past, which at once sought to appropriate families and to reshape them. For example, the propaganda (though not the practice) of the 1920s Ku Klux Klan strongly emphasized the need to transform white Christian family life along racist lines, particularly by punishing philandering husbands. The modern racist movement shows little interest in such reshaping of personal or family life despite some pressure from racist activist women to do so.

57. NSDAP/AO, *The New Order,* September–October 1994, 2.

58. From testimony of Robert E. Miles, given in the 1988 Ft. Smith, Arkansas, trial of white supremacists for sedition; in "Extremist" file, Anti-Defamation League.

59. *Viking Viewpoint: Truth and Honor,* no. 16 (1993).

60. Skingirl quoted in Mark S. Hamm, *American Skinheads: The Criminology and Control of Hate Crimes* (Westport, Conn.: Praeger, 1994), 180.

61. Quoted in *New York Daily News,* July 27, 1993; clipping in Anti-Defamation League files.

62. Quoted in *New York Daily News,* July 27, 1993; clipping in Anti-Defamation League files.

63. "Klan Kid Korp," in *Prescript of the Order of the * of the **** (distributed by Knights of the Ku Klux Klan, ca. 1997), 15.

64. "Special Information for Homeschoolers" (distributed by Scriptures for America, ca. 1996).

65. *WAR* 8.2 (ca. 1989): 6.

66. *White Sisters* 11 (1992).

67. Researchers generally assume that political socialization takes place largely within families. See Hank Johnston, "New Social Movements and Old Regional Nationalisms," in *New Social Movements: From Ideology to Identity,* ed. Enrique Laraña, Hank Johnston, and Joseph R. Gusfield (Philadelphia: Temple University Press, 1994), 271; Miriam A. Golden, "Historical Memory and Ideological Orientations in the Italian Workers' Movement," *Politics and Society* 16 (1988): 1–34; and James H. Robb, *Working-Class Anti-Semite: A Psychological Study in a London Borough* (London: Tavistock, 1954), 172–73.

68. See also Hamm, *American Skinheads,* 108.

69. Kathleen M. Blee, "Family Patterns and the Politicization of Consumption Relations," *Sociological Spectrum* 5 (1985): 295–316; Dana Frank, *Purchasing Power: Consumer Organizing, Gender, and the Seattle Labor Movement, 1919–1929* (New York: Cambridge University Press, 1994).

70. For example, see "Kosher Racket Revealed: Secret Jewish Tax on Gentiles" (pamphlet distributed by an anonymous racist group, ca. 1991).

71. Advertisement for Debbie's Crafts in *Race and Reason* (ca. 1995); see also "Aryan Women's League: Crafts, Products, and Informational Services" (flyer distributed by the Aryan Women's League, ca. 1994).

72. See the "Aryan Women's League" file, clippings ca. 1993, Anti-Defamation League.

73. *Valkyrie Voice,* no. 2 (ca. 1997).

74. On the importance of social ties in organizing and maintaining social movements, see, for example, Donatella della Porta, *Social Movements, Political Violence, and the State: A Comparative Analysis of Italy and Germany* (Cambridge: Cambridge University Press, 1995); Nigel Fielding, *The National Front* (London: Routledge and Kegan Paul, 1981); Martha Crenshaw, "Theories of Terrorism: Instrumental and Organizational Approaches," in *Inside Terrorist Organizations,* ed. David C. Rapoport (New York: Columbia University Press, 1988), 13–31; Mary G. Harris, *Cholas: Latino Girls and Gangs* (New York: AMS Press, 1988); Suzanne Staggenborg, "Social Movement Communities and Cycles of Protest: The Emergence and Maintenance of a Local Women's Movement," *Social Problems* 45 (1998): 180–204; Mark Chesler and Richard Schmuch, "Participant Observation in a Super-Patriot Discussion Group," *Journal of Social Issues* 19 (1963): 18–30; Elizabeth T. Buhmann, "Rethinking the Problem of Girls in Gangs," unpublished paper, Office of the Attorney General of the State of Texas (Austin, 1992); Anne Campbell, "Self-Definition by Rejection: The Case of Gang Girls," *Social Problems* 34 (1987): 451–66; Angela McRobbie and Jenny Garber, "Girls and Subcultures," in *Resistance through Rituals: Youth Subcultures in Post-war Britain,* ed. Stuart Hall and Tony Jefferson (New York: Holmes and Meier, 1976), 208–22; and Carl S. Taylor, *Dangerous Society* (East Lansing: Michigan State University Press, 1990).

75. Carol Mueller, "Conflict Networks and the Origins of Women's Liberation," in Laraña, Johnston, and Gusfield, *New Social Movements: From Ideology to Identity,* 237.

76. See Hank Johnston, Enrique Laraña, and Joseph R. Gusfield, "Iden-

tities, Grievances, and New Social Movements," in Laraña, Johnston, and Gusfield, *New Social Movements,* 24, and Crenshaw, "Theories of Terrorism." See also Caroline Kelly and Sara Breinlinge, *The Social Psychology of Collective Action: Identity, Injustice, and Gender* (London: Taylor and Francis, 1996), 80, 134.

77. "Preaching a Gospel of Hate," *Chicago Tribune,* May 23, 1985.

78. "Report on the Aryan Nations Youth Conference," *Aryan Research Fellowship Newsletter,* June–August 1990, 8–12.

79. Self-sufficiency is not a new idea within organized racism. The Aryan Knights of the Ku Klux Klan of Pennsylvania in the early 1970s claimed to offer its members benefits that ranged from "places to stay as you travel" to "mechanics, blood banks, and . . . AAA benefits." Bill Sickles, letter of April 8, 1972, in "Aryan Knights, Export PA" file, Special Collections, Howard-Tilton Memorial Library, Tulane University.

80. Aryan Women flyer, ca. 1992.

81. Floyd Cochran, "Sisterhood of Hate" (pamphlet, privately published, 1993); posted at ⟨http://www.evnetwork.org/sister.html⟩ (accessed January 2001).

82. See Les Back, Michael Keith, and John Solomos, "Racism on the Internet: Mapping Neo-Fascist Subcultures in Cyberspace," in Kaplan and Bjørgo, *Nation and Race,* 73–101.

83. "Report on the Aryan Nations Youth Conference."

84. Amy Benfer, "Salon Mothers Who Think: Nazi Family Values," *Salon.com,* July 15, 1999 ⟨http://www.salon.com/mwt/hot/1999/07/15/aryan_compound/index.html⟩ (accessed January 2001).

85. "Report on the Aryan Nations Youth Conference."

86. "Aryan Update" phone line, May 25, 1993.

87. Belinda Robnett, *How Long? How Long? African-American Women in the Struggle for Civil Rights* (New York: Oxford University Press, 1997), 17–32. On ties between members of organized social movements and those in their larger environment, see Clarence Y. H. Lo, "Communities of Challengers in Social Movement Theory," in *Frontiers in Social Movement Theory,* ed. Aldon D. Morris and Carol McClurg Mueller (New Haven: Yale University Press, 1992), 229.

88. *NSV [National Socialist Vanguard] Report* 5.2 (April/June 1987).

89. White Aryan Resistance, hate line transcription, October 10, 1989; see also "Earth First," *WAR* 8.2 (1989): 8.

90. "Earth First," *WAR* 8.2 (1989): 8.

91. "Report on the Aryan Nations Youth Conference."

92. See June Preston, "Women Emerging as White Supremacist Leaders," Reuters News Service article, September 12, 1999.

93. For example, Jessie Daniels overlooks the informal leadership of women when she asserts that "white women are primarily valuable to the movement for two qualities: their reproductive abilities and sexual attractiveness"; see *White Lies: Race, Class, Gender, and Sexuality in White Supremacist Discourse* (New York: Routledge, 1997), 57.

94. Karen Brodkin Sacks, "What's a Life Story Got to Do with It?" in *In-*

terpreting Women's Lives: Feminist Theory and Personal Narrative, ed. Personal Narratives Group (Bloomington: Indiana University Press, 1989), 85–95. See also Susan D. Rose, "Women Warriors: The Negotiation of Gender in a Charismatic Community," *Sociological Analysis* 48 (1987): 245–58. On the development of collective identity, see Johnston, Laraña, and Gusfield, "Identities," and Hank Johnston and Bert Klandermans, "The Cultural Analysis of Social Movements," in *Social Movements and Culture,* ed. Hank Johnston and Bert Klandermans (Minneapolis: University of Minnesota Press, 1995), 3–24. On mediation as leadership, see Luisa Passerini, *Fascism in Popular Memory: The Cultural Experience of the Turin Working Class,* trans. Robert Lumley and Jude Bloomfield (Cambridge: Cambridge University Press, 1987), 139.

95. For example, see Ezekiel, *Racist Mind,* 61–148.

96. Dick Anthony and Thomas Robbins, "Religious Totalism, Violence, and Exemplary Dualism: Beyond the Extrinsic Model," in *Millennialism and Violence,* ed. Michael Barkun (London: Frank Cass, 1996), 10–50.

97. See *The Record: North Jersey's Intelligence Report,* August 26, 1993, and "Loveland Man Heads Nazi Group," *Greeley Tribune,* February 15, 1993; both clippings in the collection of the Anti-Defamation League.

98. Katrine Fangen, "Living Out Our Ethnic Instincts: Ideological Beliefs among Right-Wing Activists in Norway," in Kaplan and Bjørgo, *Nation and Race,* 202–30.

99. See "Cookbooks and Combat Boots," *Klanwatch Intelligence Report* 56 (1991). There is little literature on women as terrorists. Two important studies are Richard G. Braungart and Margaret M. Braungart, "From Protest to Terrorism: The Case of SDS and the Weathermen," in della Porta, *Social Movements and Violence,* 45–78, and Gilda Zwerman, "Mothering on the Lam: Politics, Gender Fantasies, and Maternal Thinking in Women Associated with Armed, Clandestine Organizations in the United States," *Feminist Review,* no. 47 (summer 1994): 33–56. A more superficial account is Daniel E. Georges-Abeyie, "Women as Terrorists," in *Perspectives on Terrorism,* ed. Lawrence Zelic Freeman and Yonah Alexander (Wilmington, Del.: Scholarly Resources, 1983), 71–84.

100. Despite such violent activities, the stereotype of racist women as merely the sexual chattel of men persists. In their introduction to *Racist Violence in Europe,* the collection of essays they edited, Tore Bjørgo and Rob White insist that "female activists in racist and other right-wing groups tend to be assigned to non-fighting and subordinate roles" (11). Women in gangs are similarly either ignored or sexualized in research and journalism, though feminist studies find that gang girls, while still quite dependent on boys, have been steadily gaining independence. See Karen A. Joe and Meda Chesney-Lind, "'Just Every Mother's Angel': An Analysis of Gender and Ethnic Variations in Youth Gang Membership," *Gender and Society* 9 (1995): 412, and Meda Chesney-Lind, Randall G. Shelden, and Karen A. Joe, "Girls, Delinquency, and Gang Membership," in *Gangs in America,* ed. C. Ronald Huff, 2nd ed. (Thousand Oaks, Calif.: Sage, 1996), 185–204.

101. Farai Chideya, "Women Who Love to Hate," *Mademoiselle,* August 1994, 134–37, 186.

102. Benfer, "Nazi Family Values."

103. "Bounties Bestowing . . . Blessings Bequeathed" (ca. 1996), n.p.

104. "Bounties Bestowing . . . Blessings Bequeathed" (ca. 1996), n.p.; see also "The Jubilee's 'Captive Christian Penfriends Correspondence List,'" December 1994, n.p.

105. Lisa Turner of Church of the Creator, cited in *Poisoning the Web: Hatred Online* (New York: Anti-Defamation League, 1999), 48.

106. Luisa Passerini, "Lacerations in the Memory: Women in the Italian Underground Organizations," in della Porta, *Social Movements and Violence,* 193.

107. Although militias are outside the scope of this study, women are increasingly important in some militia groups as well, including white supremacist militias. See "Amazon Allied Forces—Holding Down the 'Homefront,'" communication from Militia of Montana, September 13, 1999.

108. White Aryan Resistance, hate line transcription, October 10, 1989.

109. Aryan Women's League flyer, ca. 1992.

110. "A Challenge to White People" (pamphlet distributed by Aryan Women's League, ca. 1989).

111. "Attention White Women."

112. "The Baby Book Is Back" (brochure distributed by the Aryan Women's League, 1992); "Make More Babies, Prepare to Survive," *White Sisters,* winter 1991.

113. "Aryan Women's League: Crafts, Products, and Informational Services."

114. Quoted in the *Greensboro Daily News,* September 12, 1982, cited in Center for Democratic Renewal, "From the Right Wing: All about Women" (pamphlet, ca. 1990).

115. "Women and the Ku Klux Klan," *White Patriot,* 1987, p. 1, in Wilcox Collection, Kenneth Spencer Research Library, University of Kansas, Lawrence.

116. Vincent Coppola, *Dragons of God: A Journey through Far-Right America* (Atlanta: Longstreet, 1996), 127–28.

117. *Aryan Mothers Inspiring Something Hopeful: A.M.I.S.H.* (New Holland, Pa., ca. 1997).

118. *Valkyrie Voice,* no. 2 (ca. 1997).

119. Miscellaneous materials from United White Sisters (ca. 1996).

120. Miscellaneous materials from Warrior Breed (ca. 1996).

121. *Right as Reina,* 1995.

122. Robyn, "Free Money," *Right as Reina,* December 1995.

123. Cheri Peters, "For Men Only," *Scriptures Holy Bible Newsletter,* June 1987, and "The Masculinized Female," *Scriptures Holy Bible Newsletter,* March 1987; see also Cheri Peters, "For Women Only," *Scriptures for America,* no. 8 (1988).

124. *Scriptures for America,* no. 8 (1988).

125. *Sigrdrifa,* no. 1, n.d., n.p.

126. Excellent discussions of fraternalism as a ideological motif are found in Mosse, *Nationalism and Sexuality;* Benedict Anderson, *Imagined Communities: Reflections on the Origin and Spread of Nationalism,* rev. ed. (London:

Verso, 1991); and Mary Ann Clawson, *Constructing Brotherhood: Class, Gender, and Fraternalism* (Princeton: Princeton University Press, 1989). Clawson's account is particularly insightful about the connections between fraternalism and masculinity.

127. See, for example, interviewees quoted in Kathy Dobie, "Skingirl Mothers: From Thelma and Louise to Ozzie and Harriet," in Jetter, Orleck, and Taylor, *The Politics of Motherhood: Activist Voices from Left to Right*, 257–67. The files of the Anti-Defamation League contain references to "white power/ women power" skinhead groups.

128. *Aryan Action Line*, no. 4 (fall 1992): 2; this is a publication of the SS Action Group.

129. For example, see Spring Leaman, "Aryan Women's Organization," *Calling Our Nation*, no. 68 (ca. 1992): 25, or "Create Conflict between the Sexes," *Calling Our Nation*, no. 72 (1994): 9 (*Calling Our Nation* is published by Aryan Nations). See also the discussion of the Women's Frontier of the World Church of the Creator in a special report published by the Chicago-based Center for New Community, "World Church of the Creator: One Year Later" (2000), 6.

130. "The Real Problem," *Aryan Nations*, no. 69 (November 1992): 17.

131. Shane Mason, "Working Mothers," *Calling Our Nation*, no. 71 (ca. 1993): 32. Though most racist leaders and literature strongly criticize feminism, some use feminist rhetoric to present racism as guaranteeing the rights of Aryan women. These white women, they insist, will gain as racist movements eradicate those religions and cultures that racists regard as oppressive to women—Muslim, Jewish, Mexican American, African American, and so on. Italian fascists also argued for a "feminism" untainted by concerns for equality but based on race, family, and tradition; see de Grazia, *How Fascism Ruled Women*, 236.

132. Martin Kerr, "On Women's Rights and White Rights," *White Power: The Revolutionary Voice of National Socialism*, no. 105 (1983): 4.

133. Hammerbringer/Baxter the Pagan, "From a Man's Point of View," *WAR* 8.4 (1989).

134. See Kathy Dobie, "Long Day's Journey into White," *Village Voice*, April 28, 1992, 22–32; *Aryan Action Line*, no. 4 (fall 1992): 2. Local skingirl groups are covered in *The Monitor*, the newsletter of the Center for Democratic Renewal, which is based in Atlanta.

135. See Randy Blazak, "The Suburbanization of Hate: An Ethnographic Study of the Skinhead Culture" (Ph.D. diss., Emory University, 1995); Dobie, "Long Day's Journey"; and Dobie, "Skingirl Mothers."

136. *The Code of the Skinhead* (ca. 1993); anonymous skinhead 'zine (n.p., ca. 1994).

137. Mrs. R. G. Skorzeny, "I Am the Wife of a Warrior," in *The Code of the Skinhead* (ca. 1993), 57.

138. "Women Skinheads," episode of *Geraldo*, ca. 1991; transcription in the files of the Anti-Defamation League.

139. White Aryan Resistance, hate line transcription, August 16, 1993; in the files of the Anti-Defamation League.

140. "Joining the Fight: 'Female Recruiting,'" *Sigrdrifa*, no. 1 (ca. 1997).

141. Hamm, *American Skinheads,* 175–76.

142. "Women Skinheads."

143. "A Woman's Opinion: (Scary Thought, Guys?!?!)," *Sigrdrifa,* no. 1 (ca. 1997).

144. Male Klan leader, quoted in Ezekiel, *Racist Mind,* 110.

145. Female racist, quoted in *New York Daily News,* July 27, 1993; clipping in the files of the Anti-Defamation League.

146. "WAR" file (ca. 1993), Anti-Defamation League; *Poisoning the Web.*

147. "Aryan Singles Pen-Pan Column," *WAR* 11 (1992); *White Sisters,* October 1992; and *Race and Reality* 2 (1994). In response to male complaints about their difficulty in finding "suitably racially aware" Aryan women as wives and girlfriends, one woman suggested that they should recruit female partners from women's prisons, arguing that the numbers of women from racial minorities in prisons "should do wonders for a lady's racial perspective." See "Brides in Chains?" NSWPP, *Resistance,* no. 41 (August 1994): 9.

148. See Anderson, *Imagined Communities,* 143; Donatella della Porta, "Political Socialization in Left-Wing Underground Organizations: Biographies of Italian and German Militants," in della Porta, *Social Movements and Violence,* 281; Jane Jacobs, "The Economy of Love in Religious Commitment: The Deconversion of Women from Nontraditional Religious Movements," *Journal for the Scientific Study of Religion* 23 (1984): 155–71; and James T. Richardson, Jans van der Lans, and Frans Derks, "Leaving and Labeling: Voluntary and Coerced Disaffiliation from Religious Social Movements," *Research in Social Movements, Conflicts, and Change* 9 (1986): 97–126.

149. Eighteen-year-old woman, quoted in "Second Wife Is Disillusioned," Associated Press article, January 26, 1994; in the files of the Anti-Defamation League.

150. Conflict over gender roles and women's place in racist movements also exists elsewhere in the world—for example, in Great Britain's National Front, in which women have been active participants. See Durham, "Women and the British Extreme Right," 280, 285.

CHAPTER 5: A CULTURE OF VIOLENCE

1. Hannah Arendt's perceptive commentary on the "banality of evil" in *Eichmann in Jerusalem: A Report on the Banality of Evil* (New York: Viking, 1965) rests on a much more sophisticated analysis of the structure of evil.

2. Anna Hamilton Phelan, "Neo-Nazi Believers—'So Average . . . It Was Surreal,'" *Los Angeles Times,* November 25, 1987.

3. Edward W. Said, *Orientalism* (New York: Vintage, 1979), 15.

4. *The Logic of Evil: The Social Origins of the Nazi Party, 1925–1933* (New Haven: Yale University Press, 1996), an otherwise excellent study of Nazism by William Brustein, is an example of scholarship that minimizes the role of culture in creating support for the Nazi Party in Germany.

5. James C. Scott, *Domination and the Arts of Resistance: Hidden Tran-*

scripts (New Haven: Yale University Press, 1990); see also Hank Johnston, *Tales of Nationalism: Catalonia, 1939–79* (New Brunswick, N.J.: Rutgers University Press, 1991).

6. Ann Swidler, "Culture in Action: Symbols and Strategies," *American Sociological Review* 51 (1986): 273.

7. Ann Swidler, "Cultural Power and Social Movements," in *Social Movements and Culture,* ed. Hank Johnston and Bert Klandermans (Minneapolis: University of Minnesota Press, 1995), 25–40.

8. I thank Clarence Lo for this suggestion, made in comments on my paper "The Ties That Bind: The Hidden Culture of Organized Racism," presented at the 1998 American Sociological Association meeting, San Francisco, August 1998.

9. For examples of research focusing on how cultural practices sustain the commitment of political activists, see Hank Johnston, "New Social Movements and Old Regional Nationalisms," in *New Social Movements: From Ideology to Identity,* ed. Enrique Laraña, Hank Johnston, and Joseph R. Gusfield (Philadelphia: Temple University Press, 1994), 270, 274, and Doug McAdam, "Culture and Social Movements," in ibid., 36–57.

10. Scott, *Domination,* 199. The authors of a historical study of a progressive reform movement make a similar point about how social movements create institutional sites for ideas outside the mainstream. See Naomi Rosenthal, Meryl Fingrutd, Michele Ethier, Roberta Karant, and David McDonald, "Social Movements and Network Analysis: A Case Study of Nineteenth-Century Women's Reform in New York State," *American Journal of Sociology* 90 (1985): 1022–54.

11. Luisa Passerini, *Fascism in Popular Memory: The Cultural Experience of the Turin Working Class,* trans. Robert Lumley and Jude Bloomfield (Cambridge: Cambridge University Press, 1987).

12. For an example of research focusing on progressive social movements, see Nancy E. Whittier, *Feminist Generations: The Persistence of the Radical Women's Movement* (Philadelphia: Temple University Press, 1995).

13. See James William Gibson, *Warrior Dreams: Paramilitary Culture in Post-Vietnam America* (New York: Hill and Wang, 1994), for a discussion of the particular salience of violence to men. My thanks to Jerome Himmelstein for this reference.

14. On young girls' use of cultural products, see Martha J. Einerson, "Fame, Fortune, and Failure: Young Girls' Moral Language Surrounding Popular Culture," *Youth and Society* 30.2 (1998): 241–57; Martha J. Einerson, "Female Preadolescent Interpretations of Popular Music Experience: An Interpersonal Perspective" (Ph.D. diss., University of Kentucky, 1993); and Lauraine Lebanc, *Pretty in Punk: Girls' Gender Resistance in a Boys' Subculture* (New Brunswick, N.J.: Rutgers University Press, 1999).

15. Susan A. Phillips notes that white supremacist graffiti is the most common type of political graffiti in the United States today; see *Wallbangin': Graffiti and Gangs in L.A.* (Chicago: University of Chicago Press, 1999), 52.

16. "Aryan Skinheads," *WAR* 7.3 (1988): 5.

17. On the role of emotion in stimulating participation in social movements, see James M. Jasper, "The Emotion of Protest: Affective and Reactive Emotions in and around Social Movements," *Sociological Forum* 13 (1998): 397–424.

18. George Eric Hawthorne, "The Essence of Timing," *Resistance Records,* spring 1995, 4.

19. According to an article in the Seattle *Post-Intelligence,* August 18, 1993, Tom Metzger of White Aryan Resistance told skinheads to "grow your hair, get rid of the boots, get an education or learn a trade . . . and work quietly within the system . . . to destroy it."

20. Paola Bacchetta argues that the "performance" of fascist ideological discourse serves to empower and unify participants in the Hindu nationalist movement in India; see "Communal Property/Sexual Property: On Representations of Muslim Women in a Hindu Nationalist Discourse," in *Forging Identities: Gender, Communities, and the State in India,* ed. Zoya Hasan (Boulder, Colo.: Westview, 1994), 188–225.

21. Mabel Berezin, *Making the Fascist Self: The Political Culture of Interwar Ideology* (Ithaca, N.Y.: Cornell University Press, 1997), 27.

22. "Aryan Wedding," *WAR* 7.3 (1988): 4.

23. "Report on the Aryan Nations Youth Conference," *Aryan Research Fellowship Newsletter,* June–August 1990, 8–12.

24. See the discussion of interpretive communities in Margaret Wetherell, "Group Conflict and the Social Psychology of Racism," in *Identities, Groups, and Social Issues,* ed. Margaret Wetherell (London: Sage, 1996), 175–238.

25. International Aryan Movement, *Aryan Action Line,* no. 8 (winter 1993).

26. See Clarence Y. H. Lo, "Communities of Challengers in Social Movement Theory," in *Frontiers in Social Movement Theory,* ed. Aldon D. Morris and Carol McClurg Mueller (New Haven: Yale University Press, 1992), 242; Micaela di Leonardo, "Habits of the Cumbered Heart: Ethnic Community and Women's Culture as American Invented Traditions," in *Golden Ages, Dark Ages: Imagining the Past in Anthropology and History,* ed. Jay O'Brien and William Roseberry (Berkeley: University of California Press, 1991), 234–52; Miriam A. Golden, "Historical Memory and Ideological Orientations in the Italian Workers' Movement," *Politics and Society* 16 (1988): 1–34; and Eric Hobsbawm and Terence Ranger, *The Invention of Tradition* (New York: Cambridge University Press, 1985).

27. Michael Lewis and Jacqueline Serbu, "Kommemorating the Ku Klux Klan," *Sociological Quarterly* 40 (1999): 139–57.

28. Michael Billig, *Fascists: A Social Psychological View of the National Front* (London: Academic Press, 1978), 103.

29. Erving Goffman, *The Presentation of Self in Everyday Life* (Garden City, N.Y.: Doubleday, 1959).

30. Benedict Anderson, *Imagined Communities: Reflections on the Origin and Spread of Nationalism,* rev. ed. (London: Verso, 1991). See also David Theo Goldberg, "The Social Formation of Racist Discourse," in *Anatomy of Racism,* ed. David Theo Goldberg (Minneapolis: University of Minnesota Press, 1990), 309.

31. Jeffrey Kaplan and Tore Bjørgo, introduction to *Nation and Race: The Developing Euro-American Racist Subculture,* ed. Jeffrey Kaplan and Tore Bjørgo (Boston: Northeastern University Press, 1988), ix–xiii.

32. Barbie Zelizer, *Remembering to Forget: Holocaust Memory through the Camera's Eye* (Chicago: University of Chicago Press, 1998), has an excellent discussion of the problems involved in collective remembering of World War II.

33. *NSV [National Socialist Vanguard] Report* 8.2 (April/June 1990).

34. The first two points about the neo-Nazi view of the past, but not the third, are made by Nigel Fielding in *The National Front* (London: Routledge and Kegan Paul, 1981), 17.

35. See Heléne Lööw, "White-Power Rock 'n' Roll: A Growing Industry," in Kaplan and Bjørgo, 126–47.

36. Similarly, even racial activists who are highly critical of terroristic actions within the movement adopt the number "14" or the slogan "14 words" to denote white supremacism, honoring the fourteen-word call issued by David Lane, an imprisoned former member of the Brüders Schweigen (The Order): "we must secure the existence of our race and a future for White children."

37. See Devin Burghart, ed., *Soundtracks to the White Revolution: White Supremacist Assaults on Youth Music Subcultures* (Chicago: Center for New Community, 1999); Kirsten Scharnberg and Achy Obejas, with Maria T. Galo, "Hate Groups Target Kids with Music," *Chicago Tribune,* December 3, 1999; and David Segal, "The Pied Piper of Racism," *Washington Post,* January 12, 2000.

38. See Michel Wieviorka, *The Arena of Racism,* trans. Chris Turner (London: Sage, 1994). It is important to remember, however, that the majority of "hate crimes" are committed by those with no clear connection to organized racist groups.

39. Ehud Sprinzak, "Right-Wing Terrorism in a Comparative Perspective: The Case of Split Delegitimation," in *Terror from the Extreme Right,* ed. Tore Bjørgo (London: Frank Cass, 1995), 17–43.

40. For explanations of racist violence that focus on internal group dynamics, see Tore Bjørgo and Rob White, introduction to *Racist Violence in Europe,* ed. Tore Bjørgo and Rob White (New York: St. Martin's, 1993), 1–16; Wilhelm Heitmeyer, "Hostility and Violence towards Foreigners in Germany," in ibid., 17–28; John Hagan, Hans Merkens, and Klaus Boehnke, "Delinquency and Disdain: Social Capital and the Control of Right-Wing Extremism among East and West Berlin Youth," *American Journal of Sociology* 100 (1995): 1028–52; and Martha Crenshaw, "Theories of Terrorism: Instrumental and Organizational Approaches," in *Inside Terrorist Organizations,* ed. David C. Rapoport (New York: Columbia University Press, 1988), 13–31.

41. Donatella della Porta, *Social Movements, Political Violence, and the State: A Comparative Analysis of Italy and Germany* (Cambridge: Cambridge University Press, 1995), 111; see also James A. Aho, *This Thing of Darkness: A Sociology of the Enemy* (Seattle: University of Washington Press, 1994).

42. Heitmeyer, "Hostility and Violence"; see also Richard G. Braungart and Margaret M. Braungart, "From Protest to Terrorism: The Case of SDS and the

Weathermen," in *International Social Movement Research*, vol. 4, *Social Movements and Violence: Participation in Underground Organizations,* ed. Donatella della Porta (London: JAI Press, 1992), 45–78, and Temma Kaplan, "Female Consciousness and Collective Action: The Case of Barcelona, 1910–1918," *Signs* 7 (1982): 545–66.

43. Goldberg, "Social Formation of Racist Discourse," 311.

44. One of many examples is the murder of a reputed skinhead with the nickname "Adolf" who was beaten to death by two alleged neo-Nazi skinheads when he started talking about cannibalism. "Police Search for Neo-Nazis near Philadelphia," Reuters News Service article, September 9, 1999.

45. On Europe, see Sprinzak, "Right-Wing Terrorism"; on the United States, see, for example, "Grand Jury in Tulsa Indicts Skinheads for Racist Attacks," *Washington Times,* October 26, 1990.

46. See Heitmeyer, "Hostility and Violence."

47. Strategic violence includes not only such widely publicized events as the 1999 murder sprees by Benjamin Smith in Illinois and Indiana and Buford Furrow in California but also smaller acts of terrorism, such as the placement of containers of medical waste festooned with swastikas and a picture of Buford Furrow in front of synagogues in Stamford, Connecticut, in August 1999; see Denise Lavoie, "Conn. Probes Hate Messages," Associated Press article, August 23, 1999.

48. Sidney Tarrow, "Mentalities, Political Cultures, and Collective Action Frames: Constructing Meanings through Action," in Morris and Mueller, *Frontiers in Social Movement Theory,* 177.

49. Wieviorka, *Arena of Racism,* 74.

50. Eric Starvo Galt, "To Kill or Not to Kill," *WAR* 12.3 (1993): 8. Italics in original.

51. The sociologist Ann Swidler's distinction among ideology, tradition, and common sense, made in "Culture in Action," is helpful for thinking about how differences between strategic and narrative violence are presented in the life histories of racist women.

52. Francesca Polletta, "'It Was Like a Fever . . .': Narrative and Identity in Social Protest," *Social Problems* 45 (1998): 137–59. See also the pathbreaking work of Patricia Ewing and Susan S. Silbey, "Subversive Stories and Hegemonic Tales: Toward a Sociology of Narrative," *Law and Society Review* 29 (1995): 197–226.

53. Polletta, "'It Was Like a Fever,'" 141.

54. For insight into how storytelling can shape a society, see Edward Bruner and Phyllis Gorfain, "Dialogic Narration and the Paradoxes of Masada," in *Text, Play, and Story: The Construction and Reconstruction of Self and Society,* ed. Stuart Plattner (Washington, D.C.: American Ethnological Society, 1984), 56–79.

55. Antonius C. G. M. Robben and Carolyn Nordstrom, "The Anthropology and Ethnography of Violence and Sociopolitical Conflict," in *Fieldwork under Fire: Contemporary Studies of Violence and Survival,* ed. Carolyn Nordstrom and Antonius C. G. M. Robben (Berkeley: University of California Press, 1995), 8, 9.

56. On the similar orientation toward action of Italian fascism, see Berezin, *Making the Fascist Self.*

57. della Porta, *Social Movements, Political Violence, and the State,* 19.

58. della Porta, *Social Movements, Political Violence, and the State,* 129.

59. Hannah Arendt is quoted in Renate Siebert, *Secrets of Life and Death: Women and the Mafia* (London: Verso, 1996), 74.

60. Tore Bjørgo, introduction to Bjørgo, *Terror from the Extreme Right,* 1–16.

61. Data from files at the Anti-Defamation League of B'nai B'rith, New York.

62. *The Rational Feminist,* summer 1994, 9.

63. Carol McClurg Mueller, "Building Social Movement Theory," in Morris and Mueller, *Frontiers in Social Movement Theory,* 15.

64. Arthur Jones, "Skinheads: National Socialists or National Bolsheviks?" *The War Eagle,* winter 1994, 24. This and similar condemnations may also reflect a sense that skinheads are unwilling to take direction from the movement's self-proclaimed leaders.

65. *NSV Report* 5.4 (October/December 1987): 2.

66. *Clarion-Ledger (Jackson, Miss.),* August 19, 1993.

67. *The Berserker: Revolutionary Voice of the New York SS Brigade,* ca. April 1993, 2.

CONCLUSION: LESSONS

1. Paul Gilroy, *"There Ain't No Black in the Union Jack": The Cultural Politics of Race and Nation* (Chicago: University of Chicago Press, 1991), 11; see also Paul Gilroy, "One Nation under a Groove: The Cultural Politics of 'Race' and Racism in Britain," in *Anatomy of Racism,* ed. David Theo Goldberg (Minneapolis: University of Minnesota Press, 1990), 263–82.

2. Chip Berlet, "Dances with Devils: How Apocalyptic and Millennialist Themes Influence Right-Wing Scapegoating and Conspiracism," *Public Eye: A Publication of Political Research Associates* 7.2/3 (1998): 1; Michael J. Sniffen, "FBI Warns of Millennium Attacks," Associated Press story, October 20, 1999.

3. See the discussion of J. Skolnick's research on leaving gangs (*The Social Structure of Street Drug Dealing,* BCS Forum [Sacramento: State of California, 1988]) in Scott H. Decker and Janet L. Lauritsen, "Breaking the Bonds of Membership: Leaving the Gang," in *Gangs in America,* ed. C. Ronald Huff, 2nd ed. (Thousand Oaks, Calif.: Sage, 1996), 103–22. Tore Bjørgo provides a useful inventory of reasons for quitting extremist groups—including negative social sanctions, loss of faith, feeling that things are going too far, disillusionment, risk of losing status or position, exhaustion, jeopardy to career or future, new family members, and aging—in "Entry, Bridge-Building, and Exit Options: What Happens to Young People Who Join Racist Groups—and Want to Leave?" in *Nation and Race: The Developing Euro-American Racist Subculture,* ed. Jef-

frey Kaplan and Tore Bjørgo (Boston: Northeastern University Press, 1998), 231–58.

4. See, for example, Greg McCracken, "Ex-White Supremacists Come Out against Crimes," *Billings (Mont.) Gazette,* January 6, 1994; see also Decker and Lauritsen, "Breaking the Bonds of Membership."

APPENDIX 1: RACIST GROUPS

1. An excellent, succinct description of racist Odinism is found in Jeffrey Kaplan, "Right Wing Violence in North America," in *Terror from the Extreme Right,* ed. Tore Bjørgo (London: Frank Cass, 1995), 44–95; see also Jeffrey Kaplan, *Radical Religion in America: Millenarian Movements from the Far Right to the Children of Noah* (Syracuse, N.Y.: Syracuse University Press, 1997).

2. See, for example, the description of a cross burning performed by a U.S. Klan/Nazi leader outside Berlin in Ingo Hasselbach with Tom Reiss, *Führer-Ex: Memoirs of a Former Neo-Nazi* (New York: Random House, 1996), 211; on the interplay of domestic and foreign groups more generally, see Leonard Weinberg, "An Overview of Right-Wing Extremism in the Western World: A Study of Convergence, Linkage, and Identity," in *Nation and Race: The Developing Euro-American Racist Subculture,* ed. Jeffrey Kaplan and Tore Bjørgo (Boston: Northeastern University Press, 1988), 3–33.

3. Flyer (no identifying information given, ca. 1994).

4. See Jack Moore, *Skinheads Shaved for Battle: A Cultural History of American Skinheads* (Bowling Green, Ohio: Bowling Green University Popular Press, 1993); Mark S. Hamm, *American Skinheads: The Criminology and Control of Hate Crimes* (Westport, Conn.: Praeger, 1994); Loren Christensen, *Skinhead Street Gangs* (Boulder, Colo.: Paladin Press, 1994); Stephen Baron, "The Canadian West Coast Punk Subculture: A Field Study," *Canadian Journal of Sociology* 14 (1989): 289–316.

5. In *The Politics of Righteousness: Idaho Christian Patriotism* (Seattle: University of Washington Press, 1990), James Aho discusses adherents who embrace a nonracist version of Christian Identity, but none of my interviewees did.

6. Kaplan, "Right Wing Violence," 52.

7. The definitive work on Christian Identity is Michael Barkun, *Religion and the Racist Right: The Origins of the Christian Identity Movement* (Chapel Hill: University of North Carolina Press, 1994).

8. A very useful overview of the call for a reformed, revolutionary "Fifth Era Klan" is found in Kaplan, "Right Wing Violence," 47–50.

APPENDIX 2: METHODOLOGY

1. The best examples of studies of members of racist groups are James Aho, *The Politics of Righteousness: Idaho Christian Patriotism* (Seattle: University of

Washington Press, 1990), and Raphael S. Ezekiel, *The Racist Mind: Portraits of American Neo-Nazis and Klansmen* (New York: Viking, 1995).

2. Lists of contemporary racist groups exist in the Wilcox Collection, Kenneth Spencer Research Library, the University of Kansas, Lawrence; but because many groups are ephemeral and constantly relocate to evade authorities, any list is outdated almost as soon as it is published.

3. Because racist groups change their names and memberships very quickly, it is impossible to tell exactly how many distinct groups are represented in this list.

4. Some groups are represented by more than one interviewee; thus published statistics in Kathleen M. Blee, "Becoming a Racist: Women in Contemporary Ku Klux Klan and Neo-Nazi Groups," *Gender and Society* 10 (1996): 680–702, on the geographical distribution of *respondents* differ from these figures on *groups*.

5. "Racists Seek to Form White Homeland in the Northwest," *Albany (Ore.) Democrat-Herald*, June 12, 1985.

6. Jeffrey Kaplan, "Right Wing Violence in North America," in *Terror from the Extreme Right*, ed. Tore Bjørgo (London: Frank Cass, 1995), 46.

7. For a discussion of the complicated ethical issues that surround issues of confidentiality and criminal sanctions in fieldwork with racist activists, see Kathleen M. Blee, "From the Field to the Courthouse: The Perils of Privilege," *Law and Social Inquiry* 24 (1999): 401–5. See also Kathleen M. Blee, "Evidence, Empathy, and Ethics: Lessons from Oral Histories of the Klan," *Journal of American History* 80 (1993): 596–606.

8. See Ezekiel, *Racist Mind,* 315. For studies that rely primarily on racist literature, see, for example, Jessie Daniels, *White Lies: Race, Class, Gender, and Sexuality in White Supremacist Discourse* (New York: Routledge, 1997), and Abby L. Ferber, *White Man Falling: Race, Gender, and White Supremacy* (Lanham, Md.: Rowman and Littlefield, 1998).

9. Tore Bjørgo, "Role of the Media in Racist Violence," in *Racist Violence in Europe,* ed. Tore Bjørgo and Rob White (New York: St. Martin's, 1993), 96–112.

10. Aho, *Politics of Righteousness.*

11. Janet Hart, "Cracking the Code: Narrative and Political Mobilization in the Greek Resistance," *Social Science History* 16 (1992): 634. See also Janet Hart, "Women in the Greek Resistance: National Crisis and Political Transformation," *International Labor and Working-Class History,* no. 38 (fall 1990): 46–62; Janet Hart, "Redeeming the Voices of a 'Sacrificed Generation': Oral Histories of Women in the Greek Resistance," *International Journal of Oral History* 10.1 (1990): 3–30. On the construction of life stories, see Carole Cain, "Personal Stories: Identity Acquisition and Self-Understanding in Alcoholics Anonymous," *Ethos* 19 (1991): 210–53; Faye Ginsburg, "Dissonance and Harmony: The Symbolic Function of Abortion in Activists' Life Stories," in *Interpreting Women's Lives: Feminist Theory and Personal Narrative,* ed. Personal Narratives Group (Bloomington: Indiana University Press, 1989), 59–84; and Diana Gittins, "Oral History, Reliability, and Recollection," in *The Recall Method in Social Surveys,* ed. Louis Moss and Harvey Goldstein (London: Uni-

versity of London Institute of Education, 1979), 82–99, esp. 92. On the narration of ideology, see Miriam A. Golden, "Historical Memory and Ideological Orientations in the Italian Workers' Movement," *Politics and Society* 16 (1988): 1–34.

12. Margaret Somers, "The Narrative Constitution of Identity: A Relational and Network Approach," *Theory and Society* 23 (1994): 606. See also Jerome Bruner, "The Narrative Construction of Reality," *Critical Inquiry* 18 (1991): 1–21, and Verta Taylor and Nancy Whittier, "Theoretical Approaches to Social Movement Culture," paper presented at the American Sociological Association's Workshop on Culture and Social Movements, San Diego, August 1992.

13. Jonathan Potter and Margaret Wetherell, "Accomplishing Attitudes: Fact and Evaluation in Racist Discourse," *Text* 8.1–2 (1988): 51–68, and Margaret Wetherell and Jonathan Potter, *Mapping the Language of Racism: Discourse and the Legitimation of Exploitation* (New York: Columbia University Press, 1992). See also Jonathan Potter, "Attitudes, Social Representations, and Discursive Psychology," in *Identities, Groups and Social Issues,* ed. Margaret Wetherell (London: Sage, 1996), 119–73, and Paul Thompson, "Life Histories and the Analysis of Social Change," in *Biography and Society: The Life History Approach in the Social Sciences,* ed. Daniel Bertaux (Beverly Hills, Calif.: Sage, 1981), 289–306. On narrative coherence, see Marjorie DeVault, "Ethnicity and Expertise: Racial-Ethnic Knowledge in Sociological Research," *Gender and Society* 9 (1995): 612–31.

14. Here, I disagree with Betty A. Dobratz and Stephanie L. Shanks-Meile, who, in *"White Power, White Pride!": The White Separatist Movement in the United States* (New York: Twayne, 1997), characterize much of the modern racist movement as separatist.

15. A very useful discussion of explanation through a "narrativized sequence" of events is found in Larry Isaac, "Transforming Localities: Reflections on Time, Causality, and Narrative in Contemporary Historical Sociology," *Historical Methods* 30.1 (1997): 4–12. See also the discussion of linking personal and social experiences in life stories in Faye Ginsburg, "Procreation Stories: Reproduction, Nurturance, and Procreation in Life Narratives of Abortion Activists," *American Ethnologist* 14 (1987): 626, and Molly Andrews, *Lifetimes of Commitment: Aging, Politics, Psychology* (Cambridge: Cambridge University Press, 1991).

16. In "Social Movement Continuity: The Women's Movement in Abeyance" (*American Sociological Review* 54 [1989]: 761–75), Verta Taylor similarly emphasizes the concept of "abeyance structures" in social movements, though my focus is on the individual's participation rather than the movement's continuity.

17. How life histories, too, can be influenced by "collective clichés" is discussed in Donatella della Porta, "Life Histories in the Analysis of Social Movement Activists," in *Studying Collective Action,* ed. Mario Diani and Ron Eyerman (London: Sage, 1992), 181.

18. Ezekiel, *Racist Mind,* 24.

19. Janet Finch argues that women are more forthcoming respondents, especially for women interviewers, because they have more experience in being

questioned about their lives; see "'It's Great to Have Someone to Talk To': The Ethics and Politics of Interviewing Women," in *Social Researching: Politics, Problems, Practice,* ed. Colin Bell and Helen Roberts (London: Routledge and Kegan Paul, 1984), 70–87. However, Catherine Kohler Reissman cautions that rapport between women is not sufficient to create a sense of shared meanings; see "When Gender Is Not Enough: Women Interviewing Women," *Gender and Society* 1 (1987): 172–207.

BIBLIOGRAPHY

This book draws on a number of written sources, including materials published or distributed by racist groups. Below, I list the main racist group periodicals analyzed in this study. Some are available at the Special Collections, Howard-Tilton Memorial Library, Tulane University, New Orleans; the Wilcox Collection, Kenneth Spencer Research Library, University of Kansas, Lawrence; or the Anti-Defamation League of B'nai B'rith, New York. Many I collected personally. The bibliography does not list the innumerable pamphlets, books, flyers, music tapes, videos, and other materials by racist groups or the many articles from mainstream newspapers consulted in this research.

SELECTED PERIODICALS BY RACIST GROUPS

!!Agitate!!
All the Way: The Fighting Journal of the Nationalist Movement
ANP [American Nationalist Party] Bulletin
ARI Reports
Aryan Action Line
Aryan Mothers Inspiring Something Hopeful (AMISH) Newsletter
Aryan Research Fellowship Newsletter
A.W.L. [Aryan Women's League] Newsletter
AWNP [American White Nationalist Party] Bulletin
The Berserker: Revolutionary Voice of the New York SS Brigade
Blood and Honor
Calling Our Nation
The Confederacy

Confederate Underground
The Cornerstone
EAEA [European American Education Association] Newsletter
International NS [National Socialist] Mobilizer
Jubilee Magazine
The Keystone American
NAAWP [National Association for the Advancement of White People] News
National Socialist Bulletin
The New Order
Northwest Imperative
NS [National Socialist] Graphics
NS [National Socialist] Kampfruf
NSV [National Socialist Vanguard] Report
NSWPP [National Socialist White People's Party] Resistance
"On Guard!"
Plexus/International Union of National Socialists
Race and Nation
Race and Reason
RAHOWA [Racial Holy War] News
The Rational Feminist
Resistance
Right as Reina
Scriptures for America
Scriptures Holy Bible Newsletter
Sigrdrifa
The Stormtrooper
The Struggle: The Revolutionary Voice of the National Socialist White Americans' Party
Valkyrie Voice
Viking Viewpoint: Truth and Honor
Voice of Revolution!
WAR [White Aryan Resistance]
The War Eagle: A Voice and Forum for Revolutionary Pan-Aryanism
We Are the Law
White Patriot
White Power: The Revolutionary Voice of National Socialism
White Raven
White Sisters
World Service Library

BOOKS, ARTICLES, AND DISSERTATIONS

Abel, Theodore. *Why Hitler Came to Power: An Answer Based in the Original Life Stories of 600 of His Followers.* New York: Prentice-Hall, 1938.

Achordate, William. "The Values of Fascism." *Journal of Social Issues* 24 (1968): 89–104.

Adorno, Theodor, et al. *The Authoritarian Personality*. 1950; reprint, New York: W. W. Norton, 1969.

Aho, James. *The Politics of Righteousness: Idaho Christian Patriotism*. Seattle: University of Washington Press, 1990.

———. *This Thing of Darkness: A Sociology of the Enemy*. Seattle: University of Washington Press, 1994.

Almaguer, Tomás. *Racial Fault Lines: The Historical Origins of White Supremacy in California*. Berkeley: University of California Press, 1994.

Anderson, Benedict. *Imagined Communities: Reflections on the Origin and Spread of Nationalism*. Rev. ed. London: Verso, 1991.

Andrews, Molly. *Lifetimes of Commitment: Aging, Politics, Psychology*. Cambridge: Cambridge University Press, 1991.

Anthony, Dick, and Thomas Robbins. "Religious Totalism, Violence, and Exemplary Dualism: Beyond the Extrinsic Model." In *Millennialism and Violence*, ed. Michael Barkun, 10–50. London: Frank Cass, 1996.

Arendt, Hannah. *Eichmann in Jerusalem: A Report on the Banality of Evil*. New York: Viking, 1965.

Bacchetta, Paola. "Communal Property/Sexual Property: On Representations of Muslim Women in a Hindu Nationalist Discourse." In *Forging Identities: Gender, Communities, and the State in India*, ed. Zoya Hasan, 188–225. Boulder, Colo.: Westview, 1994.

Back, Les, Michael Keith, and John Solomos. "Racism on the Internet: Mapping Neo-Fascist Subcultures in Cyberspace." In *Nation and Race: The Developing Euro-American Racist Subculture*, ed. Jeffrey Kaplan and Tore Bjørgo, 73–101. Boston: Northeastern University Press, 1998.

Balibar, Etienne. "Racism and Nationalism." In *Race, Nation, Class: Ambiguous Identities*, ed. Etienne Balibar and Immanuel Wallerstein, trans. Chris Turner, 37–65. London: Verso, 1991.

Bandura, Albert. "The Psychology of Chance Encounters and Life Paths." *American Psychologist* 37 (1982): 747–55.

Barkun, Michael. "Conspiracy Theories as Stigmatized Knowledge: The Basis for a New Age Racism?" In *Nation and Race: The Developing Euro-American Racist Subculture*, ed. Jeffrey Kaplan and Tore Bjørgo, 58–72. Boston: Northeastern University Press, 1998.

———. "Introduction: Understanding Millennialism." In *Millennialism and Violence*, ed. Michael Barkun, 1–9. London: Frank Cass, 1996.

———. *Religion and the Racist Right: The Origins of the Christian Identity Movement*. Chapel Hill: University of North Carolina Press, 1994.

Baron, Stephen. "The Canadian West Coast Punk Subculture: A Field Study." *Canadian Journal of Sociology* 14 (1989): 289–316.

Bearman, Peter, and Katherine Stovel. "Becoming a Nazi: Models of Identity Formation." Paper presented at the annual meeting of the American Sociological Association, Miami, August 1993.

Beisel, Nicola. *Imperiled Innocents: Anthony Comstock and Family Reproduction in Victorian America*. Princeton: Princeton University Press, 1997.

Bell, Daniel. "The Dispossessed." In *The Radical Right,* ed. Daniel Bell, 1–45. New York: Anchor, 1964.

Benfer, Amy. "Salon Mothers Who Think: Nazi Family Values." *Salon. com,* July 15, 1999 ⟨http://www.salon.com/mwt/hot/1999/07/15/aryan_ compound/index.html⟩ (accessed January 2001).

Bennett, David. *The Party of Fear: From Nativist Movements to the New Right in American History.* Chapel Hill: University of North Carolina Press, 1988.

Ben-Sasso, H. H. *A History of the Jewish People.* Cambridge, Mass.: Harvard University Press, 1976.

Beoku-Betts, Josephine. "When Black Is Not Enough: Doing Field Research among Gullah Women." *NWSA Journal* 6 (1994): 413–33.

Berbrier, Mitch. "'Half the Battle': Cultural Resonance, Framing Processes, and Ethnic Affectations in Contemporary White Supremacist Rhetoric." *Social Problems* 45 (1998): 431–50.

Berezin, Mabel. *Making the Fascist Self: The Political Culture of Interwar Italy.* Ithaca, N.Y.: Cornell University Press, 1997.

Berik, Günseli. "Understanding the Gender System in Rural Turkey: Fieldwork Dilemmas of Conforming and Intervention." In *Feminist Dilemmas in Field- work,* ed. Diane L. Wolf, 56–71. Boulder, Colo.: Westview, 1996.

Berkhofer, Robert F. *The White Man's Indian: Images of the American Indian from Columbus to the Present.* New York: Alfred A. Knopf, 1978.

Berlet, Chip. "Dances with Devils: How Apocalyptic and Millennialist Themes Influence Right-Wing Scapegoating and Conspiracism." *Public Eye: A Pub- lication of Political Research Associates* 7.2/3 (1998).

Betz, Hans-Georg. *Radical Right-Wing Populism in Western Europe.* New York: St. Martin's, 1994.

Bhavnani, Kum-Kum. "Empowerment and Social Research: Some Comments." *Text* 8.1–2 (1988): 41–50.

Billig, Michael. *Fascists: A Social Psychological View of the National Front.* London: Academic Press, 1978.

———. "Humor and Hatred: The Racist Jokes of the Ku Klux Klan." *Discourse and Society* 12 (2001): 291–313.

———. "Imagining Nationhood." In *Social Movements and Culture,* ed. Hank Johnston and Bert Klandermans, 64–81. Minneapolis: University of Min- nesota Press, 1995.

———. "The Notion of 'Prejudice': Some Rhetorical and Ideological Aspects." *Text* 8.1–2 (1988): 91–110.

Billings, Dwight B., and Kathleen M. Blee. *The Road to Poverty: The Making of Wealth and Hardship in Appalachia.* New York: Cambridge University Press, 2000.

Bjørgo, Tore. "Entry, Bridge-Building, and Exit Options: What Happens to Young People Who Join Racist Groups—and Want to Leave?" In *Nation and Race: The Developing Euro-American Racist Subculture,* ed. Jeffrey Kaplan and Tore Bjørgo, 231–58. Boston: Northeastern University Press, 1998.

———. Introduction to *Terror from the Extreme Right,* ed. Tore Bjørgo, 1–16. London: Frank Cass, 1995.

————. "Role of the Media in Racist Violence." In *Racist Violence in Europe*, ed. Tore Bjørgo and Rob White, 96–112. New York: St. Martin's, 1993.

Blazak, Randy. "The Suburbanization of Hate: An Ethnographic Study of the Skinhead Culture." Ph.D. diss., Emory University, 1995.

Blee, Kathleen M. "Becoming a Racist: Women in Contemporary Ku Klux Klan and Neo-Nazi Groups." *Gender and Society* 10 (1996): 680–702.

————. "Evidence, Empathy, and Ethics: Lessons from Oral Histories of the Klan." *Journal of American History* 80 (1993): 596–606.

————. "Family Patterns and the Politicization of Consumption Relations." *Sociological Spectrum* 5 (1985): 295–316.

————. "From the Field to the Courthouse: The Perils of Privilege." *Law and Social Inquiry* 24 (1999): 401–5.

————. *Women of the Klan: Racism and Gender in the 1920s*. Berkeley: University of California Press, 1991.

Bonnell, Victoria E. "The Peasant Woman in Stalinist Political Art of the 1930s." *American Historical Review* 98 (1993): 55–82.

Borland, Katherine. "'That's Not What I Said': Interpretive Conflict in Oral Narrative Research." In *Women's Words: The Feminist Practice of Oral History*, ed. Sherna Berger Gluck and Daphne Patai, 63–75. New York: Routledge, 1991.

Braungart, Richard G., and Margaret M. Braungart. "From Protest to Terrorism: The Case of SDS and the Weathermen." In *International Social Movement Research*, vol. 4, *Social Movements and Violence: Participation in Underground Organizations*, ed. Donatella della Porta, 45–78. London: JAI Press, 1992.

Breinlinger, Sara. *The Social Psychology of Collective Action: Identity, Injustice, and Gender*. London: Taylor and Francis, 1996.

Brereton, Virginia Lieson. *From Sin to Salvation: Stories of Women's Conversion, 1800 to the Present*. Bloomington: Indiana University Press, 1991.

Brewer, J. D. "Sensitivity as a Problem in Field Research: A Study of Routine Policing in Northern Ireland." In *Researching Sensitive Topics*, ed. Claire M. Renzetti and Raymond M. Lee, 125–45. Newbury Park, Calif.: Sage, 1993.

Brinkley, Alan. "The Problem of American Conservatism." Paper presented at the annual meeting of the Organization of American Historians, Anaheim, Calif., May 1993.

Brodkin, Karen. *How Jews Became White Folks and What That Says about Race in America*. New Brunswick, N.J.: Rutgers University Press, 1998.

Bruner, Edward, and Phyllis Gorfain. "Dialogic Narration and the Paradoxes of Masada." In *Text, Play, and Story: The Construction and Reconstruction of Self and Society*, ed. Stuart Plattner, 56–79. Washington, D.C.: American Ethnological Society, 1984.

Bruner, Jerome. "The Narrative Construction of Reality." *Critical Inquiry* 18 (1991): 1–21.

Brustein, William. *The Logic of Evil: The Social Origins of the Nazi Party, 1925–1933*. New Haven: Yale University Press, 1996.

————. "The 'Red Menace' and the Rise of Italian Fascism." *American Sociological Review* 56 (1991): 652–64.

Brustein, William, and Barry Markovsky. "The Rational Fascist: Interwar Fascist Party Membership in Italy and Germany." *Journal of Political and Military Sociology* 17 (1989): 177–202.

Buhmann, Elizabeth T. "Rethinking the Problem of Girls in Gangs." Unpublished paper, Office of the Attorney General of the State of Texas, Austin, 1992.

Burghart, Devin, ed. *Soundtracks to the White Revolution: White Supremacist Assaults on Youth Music Subcultures.* Chicago: Center for New Community, 1999.

Burkitt, Ian. "Social Relationships and Emotions." *Sociology* 31 (1997): 37–55.

Cain, Carole. "Personal Stories: Identity Acquisition and Self-Understanding in Alcoholics Anonymous." *Ethos* 19 (1991): 210–53.

Campbell, Anne. "Self-Definition by Rejection: The Case of Gang Girls." *Social Problems* 34 (1987): 451–66.

Carter, Dan T. *The Politics of Rage: George Wallace, the Origins of the New Conservatism, and the Transformation of American Politics.* New York: Simon and Schuster, 1995.

Chalmers, David M. *Hooded Americanism: The History of the Ku Klux Klan.* Durham, N.C.: Duke University Press, 1981.

Chesler, Mark, and Richard Schmuch. "Participant Observation in a Super-Patriot Discussion Group." *Journal of Social Issues* 19 (1963): 18–30.

Chesney-Lind, Meda, Randall G. Shelden, and Karen A. Joe. "Girls, Delinquency, and Gang Membership." In *Gangs in America*, ed. C. Ronald Huff, 185–204. 2nd ed. Thousand Oaks, Calif.: Sage, 1996.

Chideya, Farai. "Women Who Love to Hate." *Mademoiselle*, August 1994, 134–37, 186.

Christensen, Loren. *Skinhead Street Gangs.* Boulder, Colo.: Paladin Press, 1994.

Clawson, Mary Ann. *Constructing Brotherhood: Class, Gender, and Fraternalism.* Princeton: Princeton University Press, 1989.

Cochran, Floyd. "Sisterhood of Hate." Privately published pamphlet, 1993. Posted at ⟨http://www.evnetwork.org/sister.html⟩ (accessed January 2001).

Cochrane, Raymond, and Michael Billig. "I'm Not National Front Myself, But . . ." *New Society* 17 (1984): 255–58.

Condor, Susan. "'Race Stereotypes' and Racist Discourse." *Text* 8.1–2 (1988): 69–91.

Connell, Robert. *Gender and Power: Society, the Person, and Sexual Politics.* Stanford: Stanford University Press, 1987.

———. *Masculinities.* Berkeley: University of California Press, 1995.

Conover, Pamela, and Virginia Gray. *Feminism and the New Right: Conflict over the American Family.* Westport, Conn.: Praeger, 1984.

Coppola, Vincent. *Dragons of God: A Journey through Far-Right America.* Atlanta: Longstreet, 1996.

Cott, Nancy F. "What's in a Name? The Limits of 'Social Feminism'; or, Expanding the Vocabulary of Women's History." *Journal of American History* 76 (1989): 809–29.

Crenshaw, Martha. "Theories of Terrorism: Instrumental and Organizational

Approaches." In *Inside Terrorist Organizations,* ed. David C. Rapoport, 13–31. New York: Columbia University Press, 1988.

Daniels, Jessie. *White Lies: Race, Class, Gender, and Sexuality in White Supremacist Discourse.* New York: Routledge, 1997.

Decker, Scott H., and Janet L. Lauritsen. "Breaking the Bonds of Membership: Leaving the Gang." In *Gangs in America,* ed. C. Ronald Huff, 103–22. Thousand Oaks, Calif.: Sage, 1996.

de Grazia, Victoria. *How Fascism Ruled Women: Italy, 1922–1945.* Berkeley: University of California Press, 1992.

Dekker, Rudolf M. "Women in Revolt." *Theory and Society* 16 (1987): 337–62.

della Porta, Donatella. "Life Histories in the Analysis of Social Movement Activists." In *Studying Collective Action,* ed. Mario Diani and Ron Eyerman, 168–93. London: Sage, 1992.

———. "Political Socialization in Left-Wing Underground Organizations: Biographies of Italian and German Militants." In *International Social Movement Research,* vol. 4, *Social Movements and Violence: Participation in Underground Organizations,* ed. Donatella della Porta, 259–90. London: JAI Press, 1992.

———. *Social Movements, Political Violence, and the State: A Comparative Analysis of Italy and Germany.* Cambridge: Cambridge University Press, 1995.

DeVault, Marjorie. "Ethnicity and Expertise: Racial-Ethnic Knowledge in Sociological Research." *Gender and Society* 9 (1995): 612–31.

di Leonardo, Micaela. "Habits of the Cumbered Heart: Ethnic Community and Women's Culture as American Invented Traditions." In *Golden Ages, Dark Ages: Imagining the Past in Anthropology and History,* ed. Jay O'Brien and William Roseberry, 234–52. Berkeley: University of California Press, 1991.

Dobie, Kathy. "Long Day's Journey into White." *Village Voice,* April 28, 1992, 22–32.

———. "Skingirl Mothers: From Thelma and Louise to Ozzie and Harriet." In *The Politics of Motherhood: Activist Voices from Left to Right,* ed. Alexis Jetter, Annelise Orleck, and Diana Taylor, 257–67. Hanover, N.H.: University Press of New England, 1997.

Dobratz, Betty A. "The White Separatist Movement in the U.S.: A Look at Their Ideology." Paper presented at the annual meeting of the American Sociological Association, Toronto, August 1997.

Dobratz, Betty A., and Stephanie L. Shanks-Meile. *"White Power, White Pride!": The White Separatist Movement in the United States.* New York: Twayne, 1997.

Durham, Martin. *Women and Fascism.* London: Routledge, 1998.

———. "Women and the British Extreme Right." In *The Far Right in Western and Eastern Europe,* ed. Luciano Cheles, Ronnie Ferguson, and Michalina Vaughan, 272–89. 2nd ed. New York: Longman, 1995.

Edgar, David. "Racism, Fascism, and the Politics of the National Front." *Race and Class* 19 (1977): 111–31.

Edwards, Rosalind. "Connecting Method and Epistemology: A White Woman Interviewing Black Women." *Women's Studies International Forum* 13 (1990): 477–90.

———. "An Education in Interviewing: Placing the Researcher and the Research." In *Researching Sensitive Topics,* ed. Claire M. Renzetti and Raymond M. Lee, 181–96. Newbury Park, Calif.: Sage, 1993.

Einerson, Martha J. "Fame, Fortune, and Failure: Young Girls' Moral Language Surrounding Popular Culture." *Youth and Society* 30.2 (1998): 241–57.

———. "Female Preadolescent Interpretations of Popular Music Experience: An Interpersonal Perspective." Ph.D. diss., University of Kentucky, 1993.

Ellis, Carolyn. "Emotional and Ethical Quagmires in Returning to the Field." *Journal of Contemporary Ethnography* 24 (1995): 68–98.

Essed, Philomena. *Understanding Everyday Racism: An Interdisciplinary Theory.* Newbury Park, Calif.: Sage, 1991.

Esseveld, Johanna, and Ron Eyerman. "Which Side Are You On? Reflections on Methodological Issues in the Study of 'Distasteful' Social Movements." In *Studying Collective Action,* ed. Mario Diani and Ron Eyerman, 217–37. London: Sage, 1992.

Ewing, Patricia, and Susan S. Silbey. "Subversive Stories and Hegemonic Tales: Toward a Sociology of Narrative." *Law and Society Review* 29 (1995): 197–226.

Ezekiel, Raphael S. *The Racist Mind: Portraits of American Neo-Nazis and Klansmen.* New York: Viking, 1995.

Fangen, Katrine. "Living Out Our Ethnic Instincts: Ideological Beliefs among Right-Wing Activists in Norway." In *Nation and Race: The Developing Euro-American Racist Subculture,* ed. Jeffrey Kaplan and Tore Bjørgo, 202–30. Boston: Northeastern University Press, 1998.

Ferber, Abby L. "Of Mongrels and Jews: The Deconstruction of Racialized Identities in White Supremacist Discourse." *Social Identities* 3.2 (1997): 193–208.

———. *White Man Falling: Race, Gender, and White Supremacy.* Lanham, Md.: Rowman and Littlefield, 1998.

Ferree, Myra M. "The Political Context of Rationality: Rational Choice Theory and Resource Mobilization." In *Frontiers in Social Movement Theory,* ed. Aldon D. Morris and Carol M. Mueller, 29–52. New Haven: Yale University Press, 1992.

Field, Geoffrey G. "Nordic Racism." *Journal of the History of Ideas* 38 (1977): 523–40.

Fielding, Nigel G. "Mediating the Message: Affinity and Hostility in Research on Sensitive Topics." In *Researching Sensitive Topics,* ed. Claire M. Renzetti and Raymond M. Lee, 146–80. Newbury Park, Calif.: Sage, 1993.

———. *The National Front.* London: Routledge and Kegan Paul, 1981.

———. "Observational Research on the National Front." In *Social Research Ethics: An Examination of the Merits of Covert Participant Observation,* ed. Martin Blumer, 80–104. London: Macmillan, 1982.

Fields, Barbara J. "Ideology and Race in American History." In *Region, Race, and Reconstruction,* ed. D. Morgan Kousser and James M. McPherson, 143–77. New York: Oxford University Press, 1982.

Finch, Janet. " 'It's Great to Have Someone to Talk To': The Ethics and Politics of Interviewing Women." In *Social Researching: Politics, Problems, Practice,* ed. Colin Bell and Helen Roberts, 70–87. London: Routledge and Kegan Paul, 1984.

Fine, Gary Alan. "Public Narration and Group Culture." In *Social Movements and Culture,* ed. Hank Johnston and Bert Klandermans, 127–43. Minneapolis: University of Minnesota Press, 1995.

Finkelstein, Norman G., and Rut Bettina Birn. *A Nation on Trial: The Goldhagen Thesis and Historical Truth.* New York: Henry Holt, 1998.

Flynn, Kevin, and Gary Gerhardt. *The Silent Brotherhood: Inside America's Racist Underground.* New York: Signet/Penguin, 1990.

Formisano, Ronald P. *Boston against Busing: Race, Class, and Ethnicity in the 1960s and 1970s.* Chapel Hill: University of North Carolina Press, 1991.

Frank, Dana. *Purchasing Power: Consumer Organizing, Gender, and the Seattle Labor Movement, 1919–1929.* New York: Cambridge University Press, 1994.

Frankenberg, Ruth. *White Women, Race Matters: The Social Construction of Whiteness.* Minneapolis: University of Minnesota Press, 1993.

Frye, Marilyn. "On Being White: Thinking toward a Feminist Understanding of Race and Race Supremacy." In *The Politics of Reality: Essays in Feminist Theory,* 110–27. Trumansburg, N.Y.: Crossing Press, 1983.

Gamson, Joshua. *Freaks Talk Back: Tabloid Talk Shows and Sexual Nonconformity.* Chicago: University of Chicago Press, 1998.

Gamson, William A. "Constructing Social Protest." In *Social Movements and Culture,* ed. Hank Johnston and Bert Klandermans, 85–106. Minneapolis: University of Minnesota Press, 1995.

———. *Talking Politics.* New York: Cambridge University Press, 1992.

Georges-Abeyie, Daniel E. "Women as Terrorists." In *Perspectives on Terrorism,* ed. Lawrence Zelie Freeman and Yonah Alexander, 71–84. Wilmington, Del.: Scholarly Resources, 1983.

Gibson, James William. *Warrior Dreams : Paramilitary Culture in Post-Vietnam America.* New York: Hill and Wang, 1994.

Gilman, Sander L. *Difference and Pathology: Stereotypes of Sexuality, Race, and Madness.* Ithaca, N.Y.: Cornell University Press, 1985.

Gilmore, Glenda Elizabeth. *Gender and Jim Crow: Women and the Politics of White Supremacy in North Carolina, 1896–1920.* Chapel Hill: University of North Carolina Press, 1996.

Gilroy, Paul. *The Black Atlantic: Modernity and Double Consciousness.* Cambridge, Mass.: Harvard University Press, 1993.

———. "One Nation under a Groove: The Cultural Politics of 'Race' and Racism in Britain." In *Anatomy of Racism,* ed. David Theo Goldberg, 263–82. Minneapolis: University of Minnesota Press, 1990.

———. *"There Ain't No Black in the Union Jack": The Cultural Politics of Race and Nation.* Chicago: University of Chicago Press, 1991.

Ginsburg, Faye. "Dissonance and Harmony: The Symbolic Function of Abortion in Activists' Life Stories." In *Interpreting Women's Lives: Feminist Theory and Personal Narrative,* ed. Personal Narratives Group, 59–84. Bloomington: Indiana University Press, 1989.

———. "Procreation Stories: Reproduction, Nurturance, and Procreation in Life Narratives of Abortion Activists." *American Ethnologist* 14 (1987): 623–36.

Gittins, Diana. "Oral History, Reliability, and Recollection." In *The Recall Method in Social Surveys,* ed. Louis Moss and Harvey Goldstein, 82–99. London: University of London Institute of Education, 1979.

Goffman, Erving. *The Presentation of Self in Everyday Life.* Garden City, N.Y.: Doubleday, 1959.

Goldberg, David Theo. *Racist Culture: Philosophy and the Politics of Meaning.* Cambridge, Mass.: Blackwell, 1993.

———, ed. *Anatomy of Racism.* Minneapolis: University of Minnesota Press, 1990.

Golden, Miriam A. "Historical Memory and Ideological Orientations in the Italian Workers' Movement." *Politics and Society* 16 (1988): 1–34.

Goldhagen, Daniel J. *Hitler's Willing Executioners: Germans and the Holocaust.* New York: Random House, 1996.

Goode, Erich. "The Ethics of Deception in Social Research: A Case Study." *Qualitative Sociology* 19 (1996): 11–33.

Groves, Julian M. "Learning to Feel: The Neglected Sociology of Social Movements." *Sociological Review* 43 (1995): 435–61.

Hagan, John, Hans Merkens, and Klaus Boehnke. "Delinquency and Disdain: Social Capital and the Control of Right-Wing Extremism among East and West Berlin Youth." *American Journal of Sociology* 100 (1995): 1028–52.

Hamm, Mark S. *American Skinheads: The Criminology and Control of Hate Crimes.* Westport, Conn.: Praeger, 1994.

Harding, Sandra, ed. *The "Racial" Economy of Science: Toward a Democratic Future.* Bloomington: Indiana University Press, 1993.

Harris, Cheryl I. "Whiteness as Property." *Harvard Law Review* 106 (1993): 1710–91.

Harris, Mary G. *Cholas: Latino Girls and Gangs.* New York: AMS Press, 1988.

Hart, Janet. "Cracking the Code: Narrative and Political Mobilization in the Greek Resistance." *Social Science History* 16 (1992): 631–68.

———. "Redeeming the Voices of a 'Sacrificed Generation': Oral Histories of Women in the Greek Resistance." *International Journal of Oral History* 10 (1990): 3–30.

———. "Women in the Greek Resistance: National Crisis and Political Transformation." *International Labor and Working-Class History,* no. 38 (fall 1990): 46–62.

Hasselbach, Ingo, with Tom Reiss. *Führer-Ex: Memoirs of a Former Neo-Nazi.* New York: Random House, 1996.

Healy, Murray. *Gay Skins: Class, Masculinity, and Queer Appropriation.* London: Cassell, 1996.

Heirich, Max. "Change of Heart: A Test of Some Widely Held Theories about Religious Conversion." *American Journal of Sociology* 83 (1977): 673–75.

Heitmeyer, Wilhelm. "Hostility and Violence towards Foreigners in Germany." In *Racist Violence in Europe,* ed. Tore Bjørgo and Rob White, 17–28. New York: St. Martin's, 1993.

Helleiner, Jane. "'Women of the Itinerant Class': Gender and Anti-Traveller Racism in Ireland." *Women's Studies International Forum* 20 (1997): 275–87.

Higginbotham, Evelyn Brooks. "African-American Women's History and the Metalanguage of Race." *Signs* 17 (1992): 251–74.

Himmelstein, Jerome. "All But Sleeping with the Enemy." Paper presented at the annual meeting of the American Sociological Association, San Francisco, August 1998.

Hobsbawm, Eric, and Terence Ranger. *The Invention of Tradition.* New York: Cambridge University Press, 1985.

Hochschild, Arlie. *The Managed Heart: Commercialization of Human Feeling.* Berkeley: University of California Press, 1983.

Hockenos, Paul. *Free to Hate: The Rise of the Right in Post-Communist Eastern Europe.* New York: Routledge, 1993.

Hofstadter, Richard. *The Paranoid Style in American Politics.* New York: Alfred A. Knopf, 1966.

"Homophobia and the Christian Right." *Dignity Report* 6.1 (spring 1999). Published by the Coalition for Human Dignity, Seattle.

Hurtado, Aída, and Abigail J. Stewart. "Through the Looking Glass: Implications of Studying Whiteness for Feminist Methods." Unpublished photocopy, n.d.

Ignatiev, Noel. *How the Irish Became White.* New York: Routledge, 1995.

Isaac, Larry. "Transforming Localities: Reflections on Time, Causality, and Narrative in Contemporary Historical Sociology." *Historical Methods* 30 (1997): 4–12.

Jackman, Mary R. "Individualism, Self-Interest, and White Racism." *Social Science Quarterly* 77 (1996): 760–67.

Jacobs, Jane. "The Economy of Love in Religious Commitment: The Deconversion of Women from Nontraditional Religious Movements." *Journal for the Scientific Study of Religion* 23 (1984): 155–71.

Jankowski, Martín Sánchez. *Islands in the Street: Gangs and American Urban Society.* Berkeley: University of California Press, 1991.

Jasper, James M. "The Emotion of Protest: Affective and Reactive Emotions in and around Social Movements." *Sociological Forum* 13 (1998): 397–424.

Jeansonne, Glen. *Women of the Far Right: The Mother's Movement and World War II.* Chicago: University of Chicago Press, 1996.

Jenkins, Philip. *Hoods and Shirts: The Extreme Right in Pennsylvania, 1925–1950.* Chapel Hill: University of North Carolina Press, 1997.

Jetter, Alexis, Annelise Orleck, and Diana Taylor, eds. *The Politics of Motherhood: Activist Voices from Left to Right.* Hanover, N.H.: University Press of New England, 1997.

Joe, Karen A., and Meda Chesney-Lind. "'Just Every Mother's Angel': An Analysis of Gender and Ethnic Variations in Youth Gang Membership." *Gender and Society* 9 (1995): 408–31.

Johnston, Hank. "New Social Movements and Old Regional Nationalisms." In *New Social Movements: From Ideology to Identity*, ed. Enrique Laraña, Hank Johnston, and Joseph R. Gusfield, 267–86. Philadelphia: Temple University Press, 1994.

———. *Tales of Nationalism: Catalonia, 1939–79.* New Brunswick, N.J.: Rutgers University Press, 1991.

Johnston, Hank, and Bert Klandermans. "The Cultural Analysis of Social Movements." In *Social Movements and Culture*, ed. Hank Johnston and Bert Klandermans, 3–24. Minneapolis: University of Minnesota Press, 1995.

Johnston, Hank, Enrique Laraña, and Joseph R. Gusfield. "Identities, Grievances, and New Social Movements." In *New Social Movements: From Ideology to Identity*, ed. Enrique Laraña, Hank Johnston, and Joseph Gusfield, 3–35. Philadelphia: Temple University Press, 1994.

Kaplan, Jeffrey. *Radical Religion in America: Millenarian Movements from the Far Right to the Children of Noah.* Syracuse, N.Y.: Syracuse University Press, 1997.

———. "Right Wing Violence in North America." In *Terror from the Extreme Right*, ed. Tore Bjørgo, 44–95. London: Frank Cass, 1995.

Kaplan, Jeffrey, and Tore Bjørgo. Introduction to *Nation and Race: The Developing Euro-American Racist Subculture*, ed. Jeffrey Kaplan and Tore Bjørgo, ix–xiii. Boston: Northeastern University Press, 1988.

Kaplan, Temma. "Female Consciousness and Collective Action: The Case of Barcelona, 1910–1918." *Signs* 7 (1982): 545–66.

Kelly, Caroline, and Sara Breinlinger. *The Social Psychology of Collective Action: Identity, Injustice, and Gender.* London: Taylor and Francis, 1996.

Klandermans, Bert. "Transient Identities? Membership Patterns in the Dutch Peace Movement." In *New Social Movements: From Ideology to Identity*, ed. Enrique Laraña, Hank Johnston, and Joseph Gusfield, 68–84. Philadelphia: Temple University Press, 1994.

Klandermans, Bert, and Dirk Oegema. "Potential, Networks, Motivations, and Barriers: Steps toward Participation in Social Movements." *American Sociological Review* 52 (1987): 521–31.

Klatch, Rebecca E. *Women of the New Right.* Philadelphia: Temple University Press, 1987.

Kleinman, Sherryl, and Martha A. Copp. *Emotions and Fieldwork.* Newbury Park, Calif.: Sage, 1993.

Knowles, Caroline. "Race, Identities, and Lives." *Sociological Review* 47 (1999): 110–35.

Koonz, Claudia. "The Competition for a Woman's Lebensraum." In *When Biology Became Destiny: Women in Weimar and Nazi Germany*, ed. Renate Bridenthal, Atina Grossmann, and Marion Kaplan, 199–236. New York: Monthly Review, 1984.

———. *Mothers in the Fatherland: Women, Family Life, and Nazi Politics.* New York: St. Martin's, 1987.

Kriesi, Hanspeter. "The Rebellion of the Research 'Objects.'" In *Studying Collective Action,* ed. Mario Diani and Ron Eyerman, 194–216. London: Sage, 1992.

Lal, Jaytai. "Situating Locations: The Politics of Self, Identity, and 'Other' in Living and Writing the Text." In *Feminist Dilemmas in Fieldwork,* ed. Diane L. Wolf, 185–214. Boulder, Colo.: Westview, 1996.

Lebanc, Lauraine. *Pretty in Punk: Girls' Gender Resistance in a Boys' Subculture.* New Brunswick, N.J.: Rutgers University Press, 1999.

Lee, Raymond M. *Dangerous Fieldwork.* Newbury Park, Calif.: Sage, 1995.

Lesselier, Claudie. "The Women's Movement and the Extreme Right in France." In *The Nature of the Right: A Feminist Analysis of Order Patterns,* ed. Gill Seidel, 173–85. Amsterdam: John Benjamin, 1988.

Lewis, Michael, and Jacqueline Serbu. "Kommemorating the Ku Klux Klan." *Sociological Quarterly* 40 (1999): 139–57.

Lipset, Seymour Martin. "The Sources of the Radical Right—1955." In *The Radical Right,* ed. Daniel Bell, 307–71. New York: Anchor, 1964.

Lipset, Seymour Martin, and Earl Raab. *The Politics of Unreason.* New York: Harper and Row, 1970.

Lipstadt, Deborah E. *Denying the Holocaust: The Growing Assault on Truth and Memory.* New York: Free Press, 1993.

Lo, Clarence Y. H. "Communities of Challengers in Social Movement Theory." In *Frontiers in Social Movement Theory,* ed. Aldon D. Morris and Carol McClurg Mueller, 224–47. New Haven: Yale University Press, 1992.

Lofland, John, and Norman Skonovd. "Conversion Motifs." *Journal for the Scientific Study of Religion* 20 (1981): 373–85.

Lofland, John, and Rodney Stark. "Becoming a World-Saver: A Theory of Conversion to a Deviant Perspective." *American Sociological Review* 30 (1965): 862–75.

Lööw, Heléne. "The Cult of Violence: The Swedish Racist Counterculture." In *Racist Violence in Europe,* ed. Tore Bjørgo and Rob White, 62–80. New York: St. Martin's, 1993.

———. "White-Power Rock 'n' Roll: A Growing Industry." In *Nation and Race: The Developing Euro-American Racist Subculture,* ed. Jeffrey Kaplan and Tore Bjørgo, 126–47. Boston: Northeastern University Press, 1998.

Luchterhand, Elmer, and Norbert Wieland. "The Focused Life History in Studying Involvement in a Genocidal Situation in Nazi Germany." In *Biography and Society: The Life History Approach in the Social Sciences,* ed. Daniel Bertaux, 267–87. Beverly Hills, Calif.: Sage, 1981.

Luker, Kristin. *Abortion and the Politics of Motherhood.* Berkeley: University of California Press, 1984.

Lutz, Catherine A. "Engendered Emotion: Gender, Power, and the Rhetoric of Emotional Control in American Discourse." In *Language and the Politics of Emotion,* ed. Catherine A. Lutz and Lila Abu-Lughod, 69–91. Cambridge: Cambridge University Press, 1990.

Marshall, Susan. "In Defense of Separate Spheres: Class and Status Politics in the Antisuffrage Movement." *Social Forces* 65 (1986): 327–51.

———. "Rattle on the Right: Bridge Labor in Antifeminist Organizations." In

No Middle Ground: Women and Radical Protest, ed. Kathleen M. Blee, 155–79. New York: New York University Press, 1998.

Mayer, Arno L. "Memory and History: On the Poverty of Remembering and Forgetting the Judeocide." *Radical History Review,* no. 56 (spring 1993): 5–20.

Mayer, Milton S. "Mrs. Dilling: Lady of the Red Network." *American Mercury,* July 1939, 293–99.

McAdam, Doug. "Culture and Social Movements." In *New Social Movements: From Ideology to Identity,* ed. Enrique Laraña, Hank Johnston, and Joseph R. Gusfield, 36–57. Philadelphia: Temple University Press, 1994.

———. *Freedom Summer.* New York: Oxford University Press, 1988.

McClintock, Anne. "Family Feuds: Gender, Nationalism, and the Family." *Feminist Review,* no. 44 (summer 1993): 61–80.

McLean, Nancy. *Behind the Mask of Chivalry: The Making of the Second Ku Klux Klan.* New York: Oxford University Press, 1994.

McRobbie, Angela, and Jenny Garber. "Girls and Subcultures." In *Resistance through Rituals: Youth Subcultures in Post-war Britain,* ed. Stuart Hall and Tony Jefferson, 208–22. New York: Holmes and Meier, 1976.

Melucci, Alberto. "Frontier Land: Collective Action between Actors and Systems." In *Studying Collective Action,* ed. Mario Diani and Ron Eyerman, 238–58. London: Sage, 1992.

———. "The Process of Collective Identity." In *Social Movements and Culture,* ed. Hank Johnston and Bert Klandermans, 41–63. Minneapolis: University of Minnesota Press, 1995.

———. "A Strange Kind of Newness: What's 'New' in New Social Movements?" In *New Social Movements: From Ideology to Identity,* ed. Enrique Laraña, Hank Johnston, and Joseph R. Gusfield, 101–30. Philadelphia: Temple University Press, 1994.

Mills, C. Wright. "Situated Actions and Vocabularies of Motive." *American Sociological Review* 5 (1940): 404–13.

Mitchell, Richard G. *Secrecy and Fieldwork.* Newbury Park, Calif.: Sage, 1993.

Moore, Jack. *Skinheads Shaved for Battle: A Cultural History of American Skinheads.* Bowling Green, Ohio: Bowling Green University Popular Press, 1993.

Morgen, Sandra. "'It Was the Best of Times, It Was the Worst of Times': Emotional Discourse in the Work Cultures of Feminist Health Clinics." In *Feminist Organizations: Harvest of the New Women's Movement,* ed. Myra Marx Ferree and Patricia Yancey Martin, 234–47. Philadelphia: Temple University Press, 1995.

Morris, Aldon. *The Origins of the Civil Rights Movement.* New York: Free Press, 1984.

Morrison, Toni. *Playing in the Dark: Whiteness and the Literary Imagination.* New York: Vintage, 1992.

Mosse, George L. *Nationalism and Sexuality: Middle-Class Morality and Sexual Norms in Modern Europe.* Madison: University of Wisconsin Press, 1985.

Mudde, Cas. "Right-Wing Extremism Analyzed: A Comparative Analysis of the Ideologies of Three Alleged Right-wing Extremist Parties (NPD, NSP, CP '86)." *European Journal of Political Research* 27 (1995): 203–23.

———. "The War of Words Defining the Extreme Right Party Family." *West European Politics* 19 (1996): 225–49.

Mueller, Carol McClurg. "Building Social Movement Theory." In *Frontiers in Social Movement Theory,* ed. Aldon D. Morris and Carol McClurg Mueller, 3–25. New Haven: Yale University Press, 1992.

———. "Conflict Networks and the Origins of Women's Liberation." In *New Social Movements: From Ideology to Identity,* ed. Enrique Laraña, Hank Johnston, and Joseph R. Gusfield, 234–66. Philadelphia: Temple University Press, 1994.

Neidhardt, Friedhelm. "Left-Wing and Right-Wing Terrorist Groups: A Comparison for the German Case." In *International Social Movement Research,* vol. 4, *Social Movements and Violence: Participation in Underground Organizations,* ed. Donatella della Porta, 215–35. London: JAI Press, 1992.

Neuburger, Luisella de Cataldo, and Tiziana Valentini. *Women and Terrorism.* Trans. Leo Michael Hughes. New York: St. Martin's, 1998.

Obligacion, Freddie R. "Managing Perceived Deception among Respondents: A Traveler's Tale." *Journal of Contemporary Ethnography* 23 (1994): 29–50.

Omi, Michael, and Howard Winant. *Racial Formation in the United States: From the 1960s to the 1990s.* 2nd ed. New York: Routledge, 1994.

Parkinson, Brian. "Emotions Are Social." *British Journal of Psychology* 87 (1996): 663–84.

Passerini, Luisa. *Fascism in Popular Memory: The Cultural Experience of the Turin Working Class.* Trans. Robert Lumley and Jude Bloomfield. Cambridge: Cambridge University Press, 1987.

———. "Lacerations in the Memory: Women in the Italian Underground Organizations." In *International Social Movement Research,* vol. 4, *Social Movements and Violence: Participation in Underground Organization,* ed. Donatella della Porta, 161–212. London: JAI Press, 1992.

Patai, Daphne. "U.S. Academics and Third World Women: Is Ethical Research Possible?" In *Women's Words: The Feminist Practice of Oral History,* ed. Sherna Berger Gluck and Daphne Patai, 137–53. New York: Routledge, 1991.

Petchesky, Rosalind Pollack. "Antiabortion, Antifeminism, and the Rise of the New Right." *Feminist Studies* 7 (1981): 206–46.

Peukert, Detlev J. K. *Inside Nazi Germany: Conformity, Opposition, and Racism in Everyday Life.* Trans. Richard Deveson. New Haven: Yale University Press, 1982.

Phillips, Susan. *Wallbangin': Graffiti and Gangs in L.A.* Chicago: University of Chicago Press, 1999.

Poisoning the Web: Hatred Online. New York: Anti-Defamation League, 1999.

Polletta, Francesca. " 'It Was Like a Fever . . . ': Narrative and Identity in Social Protest." *Social Problems* 45 (1998): 137–59.

Pollner, Melvin, and Robert M. Emerson. "The Dynamics of Inclusion and Distance in Fieldwork Relations." In *Contemporary Field Research: A Collection of Readings,* ed. Robert M. Emerson, 235–52. Prospect Heights, Ill.: Waveland, 1983.

Potter, Jonathan. "Attitudes, Social Representations, and Discursive Psychology." In *Identities, Groups, and Social Issues,* ed. Margaret Wetherell, 119–73. London: Sage, 1996.

Potter, Jonathan, and Margaret Wetherell. "Accomplishing Attitudes: Fact and Evaluation in Racist Discourse." *Text* 8.1–2 (1988): 51–68.

Reissman, Catherine Kohler. "When Gender Is Not Enough: Women Interviewing Women." *Gender and Society* 1 (1987): 172–207.

Richardson, James T., Jans van der Lans, and Frans Derks. "Leaving and Labeling: Voluntary and Coerced Disaffiliation from Religious Social Movements." *Research in Social Movements, Conflicts, and Change* 9 (1986): 97–126.

Robb, James H. *Working-Class Anti-Semite: A Psychological Study in a London Borough.* London: Tavistock, 1954.

Robben, Antonius C. G. M. "The Politics of Truth and Emotion among Victims and Perpetrators of Violence." In *Fieldwork under Fire: Contemporary Studies of Violence and Survival,* ed. Carolyn Nordstrom and Antonius C. G. M. Robben, 81–104. Berkeley: University of California Press, 1995.

Robben, Antonius C. G. M., and Carolyn Nordstrom. "The Anthropology and Ethnography of Violence and Sociopolitical Conflict." In *Fieldwork under Fire: Contemporary Studies of Violence and Survival,* ed. Carolyn Nordstrom and Antonius C. G. M. Robben, 1–23. Berkeley: University of California Press, 1995.

Robnett, Belinda. *How Long? How Long? African-American Women in the Struggle for Civil Rights.* New York: Oxford University Press, 1997.

Román, Reinaldo L. "Christian Themes: Mainstream Traditions and Millenarian Violence." In *Millennialism and Violence,* ed. Michael Barkun, 52–82. London: Frank Cass, 1996.

Rose, Susan D. "Women Warriors: The Negotiation of Gender in a Charismatic Community." *Sociological Analysis* 48 (1987): 245–58.

Rosenthal, Gabriele. "German War Memories: Narratability and the Biographical and Social Functions of Remembering." *Oral History* 19 (1991): 34–41.

Rosenthal, Naomi, Meryl Fingrutd, Michele Ethier, Roberta Karant, and David McDonald. "Social Movements and Network Analysis: A Case Study of Nineteenth-Century Women's Reform in New York State." *American Journal of Sociology* 90 (1985): 1022–54.

Rosenzweig, Roy, and David Thelen. *The Presence of the Past: Popular Uses of History in American Life.* New York: Columbia University Press, 1998.

Roy, Beth. "Goody Two-Shoes and Hell-Raisers: Women's Activism, Women's Reputations in Little Rock." In *No Middle Ground: Women and Radical Protest,* ed. Kathleen M. Blee, 96–132. New York: New York University Press, 1998.

Ruddick, Sara. *Maternal Thinking: Toward a Politics of Peace.* New York: Ballantine, 1989.

Rupp, Leila J., and Verta Taylor. *Survival in the Doldrums: The American Women's Rights Movement, 1945 to the 1960s.* Columbus: Ohio State University Press, 1990.

Sacks, Karen Brodkin. "What's a Life Story Got to Do with It?" In *Interpreting*

Women's Lives: Feminist Theory and Personal Narrative, ed. Personal Narratives Group, 85–95. Bloomington: Indiana University Press, 1989.

Sacks, Oliver. *A Leg to Stand On*. New York: Simon and Schuster, 1984.

Said, Edward W. *Orientalism*. New York: Vintage Books, 1979.

Scott, James C. *Domination and the Arts of Resistance: Hidden Transcripts*. New Haven: Yale University Press, 1990.

Scott, Joan. "Gender: A Useful Category of Historical Analysis." *American Historical Review* 91 (1986): 1053–75.

Seidel, Gill. *The Holocaust Denial: Anti-Semitism, Racism, and the New Right*. Leeds, England: Beyond the Pale Collective, 1986.

Shapiro, Virginia. *The Political Integration of Women: Roles, Socialization, and Politics*. Urbana: University of Illinois Press, 1984.

Siebert, Renate. *Secrets of Life and Death: Women and the Mafia*. London: Verso, 1996.

Singular, Stephen. *Talked to Death: The Life and Murder of Alan Berg*. New York: William Morrow, 1987.

Skolnick, J. *The Social Structure of Street Drug Dealing*. BCS Forum. Sacramento: State of California, 1988.

Smith, David Norman. "The Social Construction of Enemies: Jews and the Representation of Evil." *Sociological Theory* 14 (1996): 203–40.

Snow, David A., and Richard Machalek. "The Sociology of Conversion." *Annual Review of Sociology* 10 (1984): 167–90.

Snow, David A., E. Burke Rochford, Steven K. Worden, and Robert D. Benford. "Frame Alignment Processes, Micromobilization, and Movement Participation." *American Sociological Review* 51 (1986): 464–81.

Snow, David A., Louis A. Zurcher Jr., and Sheldon Ekland-Olson. "Social Networks and Social Movements: A Microstructural Approach to Differential Recruitment." *American Sociological Review* 45 (1980): 787–801.

Solomon, John, and Les Bac. "Conceptualising Racisms: Social Theory, Politics, and Research." *Sociology* 28 (1994):143–62.

Somers, Margaret. "The Narrative Constitution of Identity: A Relational and Network Approach." *Theory and Society* 23 (1994): 605–49.

Sprinzak, Ehud. "Right-Wing Terrorism in a Comparative Perspective: The Case of Split Delegitimation." In *Terror from the Extreme Right*, ed. Tore Bjørgo, 17–43. London: Frank Cass, 1995.

Stacey, Judith. "Can There Be a Feminist Ethnography?" In *Women's Words: The Feminist Practice of Oral History*, ed. Sherna Berger Gluck and Daphne Patai, 111–19. New York: Routledge, 1991.

Staggenborg, Suzanne. "Social Movement Communities and Cycles of Protest: The Emergence and Maintenance of a Local Women's Movement." *Social Problems* 45 (1998): 180–204.

Stanton, Bill. *Klanwatch: Bringing the Ku Klux Klan to Justice*. New York: Grove Weidenfeld, 1991.

Stein, Arlene. *Sex and Sensibility: Stories of a Lesbian Generation*. Berkeley: University of California Press, 1997.

Stephan, Nancy Leys. "Race and Gender: The Role of Analogy in Science." In

Anatomy of Racism, ed. David Theo Goldberg, 38–57. Minneapolis: University of Minnesota Press, 1990.

Stern, Kenneth S. *A Force upon the Plain: The American Militia Movement and the Politics of Hate.* New York: Simon and Schuster, 1996.

Stoler, Ann Laura. "Carnal Knowledge and Imperial Power: Gender, Race, and Morality in Colonial Asia." In *Gender at the Crossroads of Knowledge: Feminist Anthropology in the Postmodern Era,* ed. Micaela di Leonardo, 51–101. Berkeley: University of California Press, 1991.

Straus, Roger A. "Religious Conversion as a Personal and Collective Accomplishment." *Sociological Analysis* 40 (1979): 158–65.

———. "A Situation of Desired Self-Change and Strategies of Self-Transcendence." In *Doing Social Life: The Qualitative Study of Human Interaction in Natural Settings,* ed. John Lofland, 252–73. New York: John Wiley, 1976.

Swedenburg, Ted. "With Genet in the Palestinian Field." In *Fieldwork under Fire: Contemporary Studies of Violence and Survival,* ed. Carolyn Nordstrom and Antonius C. G. M. Robben, 25–60. Berkeley: University of California Press, 1995.

Swidler, Ann. "Cultural Power and Social Movements." In *Social Movements and Culture,* ed. Hank Johnston and Bert Klandermans, 25–40. Minneapolis: University of Minnesota Press, 1995.

———. "Culture in Action: Symbols and Strategies." *American Sociological Review* 51 (1986): 273–86.

Tarrow, Sidney. "Mentalities, Political Cultures, and Collective Action Frames: Constructing Meanings through Action." In *Frontiers in Social Movement Theory,* ed. Aldon D. Morris and Carol McClurg Mueller, 174–202. New Haven: Yale University Press, 1993.

Taylor, Carl S. *Dangerous Society.* East Lansing: Michigan State University Press, 1990.

Taylor, Maxwell, and Ethel Quayle. *Terrorist Lives.* London: Brassey's, 1994.

Taylor, Verta. *Rock-a-by Baby: Feminism, Self-Help, and Postpartum Depression.* New York: Routledge, 1996.

———. "Social Movement Continuity: The Women's Movement in Abeyance." *American Sociological Review* 54 (1989): 761–75.

———. "Watching for Vibes: Bringing Emotions into the Study of Feminist Organizations." In *Feminist Organizations: Harvest of the New Women's Movement,* ed. Myra Marx Ferree and Patricia Yancey Martin, 223–33. Philadelphia: Temple University Press, 1995.

Taylor, Verta, and Nancy Whittier. "Analytic Approaches to Social Movement Culture: The Culture of the Women's Movement." In *Social Movements and Culture,* ed. Hank Johnston and Bert Klandermans, 163–87. Minneapolis: University of Minnesota Press, 1995.

———. "Theoretical Approaches to Social Movement Culture." Paper presented at the American Sociological Association's Workshop on Culture and Social Movements, San Diego, August 1992.

Theweleit, Klaus. *Male Fantasies.* Vol. 1, *Women, Floods, Bodies, History.*

Trans. Stephan Conway with Erica Carter and Chris Turner. Minneapolis: University of Minnesota Press, 1987.

Thompson, Paul. "Life Histories and the Analysis of Social Change." In *Biography and Society: The Life History Approach in the Social Sciences,* ed. Daniel Bertaux, 289–306. Beverly Hills, Calif.: Sage, 1981.

Thorne, Barrie. "Political Activist as Participant Observer: Conflicts of Commitment in a Study of the Draft Resistance Movement of the 1960s." In *Contemporary Field Research: A Collection of Readings,* ed. Robert M. Emerson, 216–34. Prospect Heights, Ill.: Waveland, 1983.

Tremmel, William C. "The Converting Choice." *Journal for the Scientific Study of Religion* 10 (1971): 17–25.

Tuch, Steven A., and Michael Hughes. "Whites' Racial Policy Attitudes." *Social Science Quarterly* 77 (1996): 723–45.

Van Leeuwen, Mary Stewart. "Servanthood or Soft Patriarchy? A Christian Feminist Looks at the Promise Keepers Movement." *Journal of Men's Studies* 5 (1997): 233–62.

Walsh, Edward. "Resource Mobilization and Citizen Protest in Communities around Three Mile Island." *Social Problems* 29 (1981): 1–21.

Ware, Vron. "Island Racism: Gender, Place, and White Power." *Feminist Review,* no. 54 (autumn 1986): 65–86.

Weinberg, Leonard. "The American Radical Right: Exit, Voice, and Violence." In *Encounters with the Radical Right,* ed. Peter H. Merkl and Leonard Weinberg, 185–203. Boulder, Colo.: Westview, 1993.

———. "An Overview of Right-Wing Extremism in the Western World: A Study of Convergence, Linkage, and Identity." In *Nation and Race: The Developing Euro-American Racist Subculture,* ed. Jeffrey Kaplan and Tore Bjørgo, 3–33. Boston: Northeastern University Press, 1988.

Wetherell, Margaret. "Group Conflict and the Social Psychology of Racism." In *Identities, Groups and Social Issues,* ed. Margaret Wetherell, 175–238. London: Sage, 1996.

———. "Life Histories/Social Histories." In *Identities, Groups and Social Issues,* ed. Margaret Wetherell, 299–342. London: Sage, 1996.

Wetherell, Margaret, and Jonathan Potter. *Mapping the Language of Racism: Discourse and the Legitimation of Exploitation.* New York: Columbia University Press, 1992.

White, Robert. "Political Violence by the Nonaggrieved: Explaining the Political Participation of Those with No Apparent Grievances." In *International Social Movement Research,* vol. 4, *Social Movements and Violence: Participation in Underground Organizations,* ed. Donatella della Porta, 79–103. London: JAI Press, 1992.

Whittier, Nancy E. *Feminist Generations: The Persistence of the Radical Women's Movement.* Philadelphia: Temple University Press, 1995.

Wieviorka, Michel. *The Arena of Racism.* Trans. Chris Turner. London: Sage, 1994.

Wilson, Thomas C. "Compliments Will Get You Nowhere: Benign Stereotypes, Prejudice and Anti-Semitism." *Sociological Quarterly* 37 (1996): 465–79.

World Church of the Creator: One Year Later. Chicago: Center for New Community, 2000.

Zavella, Patricia. "Feminist Insider Dilemmas: Constructing Ethnic Identity with 'Chicana' Informants." *Frontiers* 8.3 (1993): 53–76.

Zelizer, Barbie. *Remembering to Forget: Holocaust Memory through the Camera's Eye.* Chicago: University of Chicago Press, 1998.

Zwerman, Gilda. "Mothering on the Lam: Politics, Gender Fantasies, and Maternal Thinking in Women Associated with Armed, Clandestine Organizations in the United States." *Feminist Review,* no. 47 (summer 1994): 33–56.

ACKNOWLEDGMENTS

I have been privileged to have accumulated many intellectual debts in this project. Pam Goldman, Jerome Himmelstein, and Rebecca Klatch provided extensive and insightful comments on the entire manuscript. During this research, I have been guided by the suggestions and cautions of a number of colleagues, including Ron Aminzade, Vern Baxter, Chip Berlet, Dwight Billings, William Brustein, Devin Burghart, William Canak, Nicole Constable, Sara Evans, Abby Ferber, Maurine Greenwald, Carol Heimer, Norm Hummon, Claudia Koonz, Jonathan Levine, Sally Ward Maggard, Nancy McLean, Susan Silbey, Suzanne Staggenborg, Verta Taylor, Becky Thompson, Ann Tickamyer, France Winddance Twine, Eric Ward, Jonathan Warren, and Julia Wrigley, as well as students in Jerome Himmelstein's Amherst College class on the American Right. Portions of this work have been presented at the Boston Area Feminist Theory Colloquium, Boston University, Cornell University, CUNY–Graduate Center, Lock Haven State University, Loyola University–New Orleans, North Carolina State University, Northwestern University, Princeton University, Smith College, the University of California–San Diego, the University of California–Santa Barbara, the University of California–Santa Cruz, the University of Kentucky, the University of Michigan, the University of Minnesota, the University of New Orleans, the University of Pittsburgh, the University of Washington, the University of Wisconsin–Madison, Vanderbilt University, Virginia Polytechnic Institute, and West Virginia University. Comments of faculty and students at these presentations have been very useful in guiding my thinking and preventing additional errors.

I was able to interview racist activists across the country because of the generous financial support and teaching leave provided to me as the University of Kentucky Research Professor for 1994–95. Additional support for travel and research expenses was provided by the University of Pittsburgh Faculty of Arts and Sciences.

268   Acknowledgments

Most of my analysis of racist propaganda makes use of literature that I collected over a one-year period. Collections of racist publications at the Wilcox
Collection, Kenneth Spencer Research Library, the University of Kansas,
Lawrence; Special Collections, Howard-Tilton Memorial Library, Tulane University, New Orleans; the Southern Poverty Law Center, Montgomery, Ala-
bama; and the Anti-Defamation League of B'nai B'rith, New York, provided
important supplementary material, and I thank librarians and archivists at these
locations for their assistance. For a second time, I have been lucky to work with
Monica McCormick of the University of California Press, an extraordinarily
perceptive and attentive editor. The manuscript has been improved greatly by
the creative suggestions of Sue Heinemann, the project editor, and careful
copyediting by Alice Falk.

INDEX

9 780520 240551